THE (
MUNSTER
CIRCUIT

"THE JACKDAW OF RHYMES" (1913)

An impression of the Author by the late C. N. KOUGH

THE OLD MUNSTER CIRCUIT

A Book of Memories and Traditions

by

MAURICE HEALY

with Biographical Introduction
by
CHARLES LYSAGHT

London
Wildy, Simmonds & Hill
Publishing
2015

ISBN: 9780854901579

British Library Cataloguing in Publication Data.
A catalogue record for this book is available from The British Library

PUBLISHING HISTORY
First Edition Michael Joseph 1939
Revised Edition Michael Joseph 1939
Reprinted Michael Joseph 1948
Reprinted Wildy & Sons 1977
Reprinted Mercier Press 1979
Reprinted Mercier Press 1986
Reprinted with new Biographical Introduction Wildy & Sons 2001
Reprinted as paperback Wildy, Simmonds & Hill Publishing 2015

MAURICE HEALY

MAURICE FRANCIS HEALY was born at 11, Mountjoy Place, Dublin, the home of his American grandmother, Mrs Frances Sullivan, on 16 November 1887. He was eldest of the three children of Maurice and Annie Healy of Ashton Lawn, Cork, and spent his childhood in the Munster capital — his earliest memory was of being held up to see the old Cork courthouse going up in flames in 1891. His parents were cousins and on both sides of his family he was bred to the law and to nationalist politics. He later boasted that he said 'Boo to Balfour' before he could utter the words 'Mama' and 'Papa'. His father was a solicitor and a nationalist member of parliament for many years. His paternal uncle, Tim Healy, a King's Counsel both in Ireland and England, was, from 1880 to 1918, one of the leading Irish nationalist spokesmen in the House of Commons, and then became first Governor General of the Irish Free State. His maternal grandfather, A. M. Sullivan, who died in 1884, ended life as a member of parliament and barrister in London but was better known in his original calling of journalism as editor of *The Nation* and author of a much read history called *The Story of Ireland*. A. M.'s son, Alex, was appointed to the junior law officership of Serjeant by the Liberal Government in 1912 and, four years later, led for the defence at the trial for High Treason of Sir Roger Casement. The Sullivans and the Healys, who had their roots in the region of Bantry in West Cork, were the leading members of a group of inter-related political families known as the 'Bantry Band'.

Young Maurice Healy went to school at the Christian Brothers College, Cork and then, from 1901 to 1904, boarded with the Jesuits at Clongowes Wood College, Ireland's most fashionable Catholic school at that time. His mother wanted him to go on to Oxford but his father decided that this would be a handicap if he went to the Irish Bar. So Healy went on to University College Dublin which, like Clongowes, was run by the Jesuits and prepared students for the examinations of the Royal University of Ireland. In 1907 he graduated with second class honours in history, political economy and juris-prudence.

Healy was a keen debater and became active in the Literary and Historical Society which, only a few years previously, had been the early stamping-ground of James Joyce. Friction had broken out between the college authorities and some students who had disrupted the confer-ring of degrees at the Royal University in protest against the playing of *God Save the King*. This resulted in the rustication of the auditor (student president) of the Literary and Historical society, Francis Cruise O'Brien (father of Conor), who then took the society outside the college. Healy, who was on the committee, led those who attempted to carry on the society within the college. In due course he became gold medallist and Auditor. Although he described himself as a born rebel, the episode marked the young Maurice Healy as a person who was not of radical tendency.

Between 1908 and 1910 he attended lectures for Bar students at Trinity College Dublin and King's Inns. He said he neglected his legal studies because he began to write light verse. Some verses of affection lamenting a failed romance survive from this period. He was called to the Bar in 1910. Later that year he stood unsuccessfully as a candidate for West Waterford in the interests of the schismatic All-for-Ireland Party, against the official candidate of the Irish Parliamentary Party. Between 1910 and the outbreak of war in 1914 he practised in the Law Library in Dublin and on the Munster Circuit.

Like many other moderate Irish nationalists who sought home rule, he enlisted in the Army in the First World War. In 1915 he obtained a commission in the Royal Dublin Fusiliers, with whom he served both on the Western Front and in Gallipoli. He later served at the Headquarters of the 29th Division in France. He was awarded the Military Cross and retired early in 1919 with the rank of captain.

Healy returned briefly to the Munster Circuit. By this time the republican Sinn Fein, having triumphed over the Irish Parliamentary Party at the 1918 General Election, had established an embryonic government with its own parliament and courts. Assassination of policemen by the Irish Republican Army led to armed strife with the authorities and the introduction by Lloyd George's government of the 'Black and Tans' and Auxiliary cadets who were allowed to terrorize the countryside. Moderate nationalists, especially those who had served in 'His Majesty's Forces', were marginalised politically as the struggle became polarised. The Sinn Fein boycott of the official courts was effective outside Dublin, so there was little business for barristers on the Munster circuit.

It was in these circumstances that Maurice Healy told friends that he felt that there was no future for a man of his background in Ireland. He had been called to the English Bar at Gray's Inn in 1914 and he now set up practice at 1, King's Bench Walk, in the chambers of his maternal uncle, Serjeant Sullivan, who also gave him a loan of £1000 to help him on his way.

Having cut his teeth at the North London Sessions, Healy joined the Midland Circuit and built up a good common law practice, especially in Birmingham. Norman Birkett, who was a few years his senior, recalled being 'much attracted by his brogue although it was slight as compared with Lord Carson.' Healy's pleasant voice, genial smile and 'a comfortable rotundity indicative of good living' were said to have put him on good terms with juries. He also knew how to humour judges. Once, when addressing a court on behalf of a client who had made a muddled showing in the witness box, he compared her evidence to a painting by Cezanne: 'At close quarters the details are blurred, perhaps confusing, but standing back one gets a clearer view and sees it as a forceful and harmonious whole.' Healy was successful enough to be invited to become a King's Counsel in 1931. But, after that, he seems not to have reached the place in the profession to which colleagues believed that his gifts entitled him. Birkett felt that 'his richly dowered mind did not permit him to pursue the narrow path of the law with a single undeviating purpose, and that he found the tang and savour of his many sided life too attractive to be sacrificed.' Apparently, his sparkling sense of humour sometimes got out of control and created the impression that he took things too lightly.

So it was that he became known as the gastronomic leader of the Bar. He came to wine with the burning zeal of a convert for he had been a virtual teetotaler until he was thirty. He was a member of the wine committee of the Windham Club. In 1926 he was elected, together with A.J.A. Symons (author of *The Quest for Corvo*) and

Vyvyan Holland (the son of Oscar Wilde), to a dining club of lawyers and writers called *Ye Sette of Old Volumes*. It was here that he acquired his nickname 'The Prattler'. New members had to give an address and his was on Irish wine, as he called Chateau Haut Broin, claiming that Broin was really O'Brien — he liked to take a stance for the hell of it, which the English thought was charmingly Irish. Later, he was a moving spirit in the foundation of the Saintsbury Club, so called in honour of the aged wine expert, Professor George Saintsbury. Another dining club of which Healy was a founding member was the Thomas More Society for Catholic Lawyers. He was on the original Advisory Council of the Wine and Food Society founded in 1933 by André Simon, author of a hundred books on wine, who described Healy as his dearly beloved disciple, and who professed to appreciate his qualities of directness and candour. Healy contributed verse and articles to the Society's quarterly and published in 1934, as part of the *Constable Wine Series,* a popular volume on *Claret and the White Wines of Bordeaux*. In the introduction to this book he stated his conviction that 'the good talk that is inseparable from a wine dinner is even more important than the wines that are being served.' In his entry in *Who's Who* he listed his recreations as talking and listening to music. His own conversation was rich in allusion.

Healy's love of wine led him to spend his vacations in France and sometimes in Italy. After his father's death in 1923, his mother, Annie, whom he described as an imperious lady, moved to live with him in London. As long as she remained he had less occasion to visit Ireland. Doubtless, like many who had supported Home Rule in the hope of an historic Anglo-Irish reconciliation in an

Imperial context, he was repelled by the insularity of the new Irish state and the Anglophobia that came to dominate its political life. It would have been a sadness for him to see the ruins of the old Four Courts, which had been burnt down in the Civil War, or later to go to the reconstructed building and find that much, including the elegant old Law Library in which he had practised as a young man, was no more. But he was still nationalist enough to remove himself to the Inner Temple shortly before he took silk, so that he would not become a fellow-bencher at Gray's Inn of Hamar Greenwood, the Irish Chief Secretary who allowed the Crown Forces to terror-ise Ireland in 1920 and 1921. Healy also advised his old school and college friend, Thomas Bodkin, in his campaign for the return of the Lane pictures from the Tate Gallery to Dublin.

As he approached fifty in 1937, Healy's mind seems to have turned back to the lost world of his youth. He had secured a niche as an occasional broadcaster at the BBC. He was one of a number chosen to give talks on their memories of the previous coronation year, 1911, which he said had been the happiest year of his life. Later that year he gave a broadcast on his childhood. 'Looking back over those fifty years,' he said, 'it is difficult to see any but the one figure: that of my father. The poor man was under the impression that I was a genius and deserved a good education, which he undertook himself.' His father, Healy claimed, 'loved the humble and simple folk and I never visit his grave without finding some evidence that the humble and simple have not forgotten him.' He did not mention that his father had been a temperance zealot.

Out of this vein of reminiscence, which provided much of his peerless dinner-table conversation, was born *The*

Old Munster Circuit, published by Michael Joseph in March, 1939. It has gone through many editions in the last sixty years, which have seen a multitude of legal memoirs vanish without trace. Like all great writing it transcends time and place. But it had, of course, a special appeal for those who had known the circuit during what came to be looked back upon as a golden age for the practising members of the Irish Bar. One such was James Francis Meagher who reviewed it in the *Clongownian*, the journal of Healy's old school:

Our members have scattered far and wide. Jamacia knows them and Africa, so do Canada, India, Borneo and the Isles of the Sea. I can imagine an exiled Jurist before the hour of siesta, sitting down to read the latest consignment from his London bookseller. He turns Maurice's pages, and memories crowd fast upon him. The magic of sleep brings wondrous changes. The roar of breakers on the reef turns to the lapping of Shannon water round the walls of the old courthouse in Limerick. Instead of the scarlet hibiscus in his garden he sees once more the glow of rhododendron on a Kerry hillside. When the waking eye beheld the gorgeous plumage of the Bird of Paradise, the dream restores the sea gulls who swoop and circle above the Lazy Lee. The chatter of black belles on the road-way is converted to the soft brogue of Munster. For a merciful hour, his Honour the Chief Justice of Boriboola-Gha can forget that he is a weary old failure dreaming away the dregs of life in a forgotten corner of the ocean, and believe he is once more one of the gallant band of brothers who, with light pockets, and high hopes, took, twice a year, the road from Ennis to Cork.

It should be said that for all its Irish charm and the nostalgia of exile that inspired it, *The Old Munster Circuit* was not received with unmixed joy among Maurice Healy's old confrères in Ireland. Some detected the unforgiving venom of the Bantry Band lurking beneath the apparent benignity and charm of the author. It was described by fellow-Corkman Eoin O'Mahony in a review as a brilliant piece of propaganda. James Francis Meagher was moved to protest at the treatment meted out to those who, like the judges William O'Brien and Johnny Moriarty, had fallen foul of Clan Healy. Healy himself was viewed with astringent eyes by some who had known him in Ireland and thought he had sold out to the old enemy, especially when they heard reports that he had become a friend of the Duke of Kent. It was recorded sourly that Healy, a teetotaler in his Irish youth, had refused to drink wine on a visit to Ireland, saying that he did so because the Irish did not know how to drink. It was not the nastiest tale that the Irish begrudgers had to tell about him.

Another person who had reason to be displeased with *The Old Munster Circuit* was Healy's uncle, Serjeant Sullivan. He had shown Healy the draft of his own memoirs and felt 'scooped' when many of his best stories appeared in Healy's book. However, it must be said that those stories that antedated Healy's own time at the Irish Bar would almost certainly have been part of the general lore of his family circle and of the Law Library. They are told with much greater art by Healy than by Sullivan in *The Last Serjeant* (1952) or in his earlier memoirs, *Old Ireland* (1927). Although, by his financial support, Sullivan had enabled Healy to practise at the English Bar, and Healy in turn had appointed the Serjeant as his executor in a will made in 1930, their relationship had clearly soured somewhat by the time *The Old Munster Circuit* appeared. Some references to the Serjeant in the book are fairly critical. Sullivan's last surviving child, Laura, recalls that Healy seldom, if ever, visited the Sullivan family home in Kent. Of all his mother's family, he was closest to his aunt Josephine, who shared his interest in music, and who was estranged from her brother, the Serjeant. It may be surmised that Sullivan, who was rather puritanical, would not have approved of Healy's way of life.

At the beginning of the Second World War, Healy found himself called to broadcast a series of postscripts to the *Nine O'Clock News* on Sunday nights. The most memorable was on the morrow of the heroic evacuation from Dunkirk. 'The past week,' he said, 'has been in one way the most disastrous and in another way the most glorious we have experienced since the war began.' He lamented the pending entry of Italy into the war as the interruption of a long historic friendship: 'I trust,' he said, 'that we shall not visit our anger on a people that we love and can afford to forgive even when they are led astray.' He derided talk of peace and concluded, Churchill-like, that 'no triumph worth while has ever been won without tears and a victory hallowed by suffering is greater and more enduring than one secured by an easy trick or treason.' The BBC, it was said, never had a more universally popular broadcaster.

1940 also saw the publication of *Stay Me with Flagons*, a title taken from the Canticles of Canticles in the *Authorised Version*. It starts by making a case against teetotalism. It surveys the wine, sherry, port and brandy of Europe and includes chapters on beer and whiskey, which Healy seldom drank. A devotee of claret, he nonetheless declared that the Caillerets 1889 and two other wines from Burgundy were the greatest bottles he had ever tasted. The book was dedicated to 'my friend Barry Neame, sometimes the Host of Princes, always the Prince of Hosts.' Neame was the proprietor of the Hinds Head in

Bray, Healy's favourite restaurant. The epithet 'prince of hosts' could aptly have been applied to Healy himself, who was not just bountiful but also courtly and sensitive to his guests. He was famous for his generous hospitality to the young.

In 1941 Healy's chambers in King's Bench Walk fell victim to enemy bombing of the Inner Temple, of which he had been a bencher since 1938. This gave him some fellow-feeling for the bombed out city of Coventry, of which he was appointed Recorder at this time. This was the beginning of a part-time judicial career and he also sat as Commissioner of Assizes in Birmingham. In the normal course of events he would have been in line for a High Court judgeship and the knighthood that went with it.

Any such hopes were shattered by the onset of a kidney disease called nephritis in 1942. After a protracted illness, during which he was cared for by his mother's sister, his devoted Aunt Josephine, and visited by many old friends, he died in his flat at 72, Courtfield Gardens on 9 May 1943. He was only fifty-five.

The Law Times said the legal world could ill afford to lose so early the kindly, gentle, lovable company of Maurice Healy. 'In the Temple, on circuit and at many a gathering less gay for his absence,' it remarked, 'his portly stooping figure and round whimsical face will long be missed.' His old school and college friend, the art connoisseur Thomas Bodkin, who had found Healy 'suffering and lonely' on visits during his last illness, wrote that 'wherever he went he made friends, through his good talk, his brilliant topical verses, his books, his broadcasts, his genial and lavish hospitality, and, above all, through his natural kindliness and his deep sense of honour.' 'Whatever' added Bodkin, 'may be thought by some of his countrymen about some of his political views which, by the way, were never bitter, it should be realized that few, if any, Irishmen of his generation did more in England than Maurice did to earn and compel respect for his race and his religion.'

'Maurice Healy was an ideal man's man,' wrote André Simon, 'true to his friends to a quixotic degree. He was always reliable and always the same. His old-world courtesy, his sparkling wit and lively sense of humour, endeared him to all who came in contact with him, but few among his many friends knew him well and realized that he was no hedonist but a mystic at heart. He made the best of the world in which he lived; he did his best to make it a better world for others; he loved to pick all choice blooms that came within his reach — a classical concert, a fine page of prose or verse or a bottle of old Claret — but it was just by the way; he did not attach any real importance to such passing joys; he was deeply and religiously grateful for all God's mercies and gifts, and it was always the Giver and not the gifts that mattered most.'

Healy was buried privately and a Requiem Mass said a fortnight later at the Jesuit church in Farm Street. Bishop David Mathew, the auxiliary to the Archbishop of Westminster, presided. Healy was survived by his mother and also by a brother and a sister, both of whom lived in Cork. He was not well off; his gross estate, out of which debts had to be paid, was less than £2000. During his final illness he was robbed of all his silver and linen. In his will, made in 1930, he left £100 to 'his faithful friend and clerk W. E. Middlemiss.' and forgave and discharged 'a great number of friends who owe me private loans of varying amounts.'

CHARLES LYSAGHT

CYRANO: Oui, vous m'arrachez tout, le laurier et la rose!
Arrachez! Il y a malgré vous quelque chose
Que j'emporte, et ce soir, quand j'entrerai chez Dieu
Mon salut balaiera largement le seuil bleu,
Quelque chose que sans un pli, sans une tache,
J'emporte malgré vous, et c'est . . .

ROXANE: C'est?

CYRANO: Mon panache.

BY WAY OF PREFACE

SOMEBODY *who might prefer to remain anonymous when he sees the result of his conduct, sat opposite me at lunch, and encouraged me to talk. It wasn't the best kind of talk; it was a monologue, hardly interrupted by the ten seconds which Dean Swift says a gentleman should allow before once again attracting the ear of the assembly. Monologues are only interesting when they are unfamiliar; it was the first time I had held forth in that particular company. I was speaking about the old days in Ireland, and one thing was suggesting another. But there should have been two or three of us to remember in unison. The best talk in the world is to be heard in Cork, where two or three are gathered together. All speak at once; but there is both art and method in it. Talk of Haydn's Quartets! As works of art they take second place to a Cork conversation. Palestrina was a Cork man; there is internal evidence in his music. He may have been Pat Lester of Inagh; or he may have borrowed the name of some Italian under which to publish his works. But the idiom is there: one voice starts, but is almost immediately joined by a second and a third which descant about the first, adding to it, embellishing it, and sometimes even contradicting it, but never interfering with the story. Through all the apparent confusion there is pleasant repetition of the main theme; and all parts enjoy themselves thoroughly. Whether a musician would pass this as a good description of the music of Pope Marcellus's Mass, it cannot be*

15

criticised as a portrayal of a Cork conversation. And I sighed as I pursued my monologues, for they really are not as interesting to the speaker as his perseverance might lead one to think; I lacked my genial counterpoint, and I grew melancholy.

It was then that my vis-à-vis spoke the fatal word. "I wish you'd write a book," he said. I thought at first he had said a brook, which went on for ever; but he shook his head: "A book," he said, "just as you're speaking now; write it down, and I'll see that it is published for you." The man seemed to be sober and, on the whole, intelligent; he was flattering me and I knew it. So I pretended not to want to do it; discussed possible subjects; talked big about history and in a piping voice about poetry; made all the excuses, and in the end promised to think about it. I did think about it; and this was the way my thought went.

To write a book in the free and easy way that had been indicated to me as about the only sort of thing I was fit for, means that the writer must know his subject so well as almost to be oozing with it. I examined the ooze as carefully as I could; there are very few subjects of which I am as full as all that. Three or four that I suggested were turned down; I turned down three or four that were suggested to me. And at last I realised that the stories with which I have filled any stray gaps in the conversation during the last twenty years were nearly all about the old days when I used to travel the Munster Circuit; and I felt that I could prattle about that time until the cows came home. I sat down at my typewriter; and here is the book.

It is a curious production; very little of it is original. Every member of the Munster Circuit as it existed just before the war knows all these stories, and a great many more which, alas! would not pass the censor. I have told all I dared; vigour of expression was always a characteristic of the circuit, and to prune it would rob the story of its authentic foliage and flavour.

It may be that some of the tales will be recognised; they may have appeared elsewhere; I have not borrowed them from any book, but from the common talk of the circuit.

There are very few unkind pictures in these pages, and it may be thought that I have deliberately left out the unpleasant characters. But there were no unpleasant characters other than those whose depiction hereafter may call for that description.

I have set down naught in malice; and if I have revived some forgotten scandals, it is only because they were of great general interest and because I believe that everybody who could be wounded by their repetition is long since gathered to a place where such arrows cannot pierce. And it must not be thought that because I have only depicted an amusing side of a character, the person so described was lacking in more serious qualities.

Although my own memory of legal matters goes back to the burning of the Cork Court-house in 1891, tales of events behind 1904 are nearly all hearsay, and some of those of later date are subject to the same defect. The only deviations from accuracy that have been intentional are such as had already given perspective to the facts when they were told to or by me on circuit. By this I mean that a Corkman likes to tell a story as it should be told; the garb may be elaborated, but the body is not deformed.[1]

And so, let the monologue begin again.

[1] *E.g., see page 109.*

I

MY FIRST experience of a Court of Justice goes back to
the year 1893. I had attained the mature age of five;
but a small boy living in the household of a Nationalist
lawyer who was one of the Members of Parliament for
the city took an early interest in both politics and law,
two subjects at that time very much intertwined, especially
on the criminal side. Long before I ever entered a court
I was familiar with the procession of the Judges from their
lodgings to the court-house: an occasion for some little
display. Their escort was supplied in two moieties, one
by the mounted section of the Royal Irish Constabulary,
the other by one of the cavalry regiments stationed at
the barracks. First came a trumpeter and a mounted
policeman riding abreast, then two policemen, then two
troopers; then came the Judges' carriage, with the
military officer riding at one door and the police officer
at the other; then two more troopers, followed by two
more mounted police. The bravado of the street-boys
sometimes occasioned an "incident," as the escort had
no hesitation about using the flats of their sabres; but on
the whole the proceedings were accepted by the crowd
as a condescension on the part of the Government for
their amusement. Within my own memory there never
was any attempt to attack a judge, although in earlier
days some members of the Bench had narrow escapes.
The judges were not personally unpopular. Lord O'Brien
used to tell a story of a visit he had from a Clare man,
who discussed all manner of pleasantries with him, but
took his farewell with the words: "I'm taking the chair

next Sunday at a League meeting, and you mustn't mind if I take a belt at you!'' ''Belt away, Pat,'' replied the Chief Justice, and they parted with mutual esteem and affection.

The Judge whom I first saw on the Bench was also named O'Brien, but in no way resembled the genial ''Pether,'' of whom I have just spoken. William O'Brien lived and died a bachelor; he heard daily Mass, fasted and abstained on all appropriate occasions, distributed all his goods to feed the poor, and worked more injustice in his daily round than English readers would believe possible. He had a familiar named Ford, who acted as his crier, a somewhat humbler version of the Judge's Clerk, with which officer the English courts are acquainted. It was no uncommon thing to see Ford whispering in the Judge's ear, to the latter's accompaniment of: ''Oh-h! Oh-h! God bless my soul! What a ruffian!'' soon to be followed by a sentence of extreme severity. Sometimes Ford's good offices would be invoked on behalf of a prisoner; then the Judge would address the Crown Prosecutor: ''Misther Adams; Misther Adams; I think this young man has been led asthray. He is a very foolish young man; is there nobody who will be answerable for him?'' Promptly there would be observed shining upon the court from a back seat the countenance of some jolly son of Bacchus, whose name would not carry much weight in any bank or counting-house—''I will, me Lord!'' ''Oh-h! Oh-h! And who is this respectable gentleman that has so charitably come forward? Come down here, sir; I'm much obliged to you. Prisoner, you should be very grateful to this worthy gentleman, who is saving you from the disgrace of prison. Let him be bound over, Misther O'Grady; and he may go.''

Such was the man who first attracted my attention to the Irish Bench; and Mr. Ford's services had not been invoked on the prisoner's behalf on that occasion. He was a lad of seventeen; he had just been found guilty of moonlighting (an abominable offence, if he were really guilty of it—those were the days of Sergeant Sheridan and his like); and the Judge sent him to penal servitude for seven years. I can still hear the young voice calling out: "Don't be crying, Mother; it won't take so long." But I fear it took the whole seven years, save such remission as he may have earned in the ordinary way. Meanwhile, the moonlighting went on.

About the general merits of the Irish Land War, few people to-day hold any but the one opinion. In spite of the efforts of some good landlords, Irish landlordism was deservedly a byword, and the Irish tenant was treated in a way that the present generation find it hard to credit. The Nationalist leaders did their best for the tenants; but when constitutional means seemed to be securing little improvement, wild men took charge, and stained the movement with deeds of blood and blackguardism. The same causes have produced the same effects in every country in the world. The Irish were neither better nor worse in this respect than any other nation; but they at least could boast that, apart from political crime, there were practically no cases for the judges to try. Crimes of lust or greed or dishonesty were non-existent. Crimes of violence were plentiful; and were nearly all political.

In the 'eighties a fellow calling himself "Captain Moonlight" had set the fashion of threatening the inhabitants of boycotted farms, and following up the threats by raids carried out by masked men, who sometimes did much and sometimes did little harm. At its worst, moonlighting might be murder; at its best a cowardly way of frightening women and children. But it may well be imagined that convictions for moonlighting included both extremes; and sometimes a foolish lad who had never contemplated doing bodily harm to a soul, found himself doomed to seven or ten years penal servitude for his folly. The Irish could never understand why the severity should all be directed against one side, when the root evil was all on the other. A little of the modern spirit in those days might have spared half a century of trouble.

William O'Brien had in his day been mildly on the popular side in politics. He began life as a reporter on the *Cork Examiner*, and, like many another Irish journalist, turned to the Bar. He stood for the Borough of Ennis in 1879 against Lysaght Finegan, with some claim on Nationalist votes, for he had often defended prisoners accused of political crimes. Lysaght Finegan, his opponent, had fought with the French in the war of 1870–71, and was a free-lance in politics, with a leaning towards lost causes, or those supposed to be lost. He was adopted as Nationalist candidate for Clare, but all depended upon whether Parnell would take the trouble to cross to Ireland to support him. In my uncle's book he tells how he overcame Parnell's excuses, finally sitting up all night to call the Chief and cook his breakfast. Knowing my uncle and appreciating all his excellences, I still wonder whether that breakfast did not engender some of the bitterness of the Parnellite Split! As a result of Parnell's intervention, Finegan was returned, and O'Brien had to resume the humdrum life of the Bar for a little while. Through the influence of William Moore Johnson, the Attorney-General, he was made a Judge of the Queen's

Bench Division. Johnson rebuked O'Brien when the latter attacked Gladstone for declaring himself in favour of Home Rule for Ireland, saying "Gladstone turned a second-rate reporter into a first-class judge." But the praise of O'Brien's judicial eminence was more complimentary than true.

He was inclined to be lazy, a fault for which the genial Cork climate may have been responsible. Johnnie Moriarty, of whom we shall be speaking later, used to tell a story of a consultation that he had once attended in a probate action in which O'Brien was his leader. As was common on the Munster Circuit, the consultation had been located at the office of the instructing solicitor, Jeremiah Blake, a solid and slow-speaking Corkman, not over-appreciative of humour. Five o'clock had been named as the hour, at which time Johnnie and the lay client duly attended. At about a quarter to six the figure of William O'Brien was seen approaching; he strolled in unconcernedly, swinging his umbrella and whistling "The Last Rose of Summer." "Good morrow, 'Miah," said he, without a word of apology. "That man Michael Connor will be a most important witness to-morrow." "You can't call him, Mr. O'Brien." "Can't call him? B-r-r-rrrr! And why not, pray? And why not?" "He's the testator, Mr. O'Brien; he's dead. "Br-r-rrr! You know very well I didn't mean Michael Connor; I meant James Foley." "James Foley is my clerk, that served the sub-pœnas, Mr. O'Brien." An awkward pause ensued. Then Blake said reproachfully: "Mr. O'Brien, you haven't read your brief in this case." "R-read my br-rief? R-read my br-rief? And why should I r-read my br-rief? A pack of lies! A pack of lies!" On which excellent note the consultation began, and William quickly made himself acquainted with the case he was to steer to victory the next morning.

When he ascended the Bench he left behind him all trace of sympathy with the popular cause which he had once mildly supported. His attitude towards the man in the dock was one of fierce hostility. Most people are aware that, subject to certain exceptions, a prisoner must be tried without reference to his previous character, and juries are often astonished to learn after their verdict that the prisoner whom they have reluctantly convicted of an isolated case of dishonesty has in fact been leading a life of ceaseless crime. William O'Brien was subject to no Court of Criminal Appeal; he regarded the doctrine of fair play for prisoners as mere sentimentality; and when the evidence against an old lag seemed a little unconvincing he had no hesitation about saying to the jury: "Gentlemen of the Jury, by a merciful dispensation of the law I am not allowed to show you the character of the prisoner, which I have here"; and he would hold up a document and murmur to himself; "Twelve months hard labour, six months hard labour, three years penal servitude—— Oh, my! Oh, my!"; and then he would turn again to the jury and say: "But I think that if you could see this record you would not have very much hesitation about the verdict you ought to bring in." And there is a traditional story of one case where the Crown Prosecutor had rather bungled his handling of the witnesses, to the fury of the Judge, who listened impatiently to the speech of counsel for the defence and then, as the prosecuting counsel stood up to reply, waved him down angrily, saying: "Ah, leave him to me!"

Let those who deem that these tales should be taken *cum grano salis*, put them to the test. Recently the

Library of the Inner Temple received from Mr. Harold Murphy, K.C., the printed transcript of the trials of the Phœnix Park conspirators. The murder of Lord Frederick Cavendish and Mr. Burke on May 6th, 1882, was in every sense a horrible crime; it was also, what political assassinations rarely are, a cowardly crime. Usually the man who throws his bomb or fires his revolver knows that for him there is no escape, and that he will probably be torn to pieces by the crowd, before judicial retribution can reach him. But the Invincibles had been so effective in their conspiracy that they had hitherto paralysed the hand of authority; in the event it was eight months before any man was put on trial for the crime, and if the Crown had not obtained the services of informers, nobody could even then have been convicted. So wanton, so brutal, so cold-blooded were the circumstances of the slaying that I have always wondered at the halo of pity and romance with which popular opinion in Ireland endowed the murderers; and the only conclusion I have been able to reach is that the public were outraged by the conduct, not merely of the Crown but of the Judge. And, of his conduct, there stands the record. It will be appreciated by anybody familiar with the details of the crime, that, whereas none of the conspirators could hope to escape altogether, once the informers' evidence was there, for many of them there were vital circumstances, a skilful dealing with which might and in some cases did mean escape from the death penalty. Joe Brady, the first prisoner put upon his trial, was undefended; he was assigned counsel on the very morning of the trial, and, not unnaturally, the very experienced gentlemen so appointed applied for an adjournment of twenty-four hours to enable them to peruse the voluminous depositions and

B

prepare their cross-examinations. William O'Brien was the Judge; not a minute was he prepared to give. The Attorney-General demurred, and suggested that at least some opportunity must be given to the accused to confer with his counsel; the Judge rebuked him, and suggested he was failing in his duty to the Crown. This brief adjournment he unwillingly granted; but at the end of it Doctor Webb, the leading counsel for the prisoner, stated that it would be humanly impossible to conduct the defence unless he received the grace of twenty-four hours for which he had asked. The Judge refused it. " Then," said Doctor Webb, " I decline to lend myself to what would be only a farce, and I must refuse to defend the prisoner." "Your junior may have a better conception of his duty," thundered the Judge. "My Lord," said Richard Adams, "Mr. D. B. Sullivan and myself are entirely in agreement with what Doctor Webb has said." In half a dozen sentences I have summarised an unseemly wrangle which lasted for most of the morning; in the end the firmness of the prisoner's counsel prevailed and the day's adjournment was ungraciously granted. That the request was not unreasonable can hardly want proof; but if such proof were needed it was found later in the fact that young Tim Kelly, who with Brady had been the actual perpetrator of the murders, was only convicted after two juries, carefully selected by the Crown, had disagreed.

But the Phœnix Park murders were long before my time, and I am calling on tradition for nearly all my information about the first judge I ever saw. My father vouched for one story which, for its merit as an example of broad farce enshrined in tragedy, I venture to repeat. Not very long after his admission to the roll of solicitors he was retained for the defence of a man named Brown who was charged with murder. The circumstances were such as would have rejoiced the heart of any editor of a sensation-mongering newspaper. Brown and a man named Sheehan were neighbours in the vicinity of Castletown-roche, near Fermoy, County Cork. Brown had a pretty sister, and Sheehan was courting her; but his farm was a small one, and he had living with him there his mother, his sister, and his brother, all of whom depended upon the farm for their living. In an Irish country marriage the fortune that the bride brings is devoted to providing for those other than her husband whom her advent would be turning out of the home; but Miss Brown was not well blessed with worldly possessions, and not unnaturally the Sheehans were strongly opposed to a match that appeared to portend disaster for them.

At length Sheehan persuaded his relatives that a solution might be found in a new land; he proposed emigration to New Zealand, and it was arranged that the mother, brother, and sister should set out first, and that he and his bride should follow later. These were simpler days than ours, when one would expect all the details of such an emigration to be the subject of common talk; nobody seems to have bothered to ask by what route the pilgrims were to travel, or in any way to have informed themselves of the plans of the travellers. The one thing in which all the neighbours were interested was the farewell party to be held the night before their departure. And to this were gathered a large and jovial crowd, whose potations were encouraged so well that in the morning when they woke up it was to find Sheehan laughing at them for the depths of their slumbers, and telling them that the emigrants had gone off in the small hours while everybody was asleep. And this story was apparently accepted by everybody without question.

Sheehan continued to reside on the farm for some time; he wed Miss Brown, and in due course the happy pair set out for New Zealand, and had apparently said good-bye to old Ireland for ever and ever.

Years passed; the south of Ireland was visited by a drought so severe that all the habitual sources of water were inadequate to serve the public need, and long-forgotten wells were once more brought under contribution. On Sheehan's farm was such a well; it had been allowed to silt up for long years, but in this emergency the new tenant set to work to clean it out. The shaft was deep, and unpromising; but in its depths he found the skeletons of three bodies, two female and one male. Still attached to them were various fragments of garments and bits of personal property that proved them beyond doubt to be the bodies of Sheehan's relatives. When the fun had been fast and furious they had been beckoned out one by one and in the darkness felled with an axe; their bodies once down this deep deserted well, and their absence plausibly accounted for, there was little likelihood of a resurrection to trouble the married bliss of the murderer.

When I was a small boy we used sometimes to cross by ferry-boat from Youghal to Ardmore; the tolls for the ferry were collected by a white-haired, erect, and benevolent-looking man named Dunny. He was an ex-policeman; and his principal claim to fame was that he had been sent out to New Zealand to find and arrest Sheehan, which task he had successfully accomplished. On the story I have told one can easily spell out a case of murder against Sheehan, although perhaps one not free from doubts and difficulties. That such a plot could be carried out alone seemed improbable; various events were remembered which threw suspicion upon Brown, and he, too, was arrested and charged with the murders. In Ireland (and indeed in the England of those days) the prisoners could not give evidence at their own trial; it was decided to prosecute Sheehan first, and afterwards to arraign Brown.

Sheehan was duly tried before Mr. Justice William O'Brien; he was convicted and subsequently hanged. On the morrow of his conviction Brown was arraigned; he pleaded Not Guilty, and was defended by Richard Adams and my grand-uncle, D. B. Sullivan. The case against Brown was largely suspicion; but of course, although the prisoner could not be examined as a witness, it was necessary to put forward a story on his behalf, and if this story could be supported by testimony other than his there was no objection to such evidence being called. Counsel who defend prisoners have no more anxious decision to make than that of determining whether the balance of advantage lies in not calling any evidence and relying on the weakness of the Crown case (which may lay them open to the suggestion that if their tale is true it could be proved by evidence) or on the other hand in calling evidence to rebut the Crown case (in which case the witnesses so called may do irreparable damage under the hands of a skilful cross-examiner). This problem was causing the keenest anxiety to Adams and my grand-uncle and my father; for Brown *had* a story, which must be put in the cross-examination of the Crown witnesses, and it was a story which depended upon the support of quite a number of witnesses, all of whom were in court expecting to be called to expound it. So even were the advantages and disadvantages that the trial began without any determination having been reached; but at the conclusion of the Crown case it appeared to all the lawyers concerned that it was imperative to support the suggested story of the prisoner on oath.

When the Court was about to re-assemble after the midday adjournment, Adams and D. B. Sullivan and my father were sitting together, having at last made up their minds to go into evidence, when the door of the Judge's room opened, and Ford, the crier, came out with a purposeful air. Moving along the other side of the table, he halted in front of Adams, and, leaning forward, he said in a tense and meaning whisper: "Mr. Adams; *call no evidence in this case!*" Adams stiffened: "What do you mean?" he asked. "Mark my words," said Ford solemnly; "call no evidence!" And as he said these words a second time, the door opened again and the Judge returned to Court.

So strange an admonishment from Ford seemed to have no meaning at all, if it were not in fact an unofficial intimation from the Judge that he did not think much of the Crown case. So unnerved were Adams and his associates that they falteringly asked the Judge for the favour of a short extension of the adjournment, an application to which he readily acceded. He retired to his room again; but unfortunately Ford went with him, and it was impossible to probe the mystery further. A decision had to be reached. Nobody cared to ignore this strange oracle; and it was agreed that no witnesses should be called. The Judge was informed that counsel were ready; he returned and took his seat. "My Lord," said Adams, "I call no evidence." "Oh-h!" said the Judge, with a rising inflection; "a most important and momentous decision, Misther Adams; no doubt you have considered it carefully?" This was a douche of cold water; but, after all, it might be a bit of window-dressing; it could not over-ride the pronouncement of Ford. "My Lord, I have," said Adams. "Very well; address the jury," directed the Judge; and Adams began his speech for the defence. Not one word fell from the Bench as the speech proceeded; no hint of the comment that was to come. The Crown counsel replied[1]; and then the Judge began his charge. "Gentlemen of the Jury," he said in his most impressive tones, "you have listened with careful attention to the speech of Mr. Adams, and you now know full well, even if you had not known it before, the exact case which the prisoner desires to be presented on his behalf. Gentlemen, it will, no doubt, have occurred to you as it has occurred to me, not once but many times, that if there were one word of truth in that story, there must be sitting in this Court or within easy summons of it a large number of persons who could have gone into that witness-box to swear to its genuineness; and *not one witness has been called for the defence!*"

Adams gave a cry and collapsed; a pleasant fiction of the Munster Circuit insists that my grand-uncle turned to him and cried: "Oh! Richard, Richard, you've hanged the man!"—a splendid example of team loyalty, if it had a foundation in fact, which of course it had not. But all through that terrible charge to the jury the unfortunate defending counsel were as though possessed; and when the jury and the Judge had retired to their respective rooms, Adams began to rave like a man demented. He must see the Judge: he must rush to Dublin and see the Lord-Lieutenant; he must cross to London and see the Queen. But while he stormed and raged, the jury

[1] In Ireland the Crown always had last word.

suddenly ʝreturned, and before Adams could say or do anything they had brought in a verdict of "Not Guilty."

Adams fell forward, this time in something akin to a faint; he declined assistance, and, long after the Court had emptied, he sat on alone, his head in his hands. At last the Court-keeper came to lock up the building; Adams rose and staggered towards the Bar-room. As he crossed the corridor a figure came out of the Judge's room and passed in front of him. It was Ford. Adams gave a yell, and sprang at his throat; the terrified Ford screamed for help. "For God's sake, Mr. Adams; for the love of God, leave go of my throat; you're choking me." "You ruffian!" roared Adams; "you infernal blackguard! What did you mean by telling me to call no evidence," and he slackened his grip to enable Ford to reply. "Mean?" cried Ford. "Mean? Sure, Mr. Adams, you know well that I can't abide perjury!"

After such a story any other tale about William O'Brien would be an anti-climax; but I wish I could give in detail an account of the Cork Card Case, which gave the late Lord Atkinson his greatest triumph at the Bar. I have heard H. D. Conner tell the tale, and greatly regret I never made a note of the details, thinking that he himself, who had been the junior in the case, would some day publish the authentic facts. A member of one of the best-known families in Cork had been accused of cheating in the Cork Club; several eye-witnesses insisted that there could be no mistake, and his shame appeared irretrievable. But his mother was a splendid woman; she drove into her bank, armed herself with a heavy bag of sovereigns, crossed the South Mall to the offices of her solicitors, Messieurs Thomas Exham and Sons, threw her bag on the astonished solicitor's table, and said: "Mr. Exham, there's as much more as you may need; but my boy's name is to be cleared." Exham looked into the facts, but was inclined to take a gloomy view; however, he issued a writ, and retained John Atkinson to lead for the plaintiff. Apparently, the strength of the defendants' case, for they justified, was the variety of observation, each witness having a different view-point, and all agreeing in drawing a conclusion adverse to the plaintiff. Atkinson made full use of his local knowledge. Having fortified himself by getting very detailed particulars of the defence, he went into Court with exact information of the case against him and even of the witnesses likely to be called to prove it. Now, Cork is a place where everyone knows everyone else, and everyone laughs good-humouredly at everyone else's little idiosyncrasies. Atkinson had the advantage of personal acquaintance with every witness to be called; and in stating his case to the jury he pretended to forecast what each of them would say, doing an elaborate caricature of the speaker, and using his little tricks of speech. So faithfully did he do this that the jury, who had already laughed heartily at his imitations, could not restrain their merriment when the witnesses in fact came into the box, and, almost in the tones and phrases that Atkinson had used, told the story he had prophesied. The case dissolved in laughter; a tremendous triumph for the brilliant advocate who had conducted it for the plaintiff. But to laugh a case out of court is the hardest of all things to do, and cannot be done at all if the presiding Judge does not give his blessing to the process. And, whatever may have been the merits of the case, the reputation of the Bench was not improved when Mr. Justice O'Brien subsequently accepted from the proud and happy mother of the plaintiff the gift of a handsome residence at Douglas, outside the city of Cork.[1]

O'Brien was not amongst the humorists of the Bench; but he made at least one good joke. Students of the *Encyclopædia Britannica* will be aware that in the old days the police of Dublin succeeded in segregating the abodes of gay ladies, grouping them all in one district, perhaps thereby producing another illustration of the old saying, "The nearer the church, the farther from God." Not only were these ladies living under the shadow of the Cathedral of one Church; they had even acquired some property that was held in trust for the pious purposes of another. The trustees of this latter property sought to evict the damsel who presided over the revels; she put in a defence and counterclaim in which she was able to set out large sums that had been spent upon the repair and improvement of the building. This impressed O'Brien: " Misther Cherry, Misther Cherry," said he, "you appear to have taken benefit from the stewardship of this woman; don't you think you could make her some allowance?" "Oh, my Lord," said Cherry, "my hands are unfortunately tied by the fact that I am appearing for a charity." "A charity, Misther Cherry?" cried the Judge. "A charity? O-ho, I think that must be the charity that covereth a multitude of sins!"

[1] I am told there had been a bond of service between the Judge's father and the family of the donor. But the public did not thus explain the gift.

II

AT THE time when I first began my acquaintance with it, some years before I became a law-student, the Irish Bench could compare with any college of justice in any age. The Court of Appeal was presided over by Edward Gibson, Lord Ashbourne; he had as his colleagues Lords Justices Fitzgibbon, Walker, and Holmes. Sir Andrew Porter was the Master of the Rolls; he sat as Judge of first instance in the Chancery Division, his colleague being the old Vice-Chancellor Chatterton. John Ross administered the Land Court; there was no Probate, Divorce, and Admiralty Division, but Probate business was allotted to one judge of the King's Bench Division, and Admiralty business to another. The King's Bench Division was in excellent condition. It had as its Lord Chief Justice the redoubtable "Pether the Packer," more politely known as Lord O'Brien of Kilfenora. He was more remarkable as a personality than as a lawyer; but he had a good grasp of common law principles, and, when not too lazy to apply them, did very well. His strength as a judge lay in his uncanny knowledge of the minds of his countrymen; he handled both jurors and witnesses with great skill. Next to him in rank sat Christopher Palles, Lord Chief Baron of the Exchequer, the last of the Barons, appointed by Gladstone on the platform of Paddington Station as he went down to Windsor to surrender the seals of office on February 17th, 1874. Criticism is frequently directed at a government that exercises its patronage when *in extremis*. If vice this be, never did fault more remarkably burgeon into virtue.

For the next forty-four years Christopher Palles was as pattern of all that is great and good; no word could be written in his praise that would be extravagant. In the last decade of his life he was summoned specially to London to sit at the Board of the Privy Council; and English and Scottish Law Lords found out for themselves that his almost mythical reputation was well earned. John George Gibson was, I think, next to him in seniority; he was a brother of Lord Ashbourne's, sharing at least the family good looks, if not the family learning. He had an index mind, and loved to rattle off cases by name, leaving his audience to infer that he was well acquainted with their substance, and had discerned in each a bearing on the matter in hand. The credulous junior who rushed to fetch them from the Library invariably found that he had been on a fool's errand. But Gibson had dignity and a sense of justice; he was a cultured man, with a charming voice; and he was very emotional. At the hearing of the East Cork Election Petition in 1911 word suddenly arrived that his daughter was dangerously ill. His brother Judge hastened down to the Courthouse to waylay the Bar, with the result that when the Court sat the leaders on both sides, affecting ignorance of the bad news, joined in demanding a week's adjournment for the purpose of looking up legal authorities not procurable in Cork. Gibson was not deceived, and burst into tears. I thought the incident did honour to everyone concerned.

The runner-up of Palles was William Drennan Andrews. He was a descendant of William Drennan, the poet of the United Irishmen, of whom he inherited the virtues, although not his politics. In parentheses, attention might be called to the number of Sir Edward Carson's Ulster Volunteers who were the grandsons or great-grandsons of the United Irishmen of the days of the Union. William Andrews was a quiet, precise little gentleman, of wide and accurate learning, and of such probity that it used to be said of him: "When Andrews has stated a case to a jury, the only part of the verdict that remains uncertain is the amount of the damages that will be awarded to his client." His mild manner and punctilious courtesy must have added to the shock of his sentences, which were appallingly heavy. A prisoner tried by Andrews knew that his case would be put for him to the jury exactly as he would like to put it himself; but if that large measure of fair play did not avert a conviction he had to expect ten years penal servitude where another judge would have inflicted three. Andrews spoke with a thin, rather high voice, pronouncing all his words with his lips, very precisely and clearly. He was greatly esteemed by all who knew him: I think that even those who groaned under his sentences bore him no malice. One morning, shortly after his retirement, my uncle, Tim Healy, was driving through the Park to the Four Courts, and as he descended the Magazine Hill, a military convoy appeared coming up around the bend half-way down, on its wrong side of the road. My uncle, whose methods of driving were unorthodox and invariably *ad hoc*, swung over to his right, mounted the footpath, and turned the corner on the wrong side. A little old gentleman who had been peaceably taking the sun on the footpath had just time to scale the paling before we swept by. I could see him peering after us, as my uncle said to me, chuckling like a naughty schoolboy: "That was little William Andrews!"

Andrews coupled great industry with his other virtues. He was the Probate Judge, and every Friday evening he would cause to be brought home to his residence in Lower

Leeson Street the papers in every motion to be heard on the following Monday. When on the Monday the list was called, he would deal out his orders like a pack of cards, except, of course, in contested cases, which he would hear at length. Under him the business methods of the Probate Court were the admiration of the Four Courts. I think that he was assisted in these domestic labours. He had as his companion a nephew, not very long called to the Bar when I first appeared in the Library, but of sufficient standing to be able to be kind and helpful to one less experienced than himself. His uncle would take great pleasure in the knowledge that the Jimmy Andrews of those days is now the Lord Chief Justice of Northern Ireland, in which position I am told that he imitates his distinguished relative in everything except the severity. *Floreat!*

Next to Andrews must have come a warrior, beloved of all, held in esteem by everyone, but not for his judicial qualities. William Boyd in his old age was so kind to me that I fear lest what I write about him, not being read through the glasses of affection, will draw of him a picture savouring of the figure of fun, which in a sense he was, but not in the derogatory sense. Boyd had been appointed a judge in 1886, when the memory of the Invincibles was recent and when courage was the first quality needed on the Bench. Courage was by no means the least of Boyd's virtues; but his most remarkable quality was that he could smell fraud at a thousand miles. In the end this became an obsession. Boyd, once described by Dick Hennessy as "the last of the pagans," became a cynic and regarded all mankind as inspired by motives entirely base. This did not detract from his cheery good humour. He looked like Raphael's conception of Saint

Joseph; or, perhaps, what Raphael might have conceived a nautical Saint Joseph to be. For Boyd was every inch a sailor. When I was recruiting in the vicinity of Howth in 1915, I called at his summer residence. I think he had then retired from the Bench, and he was certainly well over eighty. The afternoon had been stormy to a degree; not a boat had put out. The maid said the Judge was not at home; but a roar came from an inner room: "Is that Maurice Healy? I *am* at home; don't mind that girl. I'm changing my breeches; I got soused in the bay this afternoon." He had taken his boat out, single-handed, in a storm that had affrighted younger men. I never think of him as having died; he ought to have been caught up in a fiery chariot, for never did I meet anybody so vital as he.

He had no reputation as a lawyer; he had been appointed primarily as a Bankruptcy Judge, to defeat the wiles of dishonest debtors, and he certainly raised the standard of commercial honesty. When he came to deal with the Common Law, the results were not always so satisfactory, but all the Bar liked him and helped him, and disaster was generally avoided. There was a very sensible practice at the Irish Bar, whereby as soon as the jury had retired in a civil case the counsel on either side made such objections to the Judge's charge as seemed proper to them; the matter was then argued, and when necessary the jury were recalled and further directed. Boyd was shrewd enough to recognise his errors when they were pointed out to him, if he wanted to do so ; he didn't always want to! He was full of prejudices, generally good healthy ones; and he was very obstinate, almost to the degree of stupidity. To these imperfections the advance of years added a considerable degree of deafness. I was present in Tralee about 1912, when an elderly peasant witness, having been sworn with considerable difficulty, solemnly turned to Boyd and said: "Me Lard, ye'll have to shpake up to me, for I'm very old and I'm very deaf." "And if you're only very stupid too," said the present Serjeant Sullivan, in a voice loud enough to be heard by everyone except the Judge, "you're well qualified to give evidence in this court!"

Boyd had no experience of the Criminal Law until the year 1910, when a reduction in the strength of the Irish Bench necessitated a call on his services for Circuit duties. There are so many good stories about that circuit that I must reserve them for a later stage; but the Judge returned to Dublin more firmly than ever entrenched in the affections of those who had practised before him. His uncompromising Unionism was forgiven him by those of us who were Nationalists when we remembered the loyal services he had rendered as counsel in Nationalist interests before his elevation to the Bench. In one case his firmness had drawn rebuke from Mr. Justice O'Brien, who perhaps felt wounded that a Unionist should prove a more loyal friend than himself to a cause he had abandoned. "Docthor Boyd! Docthor Boyd! Remember your duty to respect the Court!" cried the angry Judge. "I'll pay to the Court the exact amount of respect that it deserves," was the pregnant answer of the sturdy counsel who had been addressed.

William Moore Johnson might not have occupied his particular place in the hierarchy, if he had not remained sufficiently human to salute my uncle with a handshake on a morning when he appeared to prosecute him. This outrageous piece of chivalry was denounced by the Press, and poor Billy Johnson had to retire to a Judgeship paid about one-fifth as well as he had been rewarded as

Attorney-General. His vacation of the seat enabled William O'Brien (the political leader, a very different person from the Judge of the same name) to be returned for the Borough of Mallow. It was on this occasion that Johnnie Moriarty first appeared in Irish public life. He came forward as a *tertium quid,* but in consideration for a generous *douceur* from the Whig funds withdrew his candidature ; his votes, however, went to swell William O'Brien's majority. Four years later representation of the borough was abolished; Johnnie, in consideration of his chivalrous attempt to assist the Whigs, had been appointed to a Crown Prosecutorship on the Circuit. In 1886 he trimmed his sails to catch a Tory wind, and received further promotion.

Johnson in the meantime had ascended the Bench, and was acquiring a curiously mixed reputation. When he got his facts right his law was not too bad; but the difficulty was to get the facts right. In one case, the subject-matter of which was some Wyandotte hens, Johnson could not be prevented from referring to the birds as wild-ducks. In another, it was suggested that the defendant had not truly entered into a certain contract because he was drunk at the time. The plaintiff had produced the telegram he had received which was in precise terms. Johnson looked at it: "That's not the writing of a drunken man," he said. It took a great deal of persuasion to make him realise that the copy received by the plaintiff was not in the handwriting of the person who had sent it! "Wooden-Headed Billy" was his sobriquet, though " Golden-Hearted Billy " would have been a better-earned title. I have never forgotten a trial in Cork, probably in March, 1905, when a little barefoot post-boy was charged with having got a girl of less than

statutory age into trouble. Such cases were rare in
Ireland; this one was indeed a case of true love gone too
impetuously forward. I cannot remember whether there
was an actual trial or whether the accused pleaded guilty;
but I do know that Stephen Ronan, the Crown Prosecutor, thought it necessary to read a number of letters
which the lover had written to his lady; and one phrase
burned itself into my brain, and survives to this day,
although the rest which I have forgotten were all in tune
with it. Barefooted, with no education beyond what a
National School could give, this bucolic Petrarch addressed
to his Laura the following lovely words:

> "Far away from where I am now there is a little gap
> in the hills, and beyond it the sea; and 'tis there I do
> be looking the whole day long, for it's the nearest
> thing to yourself that I can see."

I watched the Judge; there was a tear trickling down his
nose. "Mr. Ronan," he said, "these young people seem
to be very fond of one another. Why couldn't they get
married?"

Stephen Ronan sniggered; there was not much romance
in his nature, and he had a trick of speech which made
every sentence seem to begin with a sneering smile.
"Heh!" he said. "Marriage is easy enough where there
is money to provide for it, heh!" "I don't suppose it
would cost a lot," said Billy. "Heh! More than these
young people could afford!" cried Ronan. "Will the
Post Office take him back if I bind him over?" asked the
Judge. There proved to be little difficulty about that.
"Come up here, my girl," said Billy kindly. The little
girl, heavy with child, came into the witness-box. "Do
you love the boy?" "I do, me Lord." "Will you

marry him?" "I will if he'll ax me, me Lord." "Now, prisoner, do you hear that? Will you marry her?" "There's nothing I'm more wishful for, me Lord." "There, now; that's all settled; are the girl's people there?" A little procession went into the Judge's room, where the bride was promptly endowed out of his own pocket; and I hope they all lived happily ever afterwards.

William Kenny was a judge of a very different stamp. For many years I regarded him with distaste, looking on him as a bitter pill, full of prejudices and fixed ideas, and without any visible kindliness. I think that the last criticism was unjust; those who knew him most intimately spoke well of him. His practice had lain more on the Chancery than on the Common Law side before his appointment as a Law Officer; his mind was dry and precise, and his oratory was devoid of the ornament that rendered the Common Law Courts more attractive than those of Chancery to the man in the street. He belonged to the ancient faith; and Hugh Holmes once said of him: "Kenny would give everything except his immortal soul to be a Protestant!" A Catholic Unionist was never a very popular figure in Ireland; and Kenny was heartily disliked by the Irish Party, who never missed a chance of girding at him in the House. Some caustic jibes of my uncle made the name of Healy sound unpleasant in his ear, as I found to my cost in the first few years of my practice. During the Tralee Assizes in March, 1915, he learned that I had been commissioned; from that moment I could not do wrong, and when I strolled into his Court at Cork during the Winter Assize of 1917, he adjourned the Court to fetch me into his room and overwhelm me by the heartiness of his welcome. I was then serving under the orders of his son-in-law, Colonel Robert Q. Craufurd, a great-grandson of Sir John Moore's General Craufurd of the Light Division; and it was good to be able to tell the Judge how my chief had distinguished himself a fortnight before during the German counter-attack at Cambrai.

If Kenny had not been bred in so narrow a stable he would have had every merit as a judge. His judicial manner was excellent; very like that of the late Mr. Justice Salter, whom he resembled in more ways than one. He was a learned and sound lawyer, and never was consciously unjust, although his complete incapacity to enter into the minds of humble people caused him sometimes to err unintentionally. He allowed his politics to influence his judgment, and was reckoned by Dublin Castle as a " safe " judge. But I am sure he faced the last assize with a clear conscience as a man that had honestly tried to do his best.

I think I ought to have mentioned before him one of the most charming of all the judges I ever knew: Dodgson Hamilton Madden, a don that had strayed into the Queen's Bench Division. Shakespearian scholars never weary of praising his wonderful book, *The Diary of Master William Silence*, wherein he has applied to the elucidation of the master's texts all the lore of deer-hunting and horsemanship which he acquired in the vacations he spent in the West of England. He pretends to have discovered a diary of the son of old Silence, the friend of Mr. Justice Shallow, in which are traced the steps of a courtship and marriage that supplied many of the incidents of the *Taming of the Shrew* and of the *Merry Wives of Windsor*. The hunting and the hawking described in the diary give occasion for much valuable textual criticism of the plays; and the whole thing is done with such friendly simplicity that the task of the critic becomes a pleasure. Madden's literary ability was of the highest order, but his legal learning, although considerable, did not attain the same level. He chirruped on the Bench, and it was always a day's pleasure to appear before him; a literary allusion would be sure to call down a compliment and give occasion for a little excursion into fields less arid than those of the law. But he tended to be diffuse in his judgments, which lacked precision; and he was not a strong judge. He was the author of a useful book on the law relating to the Registration of Deeds; and he wrote better than he spoke.

Sir Dunbar Plunket Barton was my own legal sponsor; not alone did he propose me for my Irish call, but he had been before and remained for twenty-seven years afterwards, one of the kindest friends I have ever known. The good red wine of Bordeaux informed his blood, for he was a great-great-grandson of the founder of the great house of Barton and Guestier in Bordeaux. (It may interest legal readers to know that the partnership between the Bartons and the Guestiers has gone on since 1694 without the terms having ever been defined by writing or otherwise; and there never has been even the shadow of a difference between the succeeding generations of partners. I cannot refrain from quoting this example of the admirable benignity of Claret!) Sir Plunket was rather a connoisseur in the matter of ancestors; for he had also succeeded in collecting the silver-tongued Chief Justice Bushe and the great Plunket of the days of the Union to hang upon his family tree. Although his appointment came from the Unionists, he was probably the most liberal-minded man on the Bench. "When I was a small boy," he told me once, " I was coming home from a walk with my father; and when we came opposite our house he pointed to the window of my mother's bedroom, and asked me to estimate the distance from it to the window of the corresponding bedroom in the house next door. I hazarded a guess of fifteen feet. ' Well, my boy,' said he, ' remember all your life that if you had been born fifteen feet farther east, you would have been a Roman Catholic!' '' This early lesson in tolerance was not lost on the future Judge, who had a great capacity for entering into the minds of his Catholic and Nationalist fellow-countrymen; and I never heard any criticism of his decisions on a ground of prejudice. His reputation did not stand very high when he was first appointed to the Queen's Bench; and his practice at the Bar had not been extensive. Only a couple of years before, Lord Halsbury had been very much criticised for appointing Darling to the English Bench, his practice and reputation being open to similar criticism. And it was Barton's brilliant cousin, Seymour Bushe, who made the excellent joke that was subsequently stolen for less appropriate application to Mr. George Robey. "Who's this fellow Barton that they have made a judge in Ireland?" asked a friend in the club. "What is his standing?" "Oh, my dear fellow," replied Bushe, "he's the Darling of the Irish Bar." Barton did not enhance his fame on the King's Bench side; but when Vice-Chancellor Chatterton retired he was transferred to the Chancery Division, where he built up a solid reputation. He found time in his leisure to contribute two articles to Lord Halsbury's *Laws of England*, and to write a considerable biography of Bernadotte, in which he showed a partisanship I never discerned in his legal work! He also wrote some studies on Shakespeare and upon his beloved Gray's Inn. His love of letters did not impair his diligence as a lawyer, and when he retired during the war, he carried with him the esteem of all who had practised before him. He continued to serve in various legal capacities in England until shortly before his death. He preserved his vitality to the last, including an enthusiasm for the game of golf which he had probably, more than any one man, made a popular game in Ireland.

George Wright was the last of the pre-war Unionist appointments to the King's Bench. There were three Wright brothers who came from Clonakilty in south Cork. They all had sharp noses and monocles; but there the resemblance ceased. George went to the Bar; Henry and Bob became solicitors. George had a lovely, soft Cork accent, and was a forthcoming sort of person; Henry was the coldest-mannered man I have ever met, although I have very good personal reasons for knowing that this rigid exterior covered up a great deal of kindness. Bob, the youngest, used to travel as Registrar to his brother George, a registrar being a sort of cross between the Judge's Marshal and the Associate in England. Bob was as good company as the heart of man could desire. I believe and trust that he and Henry are still alive and enjoying life somewhere in England.

George Wright was a most popular member of the Munster Circuit, and played a merry part in its revels. When the Cork Court-house was burned down in 1891 the Courts were temporarily accommodated in the Model Schools, the furniture of which remained *in situ* as far as possible. One morning George, who had only arrived the previous evening in time to take a leading rôle at the dinner to the Judges, came into Court with every appearance of not having altogether shaken off the mantle of the reveller. He polished his eyeglass with troubled assiduity, and, screwing it into his eye, proceeded to take a view of his surroundings. Never did a human countenance betray greater astonishment, and indeed he had some excuse. For, where he might have expected to see shelves of learned tomes, the walls were covered with coloured pictures of the mastodon and the ichthyosaurus and every other kind of prehistoric monster. Adams, seeing his astonishment, reassured him : " It's all right, George; they're real!" he said.

Wright's appointment as Solicitor-General gave great joy to his Circuit, coupled with the inevitable sadness of farewell; for our rule used to be that when a man was appointed to a Law-Officership his Circuit dined him; he returned the compliment; and then he must never come Circuit again without a special fee—an almost unknown thing in Ireland. When George entertained the Munster Circuit he did it in handsome style and his guests went home well content. Two of them were discussing the merits and demerits, if any, of their host, when one of them, Paddy Kelly, gripped his companion's arm and stopped him under a lamp-post. With the solemnity appropriate to such an hour and such a place he unfolded himself. "In one word I'll give you George Wright," he said. "He's on the border-line of genius; *but he never trespasses!*"

The only other member of the King's Bench that had been appointed before my call was William Heuston Dodd. He was a man of rough exterior that concealed much natural kindliness; but tact was not his strong point, although he had the saving grace of seeing and telling jokes against himself. He had a lot of good-humoured vanity, and liked to speak of himself in the third person as the Great Red Judge, or the Black-Letter Judge; and he had learning enough to justify the latter title, although it was not as well digested as it might have been. In a charming appreciation which he contributed to the *Irish Law Times* when Edward Cuming, K.C., died, he told a story of an afternoon when, having finished his day's work, he joined a pleasant parliament at the Library fire, and began to talk at some length about his younger days, when he had frequently been associated with Francis McDonagh, Serjeant Armstrong, the first Serjeant Sullivan and other notable leaders of an earlier generation. Cuming listened in grave silence; at last he said: "You were lucky." "Why lucky?" asked Serjeant Dodd, as he then was. "Why, look at the chance you had. You had all these big fellows to model yourself on; we have only you and Tommy O'Shaughnessy!"

. Dodd and O'Shaughnessy were not too friendly rivals; O'Shaughnessy invariably referred to Dodd as "the Mechanic," adding a sobriquet suggesting that the learned Serjeant's hirsute appearance was not limited to his beard. Dodd took shafts of this kind without wincing; he looked upon them as a tribute to a greatness that could not be attacked except by vulgar abuse. And Dodd had great qualities, amongst them loyalty. In the twenty years between 1886 and 1906 a surprising number of the Whigs in the Law Library shifted gradually over to Toryism; those who remained faithful knew they were cutting themselves off from promotion for an indefinite period. When Dodd at last ascended the Bench he sat junior to several men much younger than himself. He did not readily accept this secondary position, and I once heard Pether O'Brien very wantonly rebuke him and remind him that he was the junior judge. He had another great quality in that he bore no malice. I had many a fierce brush with him in Court during the very angry political squabbles of the days just before the war; and I am afraid we regarded him as a warm partisan on the side of our opponents. (It was the period when Mr. William O'Brien and his little band of Independent Nationalists were being baited by the official Nationalists with a venom they never displayed towards their Unionist opponents.) Once, when bloody war had raged all day between us, a note was flung down to me: "Dear Healy, come and dine to-night and forgive the Judge." And the dinner was as pleasant as the kindly charm of an old man encouraging a young man could make it. "Well, good night, now; don't be too hard on me to-morrow." "I'll give you all you deserve, Judge." Mutual smiles and a warm handshake; that was the way we got on in Ireland thirty years ago.

III

THE INSTITUTION which gave the Irish Bar its corporate personality was the Law Library at the Four Courts. There is no corresponding institution in England, although such places as the Library in the Victoria Courts at Birmingham are capable during the sittings of the Judges of Assize of capturing a little of that rare and precious atmosphere. The Bar in Ireland was open to very poor men, who could carry on their profession without any of the expenses which the English system of chambers necessarily imposes. Nobody can hope to survive his first few years at the English Bar unless he can gather from some source a few hundred a year wherwith not merely to keep body and soul together, but also to discharge his liability for the rent of chambers and the remuneration of a clerk. The Irish barrister had no chambers and no clerk. On the day of his call he paid a subscription to the Library and a subscription to the dressing-room at the Four Courts; I forget whether either institution exacted an entrance fee, but the annual subscriptions were two guineas and one guinea respectively. For the guinea paid to the dressing-room your wig and gown were minded and, when necessary, mended for you; clean bands were laid out every morning. When you went to Sessions or Assizes you found the robes you had doffed the evening before awaiting you in the country, having been sent by parcel post from the dressing-room, whither you posted them back when your excursion was over. As I am boasting of the economy of the system, I ought to mention that the cost was less than a shilling a time. Our brief-bags were stouter than those usual in this country, and a label with a little sealing-wax on the cords was all the packing or direction required.

The Library was still more remarkable in its services. I believe that its origin goes back to the time of Curran, when some bookseller had the idea of setting up a few shelves of books and reports in the purlieus of the Four Courts and hiring these to the barristers. Curran and his friends started a fund to purchase this library, which was afterwards handsomely housed, first in what later became the robing-room, and afterwards in a spacious building a little to one side of the central hall. The main chamber of the new library was a long hall divided by pillars into bays; a gallery ran around three sides of the room, one end being occupied by the staircase. The books were shelved in the bays, and in each bay was a desk of four seats; a similar desk, but of six seats, occupied the nave opposite the bay, so that for each bay there were ten seats. There were about twelve bays; seats were also provided in the gallery, and in a smoking-room opening off the gallery. In this way about one hundred and eighty seats were supplied; but a busy barrister would probably be in Court all day, and the juniors were glad to enjoy "seconds" on the seat of such a person. You could hold a seat against anyone except the legitimate owner; in this way accommodation was found daily for between two and three hundred members of the Bar.

Near the entrance a clerk sat at a raised desk, on which was a sheet containing the name of every practising barrister. No counsel would absent himself without informing this clerk where he would then be found, and the clerk would make a suitable note opposite his name. A solicitor desiring to imparl with counsel would ask for him at this desk; whereupon the clerk would roar

out the required name in a voice that could be heard
above the hubbub of the Library.   One's ear quickly got
attuned to react to the sound of one's own name and to
ignore all others.   If no spirit obeyed this summons from
the vasty deep, the clerk communicated to the caller the
note he had of the required barrister's whereabouts, and
the visitor followed the clue so given to him.

The Library was well stocked with reports and text-
books, several copies being taken of those in great
demand.   A number of "boys" (Mark, the "dean of the
faculty" in my time, must have been over seventy) were
in attendance to fetch the volumes required.   Some of
them were very helpful; Price, who has now become
librarian, could tell many a junior where to look for his
law.   Campion, who presided at the entrance, was always
a good friend to the newly-called.   I once returned from
some excursion to the country, to be told by Campion
of a mysterious and pertinacious visitor who had haunted
the Library all one day, looking for me.   "At least,"
added Campion judicially, "I don't know whether it was
for you or for your money he was looking; but I got rid
of him all right."   "What did you tell him, Campion?"
"Well, about the fifth time he came back we were getting
quite friendly and confidential; so I told him that you were
a very impatient sort of young man, always disappointed
because you were not getting on quicker, and talking
about going to America; 'and,' says I, 'as he hasn't been
here for the last two days, I'm thinking it's out to the
west he's gone, and you'll be wasting your time waiting
for him.'   And sure 'twas the truth I was telling him, for
where were you but in Tralee, and isn't that west enough
for anyone?"   "But you never heard me talking about
going to America!"   "I did so; when you came back

from Canada you kept telling them all that you would never be content until you had visited the States as well; so I'm not as big a liar as you think I am!'' Poor, faithful Campion, ready to perjure his immortal soul to protect my pocket!

Although the boys used to carry back the books each evening from the Courts, they never carried them down; this was the business of the junior counsel engaged in the case. None but counsel were entitled to take books out of the Library, which explains a jest dating back to my father's young professional days. At that time the Courts were plagued by a mad lady named Miss Anthony, who at first used to be represented in the ordinary way by solicitor and counsel, but soon grew impressed by her own abilities, and decided to argue her cases herself. One day she was being very troublesome to a Court presided over by the Lord Chief Baron, who at length said to her: ''Miss Anthony, I see your counsel sitting behind you; would you not be wise to leave the argument of your case in his hands?'' ''Ah, my Lord,'' replied the lady, ''that's not my counsel at all; he's only the young man I hire to bring down the books from the Library for me!''

At the conclusion of the day's work, counsel returned to the Library, which remained open until 5 p.m. One left one's papers in one's brief-bag on one's desk; at 5 p.m. the bags were collected by a service known as the ''Legal Express,'' and were awaiting one at one's residence an hour or so later. Next morning they were collected before 9 a.m. and were lying on their appropriate desks by ten o'clock. In the meantime their owners had taken an afternoon's leisure, had dined, had then settled down to a long evening's work on their briefs. We had our libraries at our homes; our consultations were usually held at 9 p.m. at the house of the leader, and sometimes gradually assumed a more sociable aspect than could easily be found in the Temple. I think that probably more solid work was done than is possible under the Chamber system. For during the day we took advantage of the proximity of others who had recently been treading the same ground, and thus saved an enormous amount of labour; while in our homes we could shut ourselves up and keep far more free from interruption than is possible in the Temple during the daytime.

The hours of the sittings of the Courts were distinctly gentlemanly: eleven to four, with a break from half-past one to two. There were no proceedings corresponding to those of the "Bear-Garden" over here; what is done by Masters here was there done by a single judge, who sat for Chamber Motions a little before his colleague joined him to form a Divisional Court. Vague memories of Boyd, J., dealing with a list of *ex partes* remain with me. A recurrent query: "D'ye swear there are documents?" suggested that the Judge was under the impression that every application was one for discovery. Kenny, on the other hand, was inclined to be pernickety, and parsed every order very carefully. George Wright cheerfully granted any application on the assurance "Well, Mr. So-and-so, if you tell me it's all right, you may take your order." Such confidence was rarely misplaced. If the Judge thought that the application required consideration he would say "Renew your application when my brothers come in." And I once heard the Lord Chief Baron say to counsel who had made an application to himself and Boyd: "This case ought not to be decided by a single Judge: renew your application next Monday!" This was not as ill-mannered as it sounds; for Boyd, who knew his limitations, usually contented himself with the words "I concur," trusting to the good sense of his colleagues to see justice done.   One day he was sitting with the Chief Baron and Madden, and at the end of the argument Palles, under the impression that there was no difference of opinion on the Bench, delivered his judgment.   To his surprise, Madden then delivered a judgment in the opposite sense.   Palles, who hadn't much an opinion of Madden, and none at all of Boyd, turned to his left and said: "Now, Boyd."   "I agree," said Boyd.   "You can't agree with both of us," cried Madden, maliciously.   "We've dis-agreed."   Boyd looked at him with lofty contempt. "Then I agree with you, Madden," he said.   Could revenge have been neater?

Another venerable story of these applications relates to one made to the Lord Chief Justice by Paddy Kelly, whose appreciation of the character of George Wright has already been mentioned.   Pether O'Brien liked it to be thought that he was, even still, a gay Lothario; a pretty witness would often turn the case before him, and a veiled reference to the weaknesses of mankind would always revive his failing interest.   And Paddy Kelly on the occasion of which I speak had not much legal support for his application, which he endeavoured to bolster up by reading the more salacious parts of the correspondence. After a while Pether lifted a deprecating hand.

"Mithter Kelly," he lisped[1] with a melancholy smile, "Mithter Kelly, it won't do; it won't do at all.   There wath a time when thuch thingth interethted me; but I regret to thay I am an exthinct volcano!"

Paddy was not in the least put out; "Begor, me Lord,"

[1] See page 200.

he grinned, "I think there's a r-rumble in the ould crathur yet!" Pether sat back, delighted; Paddy got his order!

Paddy Kelly was the most humorously witty man I ever knew. He was of humble and rural origin; somebody said of him that "he never lost the *blàs* of Barnagh," or in other words his native woodnotes wild remained with him to the last. He would not have had it otherwise, nor would we. Short and sturdy in his build, with a fine strong face, that rather recalled Danton, he had forged his own fortune, and when I joined the Munster Circuit was engaged in almost every case heard in Limerick. The wiser of the idle juniors went into whatever Court in which Paddy was to be heard. He was a good lawyer; but they did not go in to hear him arguing law. One never knew what flash of humour would suddenly illumine the dullest case. Once he was appearing before Lord Chief Justice Cherry in an action arising out of a dispute between two sections of the Jewish community in Limerick. The Judge was greatly impressed by evidence which shewed that the contributions in support of the synagogue averaged more than £5 per member of the congregation. He looked down at Paddy, who was, of course, a pious Papist, and said: "Mr. Kelly, I don't think that the members of your faith subscribe as generously as that to the support of their religion." "Ah, no, me Lord," replied Paddy, "but I understand that it takes the devil of a lot of money to save the soul of a Jew!"

On another occasion Paddy unconsciously endowed a musical comedy that was being tried out in Dublin. Some of the company visited the Four Courts, and heard Paddy opening what, in other hands, would have been a very dull Chancery action. "In this case," said Paddy, "my client resembled the young man in the Bible who wasted

D

all his substance, and was reduced to eating the husks of
swine. At last he decided to return to the bosom of his
family; he went home expecting a share of the fatted calf,
but all they gave him was the cold shoulder!'' This was
promptly enshrined in the musical comedy, and will not
sound new to London ears.

He dined one night with Pether O'Brien a few days
after the Chief had presided over a Divisional Court that
had dealt with a case of Paddy's. Pether loved the sound
of praise; and it was not long before he asked Paddy:
''Tell me now, Kelly, what did you think of my judgment in that cathe of yourth the other day?'' ''Oh, me
Lord, it was a sapient judgment, a valuable contribution
to our jurisprudence.'' ''I'm glad you thought tho; but
what part of the judgment appeared to you to be
ethpethially detherving of praithe?'' ''O me Lord, who
am I to select for special praise a part only where all was
so excellent?'' ''Ah, well, but there mutht have been
thome thpethial pathage that impreththed you.'' ''Well,
me Lord, if I had to choose one passage above another,
I'd choose that paragraph in which your Lordship pointed
out in such a lucid and mellifluous fashion that the tail
of a cow hangs down behind the cow, and not in front of
the cow.'' Pether was a little vexed by this leg-pull; he
turned the subject by asking: ''And what did you think
of my brother Madden'th judgment?'' ''Yerra, I declare
to God,'' said Paddy, feeling himself on safer ground,
'' it reminded me of nothin' so much as a pig sufferin'
from the effects of a strong diuretic—a little here, a little
there, and nothin' substantial anywhere!'' I may add
that Paddy employed one adjectival word where I have,
for politeness, been driven to use a whole phrase. Bucolic
observation had supplied a powerful analogy.

I am afraid that an appreciation of the Catholic Hierarchy, although in character, is apocryphal; its innate heresy denies Paddy Kelly's authorship. "The Irish Bishops," he is reported to have remarked, "are individually virtuous and sapient men, wise in precept and impeccable in practice. But 'tis a great misfortune that they should always fix their meetings for an occasion when the Holy Ghost happens to be engaged elsewhere!"

Paddy's opposite number from Ulster was John Bartley, who died without having achieved his life's ambition to sue out a writ of error. It was about the only process of law that he had not succeeded in employing. He had a tortuous mind; honesty itself in his personal relations with his neighbours, as an advocate he always preferred to reach his goal by the most devious of routes. During the Liberal administration before the war, a large number of Presbyterians suddenly remembered their Liberal tenets and were rewarded by appointments of greater or less profit. Somebody remarked to John, who professed that faith, but not those politics, that the Presbyterian religion was a very lucky one just now. "It isn't a religion at all," said John; "'tis a Trades Union it is!" On another occasion some of us asked him to explain to us the difference between a Calvinistic Presbyterian and an ordinary Presbyterian. "I'll tall ye," said John. "A Calvinistic Prasb'-tayrian believes all you Papishes wull be domned because ye're predástined to be domned; but we or'nary Prasb'-tayrians b'lieve all you Papishes wull be domned on yer mer'ts!" The English alphabet does not quite do justice to John's incisive northern accent.

A third of John's contributions to theology is to be found in the account of a case in which he was instructed to appear before the Lord Chief Baron, to whom he was like a red rag to a bull; for the old scholar realised that John had both learning and, as he put it, the industry to misapply it. When John stood up to open his case the Lord Chief Baron asked suspiciously: "Is there any question of religion in this case, Mr. Bartley?" "No religion at all, my Lord; all the parties are Presbyterians!"

There lived somewhere down in Connaught one of these men who deem it to be their duty to test everything by process of law. He was editor of a paper, candidate for all sorts of seats under the Local Government system, and a strong politician in every sense of the word. The result is that his name is generously scattered through the Irish Law Reports; and some case of his can be relevantly cited on almost any branch of the law. *Experientia docet;* he took to arguing his own cases; and the man who appears as his own counsel is a long-winded advocate. One day when he had held up for the entire sitting a court presided over by the Chief Baron, the old warrior grew impatient, and said: "See, sir, it is now four o'clock; would you not be well advised to take advantage of the adjournment to instruct counsel to argue your case for you?" "Oh, yes, my Lord," replied the litigant, "I'll have Mr. John Bartley instructed." "O God! no!" cried the horrified Chief Baron, determined to stick to the lesser of two evils.

John once defended a prisoner before Hugh Holmes, one of the soundest judges that ever adorned the Bench, and father of Mr. Valentine Holmes. The best way to approach Hugh Holmes was to condense your case into the shortest possible compass, cutting out all irrelevancies, and never repeating yourself. Unfortunately, counsel cannot make bricks without straw; they have to do their best with the material available. And John's client, who was charged with arson, had not deigned to supply any material at all for his defence. So John addressed the jury on his behalf, begging them to remember that his client was an orphan. The surprised Judge looked up, and saw in front of him, in the dock, a man about sixty years of age. "Ah, nonsense! Mr. Bartley," he cried. "If it comes to that, I'm an orphan myself." "And I hope, my Lord," replied John sweetly, "that should your Lordship ever have the misfortune to find yourself in the unhappy situation in which my client is now placed, full effect will be given to that fact!"

Poor John! I once saw him rise in Court when a case was called on; the present Judge Moonan stood up at the same time, and each began to address the Court. Moonan was only recently called at the time. John impatiently waved him down, and he subsided, supposing that John had been brought in to guide his 'prentice hand. The Court was obviously befogged, and at last suggested that John should read his affidavits. John demurred, and said he wanted to make his point quite clear first. After a considerable argle-bargle he consented to read an affidavit, which only made confusion worse confounded. At last the presiding Judge asked him: "What case do you think you are arguing, Mr. Bartley?" "I'm arguing M'Carron v. Quaid, of course," replied John, very truculently. "Ah!" said the patient Judge, "that explains it; the case that was called on was O'Carroll v. Lane." John turned to Moonan. "Why don't you get up and argue your own case?" he asked indignantly, making it quite plain that it was all poor Moonan's fault.

The Court known as No. 2, King's Bench was where Lord Chief Baron sat, and a very expert and very gentle officer named Yeo used to sit under him. The old Chief

Baron did not suffer fools gladly, and expected the latest called junior to discuss case-law with him as an equal. His appearance was somewhat terrifying to a neophyte. His lips were clean-shaven, but he had side-whiskers that met under his chin; his eyes were like horizontal slits behind his glasses, and his chin was his most formidable feature. He spoke with great deliberation and distinctness, and as each syllable fell from his lips his chin seemed to give it a whack to drive it home. When he grew impatient he always kicked the boards in front of his desk, and if there were no boards there he generally caught the associate's shoulders. At the same time he indulged in a strange gesture of his neck whereby he seemed to be attempting to bite his left ear. These were generally the preliminaries to a roar of: "WHERE is Mr. Yeo?" if that valuable functionary happened to be absent. Poor Norman Kough, who was a reporter in his Court, used to do wonderful sketches of him; but one of the best was a caricature by the present Professor Bodkin, showing the old man banging his fist on his desk, the legend being "Nobody gives a damn for this Court!" —a remark he actually made one day in his impatience.

Yet nobody was more patient or courteous when such qualities were appropriate. When I was first called there still appeared occasionally a more than ordinarily venerable junior, named Hyacinth Plunkett, who spoke in a round falsetto voice that in moments of stress was more piccolo than flute. Where nobody else would be allowed to waste the time of the Court, Palles always allowed this survivor from another world to divagate and extemporise as much as he liked; and he was always careful to see that the little cockle-shell was not overturned by too fierce a blast from the Bench. Not that Hycie Plunkett needed a lot of protection. A somewhat blustering opponent once tried to sweep him away by suggesting sarcastically that his knowledge of practice was out of date, and took little note of such statutes as the Common Law Procedure Act, to say nothing of the Judicature Acts. Hycie's piercing reed was heard to reply: "I admit, my Lord, that it is many years since I was called to the Bar. One of the advantages of those days, my Lord, was, that it was very difficult for anybody except a gentleman to be admitted to our profession." And he continued his argument without any further interruption.

The Chief Baron came into Court one day and began to sniff very threateningly. "There is a very unpleasant smell in this Court," he said. "O yes, my Lord," said Hycie, "we noticed it even before your Lordship came in!"

A well-known Nationalist, who had rather forsaken the Bar for journalism, used to come down to the Library from time to time, to show that he was still on the hazard as a practising barrister, hoping some day to be appointed a County Court Judge, as he afterwards was. (My uncle once caught sight of him on one of these appearances and asked: "What County Court Judge is ill now?" "Why do you ask, Tim?" "Why, look at the Banshee!") During his visits, not unnaturally, he was apt to "spread himself," as the modern phrase has it, about the old days when he had a very busy time defending political prisoners before Mr. Balfour's Coercion Courts. One day Hycie was a member of the group around the would-be judge, and took advantage of a silence to remark in piercing tones: "It must have been very dull, Mattie, when the day's work was over in those remote country towns: nobody to dine with except the magistrates?"

"Ah!" said the patriotic Mattie indignantly, "d'ye think I'd stoop so far as to dine with a couple of Removable Magistrates?" "O-o-o-o!" shrilled Hycie, with an apologetic gesture of his hands, "just to punish them, Mattie; just to punish them!"

I think that it was just before the war that an international Congress of Lawyers was held in either Paris or Brussels; the Library persuaded the Lord Chancellor to give Hycie a silk gown, and put up a fund to send him over in the magnificence appropriate to the *bâtonnier* of the Irish Bar. He is reputed to have expressed his regret to find that Malesherbes and Tronchet, who defended Louis XVI, were already dead. He, alas! followed them soon after his return.

Longevity was not uncommon at the Irish Bar. In my time Sir Francis Brady used still to come Circuit, although he was old enough to have opted to retain his practice and continue to be Chairman of Quarter-Sessions rather than become one of the new County Court Judges. What age that made him I do not know. Once he remarked that when he was a young man the railways had not penetrated to the more remote parts of the country. Our secretary, William Q. Murphy, brother of Mr. Harold Murphy, K.C., cried: "My God, man! Stephenson hadn't yet been born!" And when the Chief Baron tentatively asked during the Cork Assizes whether it would be possible to consult Siderfin's Reports in the city, the present Serjeant Sullivan replied: "No, my Lord —unless Sir Francis Brady has brought his subscription copy with him!"

Sir Francis had a passion for music, and not infrequently warbled a few notes in Court. I can remember an occasion when he was conducting a prosecution before Lord

Justice Fitzgibbon (in Ireland usually it was necessary to call upon the Lords Justices for assistance as Judges of Assize). Sir Francis, debonair and heedless of all around him, opened his brief, probably for the first time, as the witness was sworn, and the following somewhat unusual scene occurred. "Your name is Marmaduke Fitzroy?" "It is not." "And you live at Rocksavage, on the Douglas Road?" "I do not." "And you are a retired Army officer?" "I am not." Fitzgibbon had by this time recovered from his laughter at the first answer, which was hardly a surprise from the somewhat rough lips that had spoken it. "Sir Francis, Sir Francis!" he cried, "the witness doesn't agree with a word that you are putting to him!" Sir Francis lowered his brief, and for the first time caught sight of the coal-heaver who had been answering his questions, if questions they might be called. He looked at the ceiling, whistled a few bars of "Let Erin Remember," looked at the witness again and said blandly: "Then who the deuce are you? And what are you here to swear?"

IV

THE COURSE of legal education in Ireland ran on lines somewhat different from those pursued in this country. In the first place, one's arts education finished somewhat earlier; one was expected to have graduated at twenty. On the other hand, one did not enter as a law student until an arts degree had been obtained; with the result that professional life began at about the age of twenty-three, as over here. For many years the Irish law student could not be called to the Bar in Ireland without having kept a number of terms at one of the four English Inns of Court. By this regulation the Middle Temple has counted amongst its members, Curran, Grattan, Wolfe Tone, and a number of other distinguished Irishmen. The King's Inns in Dublin, always spoken of in the plural, was always one Inn, and, I think, must have owed the form of its name to the fact that when Inns were really resident colleges there were more than one group of chambers. This history of the Inn dates back to the reign of Edward I, when, of course, the King's writ hardly ran outside the city of Dublin; the new foundation was evidently subordinate, for an appeal lay from domestic rulings to the Judges at Westminster. A learned and interesting account of the troubled fortunes of King's Inns was published by Mr. Gustavus Hamilton in the year 1915, and will repay perusal. Apparently, the Society was constantly being chivvied from pillar to post; and it was not until the nineteenth century that they built their Hall and offices at the top of Henrietta Street. It had been intended that the new buildings should include sets of chambers for barristers, and some of these appear to have been mulcted of substantial contributions towards this end. In fact, no chambers were ever built; part of these premises originally intended for the Inn became the Registry of Deeds; a library was built adjacent, and it was hoped that the stately old Georgian houses which formed the quiet street would in time be let in sets of Chambers. Alas! before many years had gone by, the slums had swallowed up the surrounding area; one by one, the mansions were taken over to be turned into tenement houses; and in the twentieth century a barrister's progress to the Library, or to dinner, was not altogether free from the peril of street fights between warring bands of ragged children. The Library, once reached, was a comfortable building, and well supplied with books and reports, although I never discovered much space for their storage. Almost any afternoon one might stumble upon Archbishop Walsh, the notable prelate who exposed the Piggott forgeries, immersed in a study of some problem of the law relating to charities. But half a dozen students, and, on Saturday afternoons, a few industrious barristers, formed the entire body of beneficiaries of this valuable institution. Two servants in knee-breeches and buckled shoes were on duty daily; one of them appeared to have no charge beyond seeing that nobody ran away with the attendance book in the hall, but, the other, a genius named Horner, fetched and carried books all day, and entertained the neophytes with a vast fund of inaccurate information. Horner was as mad as a hatter, and pursued an implacable vendetta against the assistant-librarian, one Shrimpton. The Librarian, Joe Carton, did his work unobtrusively, and kept an amused eye upon the warfare between his subordinates.

The benchers of King's Inns had some rooms in the Solicitors' Buildings behind the Four Courts, as well as their premises in Henrietta Street; and a good deal of their business was transacted in these after the rising of the Courts. It was in these that the admission of students to the Bar was decided upon; the candidates were afterwards called, not by the Treasurer of the Inn, but by the Lord Chancellor, and in open court. Before achieving the status of counsel each candidate had passed through a three years course, the first year in the Law School of Trinity College, Dublin, or one of the Queen's Colleges in Belfast, Cork, or Galway; the other two years at the King's Inns. At Trinity we attended lectures from George Vaughan Hart on Real Property, from Baxter on Roman Law, from Leonard on Criminal Law, and from Bastable on International Law. I cannot imagine that they were very serious contributions to human knowledge, as I used to get over 90 per cent in my International Law examinations; on the other hand, I twice failed in those on Real Property Law, so perhaps the extremes may have merged in a golden mean, as I am quite sure that I never knew any International Law. The lectures were delivered at nine in the morning, and obviously were a mere " clocking device." On the other hand, the lectures at the King's Inns were delivered at half-past four, as they were always given by practising members of the Bar. We had the luck to have J. H. Pigott, afterwards a County Court Judge, as our Professor of Equity, and he was a really valuable instructor. The Common Law lectures were in my time given by a reporter named Thompson, who was sound without being brilliant. He had the easier subject: but he lent himself to leg-pulls. A fresh young student with a very innocent air once asked him whether one needed a licence to draw a conveyance. The reply was in the affirmative. "Then," asked the innocent student, "must every cabman have a licence?" "Yes, my young friend; but I would draw your attention to a fact that I should have thought was peculiarly familiar to you, that cabs are not drawn by cabmen, but by four-footed animals."

Once I rashly engaged him in argument. Not satisfied with his first reply, I pressed him further. "Mr. Thompson," I said, "let me put an example to you. I have an illegitimate child——" "I should never have suspected it of you, Mr. Healy," he replied, effectively putting an end to my quest for information.

But the great searcher after knowledge in our time was a certain Barney Hughes, who was old enough to be father to most of us. He had been a student when my maternal uncle, Serjeant Sullivan, had been reading for the Bar nearly twenty years before; and he had not succeeded in getting through the examinations in all the years between. He was the son of a wealthy baker in Belfast, and had no need of a profession to keep him fed and clothed. The only branches of the law upon which he ever betrayed any learning were those dealing with breach of promise of marriage and sheriff's executions; an unkind soul accused him of having taught himself by experience. When the patient John Pigott had voluntarily given us an admirable epitome of the Irish Land Laws, which took him three lectures to achieve, he asked whether there were any questions. Barney solemnly asked him whether the Wyndham Act applied to Ireland! This was native; I fear some wag put him up to asking Thompson in all seriousness: "Sir, does the phrase 'en ventre sa mère' mean the same thing as 'in loco parentis'?"

Accidentally I mentioned in the presence of my uncle, Tim Healy, that Barney had not yet been called. My uncle was indignant; he declared that Barney's father, Peter Hughes, was one of the decentest men that ever stepped in Belfast, and that something must be done about it. After the next meeting of the Benchers, Pigott called Barney up and said: "Mr. Hughes, I am instructed to give you the benefit of a special examination. Can you tell me what is a tort?" Barney unfortunately mistook the vowel, and gave a somewhat unexpected reply. Pigott tried again with several elementary questions, but without avail. At last he said: "Mr. Hughes, what is your name?" and succeeded in getting a correct answer. He made report that the candidate had answered one question correctly and with intelligence, and Barney was duly called to the Bar. He died, alas! a few years later, and a kindly source of innocent amusement was lost to us.

There was an honours examination every autumn, attached to which was a John Brooke Scholarship, and the winner of the Brooke was always excused three terms, which meant he could be called in October a legal year ahead of his fellows. Poor Poole Hickman, who died at Suvla Bay, was the runner-up one year. He was seen at dinner with W. F. Casey, the author of a successful and witty play then running at the Abbey Theatre. "Begor!" said a fellow-student, "there's the Man that Missed the Tide with the Man that Missed the Brooke!"

In England the newly called barrister usually reads for a period as pupil in the Chambers of some established junior. In Ireland such pupilage was not very common; the pupil had to go round at night to the residence of his mentor, and to sit near his desk or to follow him around the Courts during the day. The nightly pilgrimage and the risk of being ejected from the seat next his master's made perseverance in pupilage an uncommon virtue. I never formally read with anyone, although I enjoyed the run of my uncle's papers. The very day I was called Ned McElligott, then a rising junior and now Circuit Judge in North Munster, came up to me and said: "What are you doing here? Are there no Sessions to go to? Go up and hold my brief for me in Meade *v.* Aherne, and be sure to be off to Sessions to-night." So I went up to where George Wright was trying an action brought by an ex-Lord Mayor of Cork against a poor young Father Aherne, who had rashly said something that the plaintiff thought defamatory of him; I took a note there until four o'clock, and caught the 6.15 train to Cork, in order to attend Kanturk Quarter Sessions next day. I believe seals are flung into the water and learn to swim in much the same way.

Quarter Sessions in Ireland had little in common with the institution known by the same name in England. They had the same origin so far as criminal jurisdiction was concerned; but a practice had grown up whereby a plaintiff might summon a defendant before the chairman of Quarter Sessions by civil bill to answer a claim for debt or damages. Ultimately the County Court took a statutory shape very different from that it has taken in England; the County Court Judge was *ex officio* chairman of Quarter Sessions as well, and although the criminal business that came before him was a very small fraction of his total work, the name of Quarter Sessions came to be applied to his whole sitting. One day was usually set apart as Crown day; i.e. criminal work, appeals, and licensing business was heard on that day, with the assistance of such lay justices as chose to associate themselves with the Judge. The only occasion when lay justices took any part was when there was a chance of allowing a friend's appeal, or voting between two parties as to which should have a licence. On the whole, they did not interfere very often, and the County Court Judges were popular officers, possessing the full confidence of the people. Recorders in Ireland were also County Court Judges; there were only five of them. From the decision of a County Court Judge an appeal lay to the next going Judge of Assize, who reheard the whole case.

I think that all County Court-houses in Ireland were built from a single plan in the Office of the Board of Works. Some were smaller and some larger than others; but they reproduced the same discomfort in every country town. The façade consisted of a limestone wall, surmounted by a low pediment, and broken only by one large central window and two side porches. The porches were bogus; the Court itself was less wide than the façade by their width, and they themselves opened on uncovered side-passages leading to the two small rooms at the back of the principal chamber, one of which was the Judge's retiring room and the other sheltered the advocates. Sanitary accommodation was primitive, if present at all; its presence or absence proclaimed itself equally loudly. Against the back wall of the main room, or Court proper, was a raised platform which formed the bench, extending the whole width of the room save for two doors to provide access to the retiring rooms. Under the Judge's seat, but in front of the platform, was a built-in seat for the Registrar. In front of him was a table about six feet by nine; on the nearest part to him was his desk, and behind that was a chair facing the bench on which the witness sat. At either side of the table sat the advocates. Behind them their clients crowded; behind the table was the dock. Behind that again was a space and then some seats generally unoccupied, for it was hard to see or hear anything from them.

The County Court Judge generally went his round four times a year, and each judge usually was followed by a bar of some half-dozen members, who would thus be enabled to face the next Judge of Assize with a number of appeals from two sittings of the County Court Judge. The Munster Circuit covered the areas adjudicated on by five County Court Judges, those of Clare, Limerick, Kerry, and the East and West Ridings of Cork. It was permitted to all counsel to appear in the County Court; but only members of the Circuit could appear on Assizes, unless when paid a special fee. It was difficult to follow the Courts of more than one County Court Judge; sometimes a neophyte got rid of his shyness in one county and then transferred to another, hoping to do something at the Assizes in both. I never ventured to invade Clare or Limerick except at Assizes; I never held a brief of any description in Clare. I cut my teeth in East and West Cork; then I moved to Kerry, the fact that my father was a solicitor in Cork ensuring me a certain amount of work there as well.

My first experience of a County Court was in Kanturk, in North Cork: hard by the birth-place of John Philpot Curran, and, of more practical importance, close to Lonesome Lodge, Banteer, the residence of Mathew J. Bourke, K.C., Recorder of Cork and County Court Judge of the East Riding of Cork. The proximity of his residence to Kanturk rather inclined to make the local Sessions a "linked sweetness, long drawn out." But

E

I had committed the *gaffe* of mistaking the date, and arriving the day before he sat. An old-world solicitor, named Beytagh, saw me hanging around the Court-house and sent his clerk to rescue me. It was, I fear a break in the idleness of that office ; for the Land Purchase Acts had swept away all poor Beytagh's clients, and a man that would have found his proper setting in Boodles, was marooned in a quiet country town without a soul of his own kind to talk to. He and I became very good friends, and I think he took a sort of personal pride in such little success as I enjoyed. But on this fine summer morning he made a brilliant suggestion: why shouldn't I stroll over to Lonely Lodge, where I would be sure of a warm welcome from the Recorder?

I had no need of Beytagh's assurance of a welcome at Lonely Lodge. Matt Bourke, as everyone affectionately called him, was an old friend of my father's, and had already found several opportunities of shewing personal kindness to myself. Although far from an old man (he cannot have been sixty at this time) he also was a survivor from another world. He still employed the polished oratory of the eighteenth century; he was a well-read scholar, and his reading supplied ornament to his judgments. Not by any means lacking in humour, he, nevertheless, reserved his smile for the more classical jest; buffoonery was abhorrent to him. A touch of pomposity only served to endear him to us; he looked the part and needed the appropriate manner. He had a very shrewd, wine-coloured face, with iron-grey hair, and eyes that were perpetually twinkling. He had a pleasing voice, and it was one of his amiable vanities that he knew it, and played a little with it. Consciously or unconsciously, he modelled his speeches upon Edmund Burke; I had heard him being truly magnificent on more than one occasion in Cork Court-house. But, alas! the days of leisure had passed away; just as Napoleon snapped his fingers at the stately movements of the Austrian armies in Italy, so did the .young blades of the Munster Circuit outmanoeuvre Matt Bourke, who was constitutionally incapable of changing front in the course of an action. He, however, remained securely entrenched in the affection of his colleagues, nor would anybody have ever thought of making any attack upon that position. He had attained the three objects of his ambition, declared by him at his first Sessions in Mallow many years before to his friend Thomas Keppel: a competence, a house by the Black-water, and the Recordership of Cork.

As we strolled by the river after lunch that summer afternoon an eavesdropper would have thought that father and son were discussing the future of the younger man. In particular, he recommended me to study the art of cross-examination, and especially recommended to my attention the chapter in Serjeant Ballantine's Memoirs on this subject, a volume that he took the trouble to send me a few days later. Looking back on it now, I am not sure that I agree with him. All that can be learned about cross-examination is contained in a few principles; these must be applied to the particular circumstances of the case, but the fact remains that in nine cases out of ten a successful cross-examination depends upon the ammunition available. On the other hand, the examination-in-chief of a witness gives the artist full scope every time. Most beginners make the mistake of thinking that all they need do is to hold up the proof which the solicitor's clerk has taken from the witness, and ask questions out of it as though they were examining a child in his knowledge of the catechism. If the witness fails to repeat in the box something which the clerk has written down in the proof, these diligent advocates will go back again and again to try and hook the missing fish, thereby destroying the spontaneity of the witness's story. A good advocate will appear to be examining the witness "out of his boots." He may have a note; it will be better if he has not even that. And, by appearing to hold a natural conversation of question and answer, he will remove the witness's nervousness; he will make the jury think that this is not a story learned by rote; he will be enabled to keep his eye on the witness and by that magnetic control prevent any wandering. Only one art is more difficult; that is the art of re-examination. Herein the object of the advocate is to overcome the effect of a destructive cross-examination. This object is attained by a miracle; if you can't perform them, you had much better allow your witness to go out of the box without further question. I once heard Sir Edward Carson perform that miracle in this country, shortly after the war. His client had been grievously defamed; the defendants had justified, and in furtherance of their defence endeavoured to shew that he was something of an adventurer, living entirely upon his wife's fortune. Carson's case was that there is every difference in the world between the man who exploits his rich wife and the man who, having married a rich wife, allows her to help him. The plaintiff had been handled very severely; his wife was asked on the threshold of the cross-examination: "When did your husband last do a day's work?" and she had to answer that she didn't know. Then began a terrific bombardment. "Your husband is wearing a very handsome astrachan coat; where did he get it?" "I gave it to him." "Who paid for the Rolls-Royce you arrived in this morning?" "I did." "How much money did he put up towards the purchase of your mansion in the country?" "Nothing." And so on, through a minute examination of all the daily expenses of the married couple. Cross-examining counsel sat down with a very satisfied expression. Carson slowly lifted up his long, lean body, smoothed his silk gown, turned his melancholy face towards the lady, and said: "Mrs. X." He paused a moment to let the musical voice obtain its effect. Then in a sad, weary tone, as though the whole matter were very painful to him, "Mrs. X," he asked, "were you in love with your husband?" In the circumstances, no answer but one was possible, and therein lay the skill of the advocate. "I was," she replied, faintly. Carson looked at the jury for a moment; then lifting his eyes towards her he asked gently: "Is there any one of these things about which my friend has asked you which you regret?" Once again, only one answer was possible. "No," she replied. Carson paused for a moment; he appeared to be thinking. "Mrs. X," he said, "if the opportunity arose again to-day, would you be proud and happy to do it all again?" "I would," she cried, lifted by her advocate to enthusiasm. "Thank-ye, Mrs. X," said Carson, and sat down. The jury gave his client £5,000, and it was those three questions that won the verdict. Of course, the last was, technically, a leading question, and one which, by exalting the witness, achieved its object; but it was excusable in the circumstances, for he was only putting into words what it was already obvious to everybody in Court the lady was desirous of saying.

That story is not as irrelevant as it may seem; for whenever I tell it I am put in mind of that afternoon by the Blackwater, and a story that my kind host then told me of another case, in which the genius of the advocate, expressed in two questions, won a verdict for his client. The case in question achieved international renown, and the question at issue between the parties was litigated in English and Scottish Courts, as well as in the Irish. The net question was whether a Major Yelverton had legally married a lady named Teresa Longworth. Miss Longworth was a beautiful girl, of good family, who had volunteered to go out as a nursing sister to the Crimea; in the course of her travels she had met the Major, and love at first sight was followed by a form of marriage. The parties lived as man and wife for some time; then the Major, who had unexpectedly inherited a fortune, saw the opportunity of making a very splendid match for himself if he could only disembarrass himself of poor Teresa. I forget how the matter came to be litigated in England and Scotland; in Ireland an obliging butcher sued the Major for the price of meat supplied to the lady; if he were her legal husband, he would be liable to pay for her necessaries. He set up the defence that any relations between himself and the lady amounted to nothing more than a mere flirtation, and the alleged marriage ceremony was only a joke incidental to the pleasant dalliance.

At the conclusion of the defendant's examination in chief, Serjeant, afterwards Sir Edward, Sullivan, Master of the Rolls and later Lord Chancellor, arose. He was always known as "The Little Serjeant," in contrast to Serjeant Armstrong, the "Big Serjeant." But Sullivan was big enough to be imposing. He looked at the witness, and said, very slowly and deliberately, "Major Yelverton: did you ever love Teresa Longworth?" The Major started; he had not expected this, and he foresaw a trap. But only one answer was possible, so he straightened himself, and said: "Yes, of course I did." The Serjeant looked at him quietly; then, after a slight pause, more deliberately than ever, he asked: "Did you ever love her honourably?" And there was the Major, impaled upon the horns of a dilemma from which there was no escape. In fact, he twisted and turned through several answers; but the upshot of it all was that, unless he were to admit himself to be a designing seducer devoid of all honour, he was bound alternatively to admit that he had gone through this ceremony of marriage because without it Teresa Longworth had refused to be his. An Irish jury found no difficulty in returning a verdict for the butcher, which meant the establishment of the honour of the lady. The Courts of England and Scotland, unfortunately, took a different view. This hardly detracts from the triumph of Serjeant Sullivan, whose questions have always seemed to me a model that every cross-examiner should study. They have the inevitability of a master's moves in a game of chess.

On the day following this pleasant excursion to Banteer I held my first brief. My client's cattle had been seized to satisfy a judgment against her husband. Matt Bourke knew his fellow-countrymen in and out, and he disbelieved the lady and gave judgment against me. I wonder was he unconsciously avoiding any suspicion of bias in my favour? For, a month later Lord Justice Cherry reversed his decision and gave me judgment for the value of the cows. Cherry was not at all as shrewd a judge of human nature as was Matt Bourke; and I have often wondered where the truth indeed lay.

V

GOING SESSIONS in the old days in Ireland involved various discomforts and inconveniences, but the delights would have outweighed much more discomfort than we ever suffered. Oddly enough, we were worse off in East Cork than elsewhere. Hotels were very bad, trains were inconvenient, and the motor-car was not yet sufficiently established to provide an alternative means of progress. At the end of a twenty-mile drive over the old limestone roads of County Cork, you could collect about two pounds weight of dust from your clothes. The last time I drove through the county I found roads that would compare favourably with any roads in the world. In the same way progress has been attained in the provision of comfortable hotels and restaurants; we were dependent upon hostelries closely resembling those described by George Birmingham, and in the Somerville and Ross books. West Cork and Kerry were better provided; the tourist traffic encouraged a higher standard of comfort, and we had the benefit. But the cinematograph theatre had not yet established itself in the country towns; we had to be self-contained as regards our amusements, which rarely got beyond a country walk, or the perusal of such books as we had the forethought to bring with us.

The local Bar were once stranded for the night at Kanturk, Matt Bourke having risen early for some reason; and grief and desolation were to be seen on every countenance. The venerable proprietor of Johnson's Hotel was profoundly concerned that his guests should thus be marooned without amusement; he produced the best dinner his house could provide, and that is to be read as a term of high praise. But Edward Camillus Ronayne, dean of our local faculty, refused to be comforted; he wanted amusement, new faces to look upon, something other than the perpetual discussion of the cases that had just been heard, or the stories of what Tim Doolan had said when Tom Duffy sued him for the price of the horse, and suchlike. Camillus was in a heavy sorrow; even that delectable brew yclept Guinness, seemed to be bringing him slight comfort.

And suddenly in came James Comyn with the news that there was a penny gaff in the town, and that they were playing *Maria Martin*, or some such play. Instantly all was confusion, as hats and coats were sought. An eager throng of learned counsel were soon to be seen making their way into the building that had been temporarily turned into a theatre. The play was already well under way; a critical moment had arrived, for the villain, a horrible-looking elderly man in a rusty coat, was explaining to the heroine that she was be-trrayed; for by this deed which he held in his hand all her prroperty had passed under his contrrol, ha! ha! ha! And the beautiful maiden threw her eyes up to Heaven and wailed: "What shall I do-oo? What shall I do-oo?" And, the age of miracles not being past, an answering voice, the voice of Edward Camillus Ronayne, rang through the building uttering the unexpected advice: "Object that the document is insufficiently stamped!"

Poor Edward Camillus! His soul went out in glory, for he caught the cold that killed him when heroically handling the Youghal lifeboat in a bad storm. His father was a doctor, and sufficiently comfortably off to keep Camillus above the hunger-line. "That fatal four hundred a year!" as the old Lord Chief Baron used to say. Not that

Camillus enjoyed any such private fortune, which would have been untold wealth in pre-war southern Ireland. But he had enough to keep him from throwing himself into the arena with the enthusiasm necessary for great success; and he limited his forensic efforts to attendance at the East Cork Sessions and the Cork Assizes, which left plenty of time for sailing a yacht, and encouraging the youth of Youghal to man a lifeboat. He was a fellow upon whom the smallest quantity of alcohol had the most extraordinary effect; it turned him into a sort of Puck, mischievous and witty, but always good-natured (although he sometimes displayed his affection in these moments by the most painful grips and tweaks). He appreciated good literature and spoke well; he hated hypocrisy. Once when a certain Attorney-General was dining with the Munster Circuit, and was endeavouring to attribute his promotion to something other than the political hack-work that had really procured it, Camillus rose in his seat and, with a marksmanship that paid tribute to his sobriety, planted a dinner-bun just where the Attorney's waistcoat met his trousers, thereby bringing that particular speech to an effective close. As the law officer in question had formerly belonged to the Circuit, he knew better than to complain of this rough justice.

On the occasion of my first appearance at Kanturk Sessions my opponent was an elderly barrister named George Lawrence, bearded and gruff in appearance, but quite prepared to be friendly with anyone he thought worth knowing. Whether because he was already an old friend of my father's or not, I do not know, but he admitted me to the charmed circle at once. It was advisable not to get across him; he was a very learned lawyer, and he had a sharp and ready tongue. I remember that on the day he defeated me in my first case he had a passage at arms with an expert witness who would not agree with him. After some warm exchanges George asked: "What did you say your profession was?" "I'm an engineer." "Yes, yes, I know; but what kind of an engineer? For you're making no show as a mechanical engineer—and you're certainly not a civil engineer!" Then the fur flew.

Lawrence had a very high reputation with the Judges, and it was always a matter of surprise to me that he never took silk. He preferred to remain a stuff gownsman, living in Cork and confining his practice to the Courts in the vicinity of that city. I have no doubt at all that if he had chosen to seek practice as a leader in Dublin he would have met with a large measure of success, for he had that real essential to a lawyer's reputation, a sound foundation in the principles of the Common Law, and he could always be relied upon to deliver a learned argument upon any point that emerged without warning in the course of a case. I suspect that there were domestic reasons; I know that he suffered a sad bereavement which greatly affected him. One night as we changed trains at Mallow station, we found on the platform a scrap of a child that had momentarily lost its parents, and was crying bitterly. The great rough barrister that had been snarling and growling all day in Court snatched up the little tot and set to comfort it with a tenderness and confidence that were very moving. In a moment the tears were forgotten and the child was laughing happily at the jokes of the new father that had so surprisingly appeared. The real parents soon claimed their offspring; but I noticed that George Lawrence remained silent during the journey to Cork.

Much of the fun of the East Cork Sessions was due

to the good humour of the Registrar that Matt Bourke had inherited from his predecessor, Sir John Chute Neligan, who had appointed his nephew David to the post. David Neligan always adopted an attitude of appalling ferocity towards all who approached him in Court; but the request that appeared to be fiercely and finally repelled came to be granted silently in some miraculous fashion a few moments later. Once he contrived to have a pair of trousers stolen. It was the most humdrum example of larceny that could have been imagined, the thief having by some pretext entered David's room and walked off with the garments in question. But he had chosen a moment when there was not very much doing on the East Riding; and the wits of our fraternity set to work. Poor David's character was fortunately above suspicion; otherwise the embroidered version of the rape of his trousers would have cost him his position. In one rendering he was made pursue the thief through the streets of Cork, clad only in his shirt and a blanket, the poet blissfully overlooking the relevant fact that at the time of the larceny David was away from home. He had to abandon the comfort of wrapping himself in a rug in Court, as some officious member of the Bar would be seen to go pulling at the folds of the plaid to see if there really were a pair of trousers underneath. Through all this almost literal leg-pulling David Neligan kept his temper, and took vengeance on none of his tormentors. It is only to be added that his efficiency was equal to his good humour, and it will be appreciated what an excellent official he was, and, I hope, in some exalted sphere, still is. I have a suspicion that the last dread Assize may be interrupted at the outset by a cry from David: "You must prove service first!"

But far and away the most remarkable of the old familiar faces that I associate with Kanturk Sessions was that of James Rearden, too soon gathered to his fathers, and remembered with commiserating affection by all who ever knew him. At the time when I first met him he was about twenty-eight; he had served his apprenticeship and knocked off his corners, and was beginning to enjoy one of the best practices on the Munster Circuit. Of middle height, he bore himself with dignity; his black hair, dark complexion, rather high cheek-bones and prominent straight nose gave him a markedly Jewish appearance, which he regarded as a joke to be kept up, and carefully cultivated the habits and mannerisms of the Jew of the jest-book. I am sorry to say he was the most complete cynic I ever met. The ancient faith in which he was born and brought up never sat heavily on his conscience; I think that this emancipation caused him to choose a false set of values, and he determined every problem by the touchstone of the relative personal advantage to himself of either course. "Debonair" is the portmanteau-word I should choose to describe his appearance; he had tremendous charm, and was always an amusing and agreeable companion. His methods of advocacy, in the main entirely admirable, sometimes could not command my approval. Once, when cross-examining an expert on handwriting he was seeking to get from the witness an opinion in a centre direction. He adopted the device of going through "Best on Evidence," and picking out several passages that appeared to contradict what the expert had sworn in his depositions. He cross-examined the expert on these points, and when the witness expressed surprise that Best should have expressed such views, handed him the textbook to see for himself. After three such surprises, the witness was prepared to modify his evidence in view of what Mr. Best had written; on the fourth point he did not even ask to see the book. "And," said James, "I suppose that you would also agree——" and he read out the proposition for which he was seeking authority, but from a slip of paper he had concealed in the book. The witness fell into the trap and agreed. When James told me that story, I asked him what he would have done if the witness had asked to see the book again. "Oh," said James, "I should have told him that I was only trying how far he would go." I do not think he would have escaped censure from the Bench. But this kind of trick was not native to James; he learned it from Johnnie Moriarty, of whom more anon. Another, but perhaps less reprehensible, performance of James's took place at the Limerick Summer Assizes in 1910. This was the first occasion when Mr. Justice Boyd had tried crime; and he had been ladling out the sentences with such a heavy hand that the juries had ceased to convict in even the plainest cases, lest some prisoner that another judge would send to prison for six months might languish in penal servitude for many years. After a while Boyd perceived this, and in a case where James Rearden was appearing for the prisoner, he began to wheedle the jury. "Now," he said, "don't hesitate to convict this prisoner if you think him guilty, merely because you are afraid that I will give him a heavy sentence. There are degrees in every crime, and in this case if he were convicted I think I could see my way to give him a comparatively light sentence." James was sitting under the jury-box, with his back to the jury. He took his brief and wrote inside the fold in enormous letters: "He will give him at least seven years!'' and passed this missive, in full view of the jury, to his solicitor. The jury disagreed.

In all the years I knew him, and in the old days we were meeting several times a week, those were the only two incidents in his forensic conduct of which I did not approve. Normally, he was unbelievably good. He affected to know no law, although he was a Brooke scholar; but he always had the relevant case on the tip of his tongue and within reach of his hand. He pretended to despise oratory; I have heard him make the most powerful and eloquent speeches, using all the arts of the orator, choosing his words with literary judgment, and adorning his delivery with simple but graceful gestures. He was one of the best cross-examiners I ever knew; and he always knew how to leave well alone. How often does one see an inexpert advocate, who has had the good luck to extract from one witness an admission of value, put the same matter to another witness, who thereupon puts such a qualification on the admission as destroys its worth! He had a magnetic personality, and the smile on his handsome face seemed to destroy the confidence of the witness opposed to him. I know no advocate who ever defended prisoners with greater judgment or greater skill; when he prosecuted, he was fair, but deadly. If it had not been for his cynicism and opportunism, I think he would have had more of my heart than any other of my brethren on the Circuit; and nobody has grieved more over the last sad chapters of a life that appeared to be destined to such great things.

He had a delightful and delicate sense of humour; but he preferred to draw out the humour of others rather than play the leading part himself. He saw the funny side of every situation, and faithfully recounted it afterwards, no matter at whose expense. Bred in surroundings of more or less Nationalist tendency, he came to the Bar when it was plain to all that the Tory administration of Ireland was nearly at an end; at the same time what would in modern parlance be described as a "come-back" was being attempted by one of the most remarkable and one of the most unscrupulous advocates that ever practised at the Irish Bar. The success of Moriarty's efforts attracted the cynical appreciation of James Rearden; a great friendship set in between them which was only broken by death; yet it was from James Rearden that I heard many of the stories which caused me to look upon John Francis Moriarty as the danger-spot in the Law Library.

Johnnie Moriarty, as everybody called him, was called to the Irish Bar about 1877. He was born in Mallow, where his father practised as a solicitor; Dick Hennessy used often to tell in his presence the pleasant legend that his grandfather had been a highwayman in command of two gangs of robbers, one of which operated between Mallow and Charleville, and the other between Mallow and Kanturk. Any trouble with the first band was promptly suppressed by punitive measures undertaken by the second and *vice versa*; the result was a steady and lucrative business which enabled the chief not merely to article his son to an attorney but also to give him a good grounding in the principles on which he should conduct his business! Johnnie always smiled when this tale was told, and I do not suppose that anybody paid much attention to Dick's pleasant malice.

Johnnie had been a bit of a firebrand as a student; but his first entry into politics showed him in a better-governed light. The borough of Mallow had been represented by a Whig from time immemorial; the voters did not number more than a couple of hundred, and, election law being then by no means as strict as it subsequently became, there had been no difficulty in maintaining the party majority. True, in 1874, a Home-Ruler, Mr. John George McCarthy, had got in on a badly-split vote; but William Moore Johnson had recovered the seat in 1880, and retained it with an increased majority when appointed Solicitor-General. But, as has been told in a previous chapter, he was exiled to the Bench in 1883; and John Naish, Q.C., was sent down to take his place. In the fierce struggle then taking place in Ireland a notable part was being played by William O'Brien, probably the most brilliant journalist of a brilliant age in journalism. O'Brien, himself a Mallow man, decided to stand for the borough as a Nationalist. At first his advent occasioned little alarm to the Government candidate, who was confident that he would win in a straight fight. But at this stage Johnnie Moriarty made his appearance. He professed to be shocked by the extremism of William O'Brien, but to be unwilling to allow the seat to go to a Coercionist candidate; and he therefore offered himself as a Moderate to the good burgesses of Mallow. Then indeed did confusion and alarm break out in the Whig headquarters; O'Brien was proving a formidable speaker, and a split vote might be as fatal as it had proved nine years before. So ambassadors were sent to Moriarty; at that time it was not an offence to buy off a candidate; Johnnie accepted a handsome present and withdrew; the malicious say that he then transferred his supporters to the service of William O'Brien, who won by a large majority. This may be doubted, for if one person learned of it another would

F

also; and the fact remains that a Liberal Government, grateful to Johnnie for his patriotic self-abnegation, appointed him to a Crown Prosecutorship on the Munster Circuit within a few months of the election. This did not prevent him from assuming the mantle of Toryism in time to secure a more valuable prosecutorship from Lord Salisbury's Government when it assumed office.

About this time he married a wealthy widow; and for a while other interests occupied his mind. The newly married couple both liked good living and sport; they frequented all the leading race-meetings and backed their fancies freely, with the usual consequences. At last, at the beginning of the naughty 'nineties, Johnnie, who was deeply embarrassed by this time, made a bet with a book-maker named Silke, whereby he stood to win some five hundred pounds if the horse finished first. The horse did finish first; but an objection was lodged. Johnnie persuaded Silke to pay him his winnings before he left the course, Silke understanding that the cheque would not be drawn against until the ruling on the objection had been obtained. Moriarty sent the cheque by post to his bank, and by the same post sent off other cheques to other creditors, which cheques the bank paid out of the proceeds of the Silke cheque. When the ruling was made it was found that the objection had been sustained. Silke then sued the bank, or the bank sued Silke, I forget which; at any rate the whole story is to be found in the Law Reports, where the National Bank v. Silke figures as a leading case. It is right to add that Moriarty was not a party to that action, so that the statement in the report, that he obtained the cheque by fraud from Silke, must be read as *ex parte* and not evidence against a man who died a Lord Justice of Appeal.

After the Silke incident the only thing for Johnnie to do was to go bankrupt. At what stage his wife died I do not know; but it appeared that all her fortune was gone. His public examination took place before Boyd, who many years later told me how shocked he was by Johnnie's callous disregard of the interests of his smaller creditors. One of these produced a bill of more than £100 for goods supplied, and told a pitiful tale of the ruin this defalcation would mean. "I turned to Moriarty," said Boyd, "and I asked him could he do nothing for this poor man. Moriarty pulled out of his pocket a handsome cigar-case and said: 'I can offer him a cigar!' I nearly committed him? I wish I had now!" This was said at a period when Johnnie had become Serjeant-at-Law.

It is the general belief that Johnnie never was discharged from his bankruptcy. Every document lost in Ireland used to be accounted for by the allegation that it had been burned in the Cork Court-house fire in 1891. Johnnie's supporters always said that his certificate of discharge had probably caused the brightest of the coruscations in that holocaust; but nobody believed them. Johnnie did not worry about such matters; he went back to the Bar, and by sheer ability and force of character he soon fought his way to the very front rank of stuff gownsmen. Just after the Boer War the Government were unwise enough to prosecute a Major Stoddart in connection with some transactions in the Remount Department. Johnnie defended him so brilliantly and successfully that the entire profession felt he ought to be appointed King's Counsel, and he accordingly took his place in the front row about 1903 or 1904. He was once again playing about on the edge of Nationalist politics; and he appeared against the Tory Government in some important political

cases in the last days of their power. He made a brilliant
attempt to commit Mr. Walter Long for Contempt of
Court just before Mr. Long ceased to be Chief Secretary;
the attempt would have been successful if the decision
had not gone on party lines, three judges appointed by
the Tories voting against the old Lord Chief Baron, who
fairly flayed his colleagues in his judgment. Such services
as this by Moriarty were not forgotten when the Liberals
came into office, and he was appointed Serjeant-at-Law.
(There survived in Ireland three King's Serjeant's, who
had precedence over all except the Law Officers, and
were precluded from ever holding a brief against the
Crown. They received no salary, but they were supposed
to be briefed to assist the Crown when the Law Officers
were not available.)

Johnnie remained on the outskirts of Nationalism until
1910, when the result of the elections was to give John
Redmond a dominating position. Moriarty promptly
burgeoned forth as a full-blown Nationalist, but it was
obvious that he was only seeking promotion. He was
at length appointed Solicitor-General and after a short
interval he became Attorney-General. He held that
office during the most difficult period of Irish pre-war
politics, and no man could utter a word of criticism of
the way he discharged the duties of his office. He had
to deal with the Dublin Strike, with the beginning of the
trouble about the Volunteers, and with a number of other
ticklish situations. He put an end to an old agrarian war
in Kerry; and he achieved the paradox of keeping Ireland
in the most peaceful and law-abiding state ever attained
during the history of the Union, at a moment when three
different organisations were drilling and arming to
slaughter one another. At length he was appointed a

Lord Justice of Appeal; but he only survived his appointment for a couple of years. He died in 1916; and rumour has it that his last remark was "What won the 3.30?"

Moriarty was an advocate of amazing ability. Tall and powerfully built, he made full use of his height when dominating a witness. To see him slowly rise like a great snake uncoiling was calculated to make the stoutest witness quail; and as he screwed in his monocle he seemed to be capable of looking into the innermost secrets of your heart. He had a number of mannerisms, amongst them an uncomfortable, mocking laugh, with which he pleasantly led a witness along the path to a trap, only to fly at him as soon as he was in the toils. In the last week of September, 1918, I returned to France from leave, and crossed the Channel on the same boat as the late Field-Marshal Sir Henry Wilson, then General, who as senior officer on board took station on the bridge. I was immediately underneath him; he had a lot of the actor in him and he assumed a new attitude every half-minute. I kept watching him, wondering of whom he kept reminding me. Suddenly I realised that he had every trick of Johnnie Moriarty. I should not care to make too close a comparison, but undoubtedly Wilson had some of Johnnie's weaknesses, which did not help to improve the relations between England and Ireland.

Johnnie, however, was entirely unscrupulous in his conduct of a case. I remember seeing him uncoil to cross-examine a witness, whom he hypnotised with his monocle as he asked him: "I suppose you know that every word which you have just sworn has been taken down in shorthand?" "And *that's* a lie," remarked his opponent pleasantly. "Ah, I do wish you would not be interfering with my cross-examination!" cried Johnnie angrily. The spell had been broken; he never got back into his stride after an incident of the sort, and I always marvelled at the rash way he courted such disasters. Once, when convicted of completely misrepresenting the evidence, he plaintively said: "My Lord, I hope I may now continue my speech without any further wanton interruptions of this kind!" Another time he conducted in the hearing of the jury, and quite close to the jury-box, a long argument about the admissibility in evidence of a letter which he desired to prove. The Judge, Kenny, was rather deaf; a good lawyer, he ruled against Moriarty's contention. Johnnie immediately turned to his colleague, who was sitting between the jury-box and himself, and said in a whisper quite loud enough to be heard by all the jury, for it was heard by me at a great distance behind him: "It doesn't matter, the only value of that letter was that it contains an admission of So-and-so." And when Johnnie purported to read from a document when he was cross-examining a witness, it was always prudent to call for the document and make sure that it was being accurately read. Johnnie loved a *finesse*, and was not very particular if it was permissible or not. He seemed to me to prefer to lose a case by a trick than to win it by fair means.

He was devoid of religious principles, but he had a lot of superstition. James Rearden once met him unexpectedly in a Turkish bath, clad only in a towel and a pair of scapulars, the latter being the badge of a religious belief which Johnnie certainly never bothered to hold. When the Liberals returned and Johnnie became a suitor for office, he began to cultivate the outer signs of religious orthodoxy. Joseph O'Connor once went out to play golf with him at Dollymount, and as the tram passed a certain church Joseph was astonished to hear Johnnie break out into a torrent of abuse of the inoffensive temple. "What on earth is wrong?" asked Joseph. "For years," said Johnnie, "I have been taking off my hat when passing that building; and it was only yesterday I learned that it is a Protestant church!" He was once conducting a prosecution at Green Street at a time when he was Attorney-General; the prisoner was accused of murder, and was defended by Joseph O'Connor, the presiding Judge being the present Sir Thomas Molony, as well known for his piety as for his learning. In the middle of Johnnie's opening speech the *Angelus* bell rang, and several of the jurors were seen to cross themselves. Johnnie, who, it would be safe to bet, had not said the *Angelus* for forty years, solemnly turned to the Judge, saying: "Your Lordship will excuse me for a moment;" then he blessed himself and, covering his face with his hand, appeared to be deep in prayer. It is right to add that his irreverent opponent repeated the demonstration the next day, "so as to even matters out," as he said.

Johnnie's play-acting was not limited to religion; and was usually elaborately thought out. James Rearden called upon him one Saturday morning about eleven o'clock, and found him still in bed, reading Catullus. He could hardly have chosen a poet to whom he would have been more unsympathetic; and he must have known that this affectation of classical tastes would not deceive James Rearden, who knew him through and through; but he counted on James repeating the story to an audience, some of whom would be taken in and would help to build a reputation for him.

Once I was opposed to him in an action in the course of which he was completely overwhelmed by a single answer of a witness. Everyone who visited Cork in the first quarter of the present century will remember Flurry O'Donoghue, the porter at the Imperial Hotel. He practically owned the hotel, but accepted your tip with gratitude. He put his savings into the purchase of another hotel at Killarney, which was managed by his wife, who had the misfortune to have an accident when out driving one day. Out of the accident an action arose. In the course of her story Mrs. O'Donoghue happened to describe her little hotel with some satisfaction and pardonable complacency. Johnnie unwound himself with a sinister smile. " So you live in this earthly paradise?" he asked. "A regular Garden of Eden—tell me, have you any serpent there?" "No, Serjeant, but we'd always be happy to see you!" replied the lady, bringing the cross-examination to an immediate and ignominious conclusion.

VI

THE MUNSTER CIRCUIT was the only open circuit in Ireland—a noble argument for Free Trade, for its standards were probably the highest in the country, and it certainly produced most of the names that have lent lustre to the Irish Bar. The newly-called barrister sent a cheque to the Secretary in settlement of his entrance fee, and *ipso facto* became a member. But if a member of another Circuit desired to transfer to the Munster, he had then to be elected in the usual way; otherwise, anybody who had "blotted his copy-book" elsewhere could treat the Munster Circuit as a City of Refuge. It was not because of any trouble with his own Circuit, the Leinster, that Carson sought to transfer to the Munster; in the Courts open to the entire Bar he had done a considerable business for the Crown, and had made a good connection in the south-west. But the stern rule of the Circuits is the same in England and in Ireland; unless there is a very special reason, a man must stick to the choice he first made, and the mere fact that he would do better on another Circuit would be no ground on which to base an application for a transfer. Carson's application was refused, a refusal that cast no slur upon his character, forensic or otherwise. I am sure that many of my old colleagues share my own regret that a splendid exception was not made to the rule. Not that Carson in those days had built up any outstanding reputation; his phenomenal success in England was always a puzzle to his best friends in Ireland, most of whom rated James Campbell much above him. I think the explanation is to be found in the difference between the forensic methods peculiar to the two countries. Carson was quiet, sarcastic, and imperturbable; Campbell was flamboyant, hectoring, and excitable. Carson scored his points because he had read and re-read his brief; Campbell was a superb improviser, and trusted to his magnetic contact with the witness to guide his most daring excursions. But in the long run it came down to a question of character. Carson was a strong and sincere man; Campbell was a lath painted to look like iron. It was the difference between Rupert of the Rhine and Cromwell's Ironsides.

Now, Carson's manner suited the English Bar, and Campbell's manner suited the Irish Bar. Why? Because of the *personnel* of litigation in the two countries. The Englishman goes into a court of law unwillingly, fearfully, and especially apprehensive of cross-examination. No doubt there are occasional witnesses of that kind in Ireland, too; but the vast majority go to give their evidence as a cricketer walks to the wicket. Each is confident he will not be bowled until he has knocked up a good score; each is very disappointed if the bowler limits his efforts to preventing the score from rising, and does not attack his wicket. To see a Kerryman climb onto the table and take the oath would inevitably recall Macaulay's lines:

> But hark! the cry is Astur;
> And lo! the ranks divide,
> And the great Lord of Luna
>   Comes with his stately stride.

The witness would settle himself in the chair with which every Irish witness is accommodated, and would turn upon the enemy "a glance serene and high," which he would renew from time to time during his examination, especially when he thought he had scored a hit.

He would answer his own counsel condescendingly, much as the gardener might explain to you about the roses; and every now and then he would turn to the Judge in a friendly way and explain the effect of his last answer so as to make it easy for him. As the opposing advocate stood up to cross-examine him, he would stiffen; every faculty brought under strict control, he would listen to the first question, to see if he could not get in something really contemptuous in his reply. Sometimes he would merely turn to the Judge with a pitying smile, as much as to say: "Will you listen to what this poor omadhaun is asking me!" At other times his eye would sweep around the galleries, much as Mr. Gladstone might have emphasised a point by turning a flashing glance towards his supporters. To attempt to overthrow the testimony of such a highly-skilled partisan by the usual "I-suggest-that-you-are wrong?" kind of cross-examination, would be to court disaster. An apparent preparation for a frontal attack, very quietly made, would be followed by a thundering charge upon an unsuspecting flank; and then in the confusion of this surprise, some vigorous cut-and-thrust might well take place. Carson was not good at this; and Campbell was. In the late Edward Marjoribanks' *Life of Carson*, he cites a number of instances of English witnesses being bowled out by a cross-examination, deadly over here, but which would not have knocked a feather off a Kerryman. Instead of the awkward silence chronicled in the biography, there would have been an indignant repetition of the question, followed by an immediate turn towards the Judge, who would be swamped in a deluge of irrelevant matter, as though it were a complete explanation of the problem under examination; and by the time the witness would be brought back to the point he would have thought of a plausible answer to the actual question he had been asked. The difference of atmosphere between the two countries was twice exemplified in a case of my father's which came to be tried in London before the late Mr. Justice Darling. The point at issue was the identity of a valuable picture, and hosts of witnesses, many of them humble Irish folk, were examined on either side. One of these Irishmen, who had tuned his harp to the romantic air of his own County Court, was a shock to a judge of pedestrian imagination. Darling at last turned to him sternly and said: "Tell me, in your country what happens to a witness who does not tell the truth?" "Begor, me Lord," replied the Irishman, with a candour that disarmed all criticism, "I think his side usually wins!" A little later on, a very decent joiner was being examined as to happenings of a very long time ago. He confessed himself unable to answer a particular question, adding in a friendly way, "'Tis me mother that could tell you that. She often told me——." An immediate objection was taken to hearsay evidence, and a long and learned argument took place as to whether under some rule this answer could not be evidence. The witness followed the legal discussion with obvious pleasure and interest; but he most correctly refrained from interposing. At the end of twenty minutes counsel said: "Well, my Lord, I must only go to the trouble of calling the lady herself." He turned to the witness and asked: "Where is your mother at present?" "Oh, I don't know, sir; she's dead this thirty years!"

The art of cross-examining a witness of that mentality is obviously completely different from the skill ordinarily suitable to English Courts. And the Irish tribunals, judges, and jurors, knew their witnesses, and knew exactly how much to believe and how much to discount. One of the most skilful of English cross-examiners, now a judge, once told me a story which showed me two things, first, that he himself had not appreciated the necessity of adjusting the idiom of your cross-examination to the country in which it is set, and secondly, that an advocate may sometimes forget that he is cross-examining before a tribunal that may not understand the idiom of his cross-examination. The English barrister was prosecuting several prisoners before Courts-Martial in Dublin; the Attorney-General, Denis Henry, was briefed with him in all the cases, but was engaged elsewhere. One day Denis slipped into the Court; the Englishman did not even know him by sight, but on learning that he was the Attorney-General, he said: "You had better cross-examine this witness." At first Denis Henry demurred; then he agreed to do it. The witness came to the end of a long and elaborate story which, if true, proved a complete alibi for the prisoner. Denis stood up and said very quietly: "Where did you say you lived?" The witness repeated his address. "How many doors from the prisoner's house?" "Next door." Denis sat down.

Now the Englishman could not understand that this was, in fact, an excellent cross-examination—or rather, it would have been, if the tribunal had been Irish. Denis knew perfectly well that the alibi witness had probably been taken through his story by his own friends a hundred times, and cross-examined each time. As each weakness in the narrative would appear, a remedy for it would be found; and the most skilful questions in court would only produce prepared answers that would seem to strengthen the tale. On the other hand, every Irish judge or juror would know this quite as well as Denis; all that would be necessary to direct their attention to the probable falsity of the story would be to draw attention to some link between the prisoner and the witness. Denis had done that. But he had forgotten that the tribunal consisted in this case of five poor Englishmen, to whom the condensed cross-examination meant nothing at all!

However, we have wandered a long way from the Munster Circuit, about which I had intended to speak in this chapter. I am told that some at least of the charm of Irish conversation lies in the fact that the speakers are always prepared to follow any red herring drawn across the trail; without laying claim to the charm, I must plead guilty to frequent irrelevance. Let me now return to my theme. At the time when I joined the Circuit many of the old customs were dying out. In the old days nobody, no leader at any rate, would have ventured to travel without his silk hat; it was legitimate to advertise his arrival in a Circuit town by making an afternoon promenade of the streets, where a silk hat was apt to attract attention, silk hats in provincial Irish towns being the outward sign of a wedding, a funeral, or an Assize. Easier manners gradually banished the silk hat; but Matt Bourke continued to wear his until very shortly before I was called, when Edward Camillus Ronayne and some of his friends seized the offending tile one day in the Bar Room in Cork, and danced upon it. Again, it was *de rigueur* to travel first class, if the Judges happened to be travelling on that train; until some great man, just after I was called, arranged with the Great Southern and Western Railway Company to attach to the Judges' train a third-class saloon coach, into which the Bar were shepherded. The Judges and their Associates travelled first class; their criers travelled second; and the Bar went third. No doubt we lost in dignity, but we gained in privacy and good-fellowship. It amazes me that we were not able to arrange for first-class travel at third-class fares.

Once arrived in the County town, and duly settled in the Bar Hotel, the next episode was a stroll through the streets to let it be known that you were on the hazard. How any young man got going in a strange town I cannot guess. In England the less important prosecutions are conducted by counsel instructed by the clerk to the justices who committed the prisoner; frequently the sight of a forlorn young man in a white wig and new gown will awaken his commiseration and he will " give the boy a chance." A chance ought to be all that a young man should need. In Ireland I find it very hard to suggest how that chance came; for all prosecutions were conducted by specially appointed Crown Counsel, two being appointed for each county, much as the Treasury appoint their counsel at the Central Criminal Court. A dock brief was a great rarity; in England it is by no means uncommon to see a prisoner calling on the services of "any counsel robed in court, other than the counsel for the prosecution," and he is entitled to such services for the sum of one guinea. I remember a barrister at the Old Bailey who was thus selected by one of the accused in a housing fraud case which subsequently lasted twenty-four days. Furthermore, it had been adjourned to the following sessions immediately after his selection; a similar case was taken instead; and the poor barrister, since tragically dead, deemed it his duty to sit through the nineteen days of that case as an apprenticeship for the proper discharge of his duties towards his client! And, by the way, it is not generally realised that, since his late

Majesty, King George V, was pleased to dispense his
counsel from the obligation to obtain a licence to appear
against the Crown, leaders as well as juniors are liable
to be called on to serve the man in the dock for this
nominal fee. But I cannot remember a single dock brief
during my time at the Irish Bar.

I am tempted to tell one story which must sound like
a blast upon my own trumpet, and which, quite frankly,
I cannot expect anyone to believe. But there are at least
two of the actors alive to call me a liar if time and memory
have conspired to distort the facts; and as regards the
part of the transaction that took place in public, there
are records in the papers of the day. I shall therefore
tell my tale according to my honest recollection, and
await the results with interest. The Spring Assizes of
March, 1911, were my second circuit (for I had missed
the Winter Assize of 1910 through my unsuccessful effort
to sit for West Waterford in the new parliament). At
the age of twenty-three I had a good conceit of myself;
I was a glib speaker; my practice had already attained a
size far in excess of my deserts; and I wish that to-day I
could muster up one half of the confidence in myself that
I then possessed. The Circuit Judges were the old Lord
Chief Baron and Mr. Justice Dodd. The former was
President of the Old Boys' Union of my former school,
and in that capacity I had met him at committee meetings,
and, as the phrase goes, he knew who I was. I determined
to go the whole Circuit, confident that I was about to
overgild an already glorious name. I am happy to think
that the three weeks' experience effected some modifica-
tion of this view.

I drew a blank at Ennis; and it was in a somewhat
mortified frame of mind that I set out with a colleague,

Redmond Naish, to perambulate the streets of Limerick shortly after our arrival in that city. It was really very provoking; nobody seemed to recognise us here, either. And then I suddenly ran into Hugh O'Brien Moran, who had been a fellow-student of mine in Dublin, and who had just joined his father, who was a well-known solicitor in Limerick. He greeted me warmly; asked me was I free, and invited me to come and meet his father. Assuming this to be a mere social courtesy, I went with him, and we found the old gentleman sitting in his office, writing. He continued to write as Hugh said, "This is Mr. Healy, Father." There was quite an awkward pause; I made some banal observation, which was apparently unnoticed and remained unanswered. Just as I was about to suggest that my visit had occurred at an inconvenient moment, Mr. Moran looked up, blotted what he had been writing, and handed me three briefs: "There you are, Mr. Healy, that's all we can find for you this time," and he added a cheque for four guineas to the briefs. "There's nothing in the murder case; but the two civil bill appeals are nice little cases, and I want you to win those if you can." And he bowed me out, after a few civilities.

I was aghast. Cock-a-hoop as I was, a murder case was somewhat alarming. And when I read the brief my uneasiness was only increased. My client was an elderly woman who had lived for years with her invalid husband. He was not a pleasant companion, but their quarrels had been limited to words, perhaps because he was bedridden. And then as she was sweeping the room one day he called her a name, and she flew at him with the broom and battered him to death in the bed. The only glimmer of hope seemed to be that it was unlikely that they would

G

hang a woman of close upon seventy. But defence there seemed to be none. I feverishly searched the pages of "Archbold" that deal with cases of provocation; but I could find nothing to lead me to hope that I could expect to reduce the crime to manslaughter. Incidentally, I learned, by breaking it, one of the strictest of our Circuit rules: we were never allowed to work in the Bar-room of the hotel; work must be done in our own room or at the court-house.

At that time the prosecuting counsel for the city of Limerick were Wood G. Jefferson, K.C., and Laurence O'Brien Kelly. "Jeffy," as we all called him, was very fond of his own comfort, and was not attracted by the amenities of Circuit life. He arrived from Dublin that evening, and I overheard him telling Larry Kelly that he must catch the four o'clock train next afternoon. This gave me my cue. The defence of insanity had not then become the common form it has become in recent years; and there was just a scintilla of evidence of a mad strain in the case of my old lady. I had sent word to my client to hunt up all the evidence he could on this point; I also informed him of what I proposed to do, and of the part I wanted him to play.

It was not long before Jefferson approached me. It was the first time we had met on Circuit, although I had known him before; and he was only being natural when he greeted me with a warmth that was very pleasant to a young recruit. After a few minutes he said: "You're for the defence in that murder case, aren't you? I suppose it won't take more than an hour?" "An hour?" I said. "But I'm afraid it's going to go into a second day!" "What do you mean?" he cried. "Sure, it's the plainest of plain cases; you've no defence, and the whole thing is to put a complexion on the facts that will enable them to reprieve the woman." "Oh!" I said, "there's much more than that in it. My solicitor suggests that she was insane; he has already got some evidence to that effect, and he hoped to have more to-morrow." Jefferson's face darkened: "If that be so," he said, "good-bye to my four o'clock train." "Did you want to get back to Dublin?" said I anxiously. "Oh! I'm sorry; but you know, I could hardly shorten an important case like this just to help you, much as I should like to." "No, of course not, my boy; you must do your duty to your client. But it's most unfortunate; most unfortunate. I have a very important political engagement in Dublin the day after to-morrow; I don't know what I shall do." "Well, Jeffy," said I hypocritically, "if there's anything I can legitimately do to help you, be sure to let me know." "Thank you, my boy; I'm much obliged to you." And Jeffy went off to see what could be done about that important political engagement.

Next morning I was over at the Courts as early as possible; and to my delight I found that my solicitor had dug up a number of witnesses to various acts of eccentricity on the part of the prisoner. This was no time to remember the quotation:

> La gloire ne compte pas les voix;
> Elle les pèse quelquefois.

And, brigaded outside the Court where Jefferson would see them as he came in, the "evidence" looked very imposing indeed. So that I was not in the least surprised when he appeared shortly after, and, coming straight over to me, said: "Maurice, my boy, I have a great sympathy with you in this responsible case; it's not fair to put a heavy burden like that on your young shoulders. I've been thinking it over; of course, there's no legal ground to reduce the charge to manslaughter, but there was some provocation, and I've decided to take the responsibility of sending up a bill for manslaughter only to the Grand Jury." "Oh! Thank you, Jeffy," I cried gratefully; "I shall never forget your kindness; you have taken a terrible responsibility off my mind." "Not at all, not at all, my dear boy; delighted to do it; it's the right thing to do; it meets the justice of the case." There was a pause. "I suppose you will plead to manslaughter?" I looked at him in astonishment. "Oh, no," I said, "I can't. My solicitor has taken up this defence of insanity with great zeal; you might have seen outside the battalion of witnesses he has gathered, and I am sure he would not allow me to plead guilty to manslaughter, when the act was done in a spell of insanity." Jefferson gloomed; the four o'clock train seemed as far away as ever. He went off to talk to Larry Kelly, who plainly did not approve of his leader's line of conduct. Not finding any comfort there, he went out on the terrace overlooking the Shannon, and spent some time in uffish thought. Finally he came back to me. "Maurice," he said, "you know, this isn't a bad case of manslaughter. One must remember, not merely the words spoken that day, but also the nag-nag-nagging of several years; her husband had been a constant annoyance to her for the last ten years, or whatever the period of his illness was. And she only used the broom because she had it in her hand; she wouldn't have gone to look for it to beat him. No, it's not a bad case; and I'll tell you what I'll do. I'll go in and see the Lord Chief Baron, and I'll ask him is he willing to let her out with a light sentence if she pleads guilty to manslaughter; and then you'll avoid all the unpleasantness of a verdict of insanity and perhaps a life of detention in a criminal lunatic asylum.''

I was naturally delighted; and I so expressed myself. But I said I must consult my solicitor, and it would be better to know what view the Judge would take before going on what might be a fool's errand. So Jeffy went off to see the Chief Baron, having first armed himself with the important information that my old lady bore an excellent character. He must have made an admirable speech in mitigation, because he came back to tell me that the old man was most sympathetic, and that the largest sentence I need fear would be about six months hard labour!

I made my way to the cells, accompanied by my solicitor. Of my interview with my lay client I only remember that she was lachrymose, and that I drew the attention of my solicitor to the importance of exact timing in the control of the tear glands. She herself was only too willing to do anything she was advised to do. I came back and told Jeffy that the four o'clock train was all right.

Then came the final act. When the lady pleaded Jeffy stated the facts more as though he were mitigating her offence, and the prisoner worked in a suitable accompaniment of gentle sobs. When it came to my turn to speak I had prepared a somewhat careful appeal to the emotions, and I am told that I did it reasonably well. And at the culminating point, so well had my solicitor done his work, my client burst into a storm of passionate weeping, during which I sank rather incoherently to my seat. I ventured an upward glance at the old Lord Chief Baron; he was obviously very much moved.

He bound my client over. Brought into that building under a charge of murder, pleading guilty to manslaughter, she left the Court, a free woman; and Jefferson caught his train to Dublin. But I am afraid I lost the civil bill appeals. Certainly, old Mr. Moran never instructed me again.

VII

THE CIRCUIT during which I had the surprising adventure I have just described was not my first. I was called on June 8th, 1910; and on July 1st Lord Justice Cherry and Mr. Justice Boyd started off together on what was pleasantly christened "the Mad Assize." Up to 1909 there had been no difficulty about furnishing judges for all five circuits, which all went out and finished at the same time; I never remember any "remainders." For some reason, perhaps because for many years there had been an ex-Lord Chancellor to augment the personnel of the Court of Appeal, that Court had been laid under contribution for one or more Judges of Assize; and it had not been considered necessary to interrupt Mr. Justice Boyd's attention to the Bankruptcy Court. But when William Andrews and William Moore Johnson retired, the King's Bench, strong enough for its ordinary work, was not equal to the strain of Assizes; even the appointment of Mr. Justice Dodd left it short. So Boyd was for the first time let loose on the country. He had not had any experience of the Criminal Law since his appointment a score of years before; I doubt he had ever seen a prisoner enter the witness-box to give evidence, a privilege first conferred by Stead's Act in 1885, but limited in Ireland to cases under that Act, the Criminal Evidence Act not having been applied to Ireland. Boyd was possessed of shrewd common sense, a flair for the discovery of chicanery, a mind that suspected everybody of fraud, and good healthy prejudices in favour of Unionists and Protestants and against members of the United Irish

League and similar institutions. It is only fair to say that those who were the objects of his antipathy liked him well, so that he cannot have allowed prejudice to work much mischief. When he went out with a strong judge as his colleague, he had the good sense to discuss his difficulties and to accept advice; but he had a terribly poor opinion of Cherry, in which he was unjust, and declined to take counsel with a man whom he regarded with contempt. Cherry had owed his appointment to his fidelity to the Liberal Party. For twenty years, Tories had governed the country before Sir Henry Campbell-Bannerman formed his administration in December, 1905; most of the old-time Liberals were dead. I forget why Serjeant Dodd was not given a Law-Officership; perhaps because he had only secured a majority of nine in North Tyrone, and the seat was considered too unsafe to be made the scene of a by-election. Incidentally, when Dodd became a judge, Redmond Barry succeeded him in the representation, and in the next two elections the majorities were seven, and nine—surely a record in the matter of consistent voting! Of the other Liberals of the "Old Guard," Serjeant Hemphill was considered too old for office, and was given a peerage to get him out of the way; most of the others were cripples, and there had been the greatest difficulty in finding law officers. Redmond Barry was appointed Solicitor-General because it was assumed he was a relative of John Redmond's, and because he had had a hat broken when as a young student he went to heckle the speakers at a Unionist meeting. However mistaken the Government were about his political antecedents, they secured the services of a cultured and able lawyer who was an ornament to the Irish Bar, and who left behind him more affectionate memories than any of his contemporaries. It might well be said that Redmond Barry was the Frank Lockwood of the Irish Bar; no greater compliment could be paid.

Richard Cherry had not been a notable figure at the Bar. He was a conscientious plodder, with few forensic graces; but he had written a notable textbook upon the Irish Land Acts, and this had become as essential a part of the Irish barrister's equipment as the Annual Practice would be to an English lawyer. He did not enjoy a large court practice, and his mind was slow and philosophical rather than practical. His knowledge of his fellow-men was not extensive, and erred towards charity; a virtue in a saint, but not in a practising barrister. However, he had continued to fight hopeless seats in England, and in 1906 he captured the Exchange division of Liverpool. So he was appointed Attorney-General; and, although he did his best and gave offence to none, he can hardly be reckoned as one of the outstanding successes in that office. In 1909 when Lord Justice Fitzgibbon died, Cherry went to the vacant chair in the Court of Appeal; on the resignation of Pether O'Brien he succeeded him as Lord Chief Justice. He had been about a year in the Court of Appeal when I was called; I think that this was his second Assize, and his familiarity with the Criminal Law was entirely academic; although, if I mistake not, he had published a very useful little book on the subject. A less effective bridle upon the exuberance of Boyd could not be imagined.

The fun began at Ennis. Amongst the civil bill appeals listed was one wherein the plaintiff had brought an action for seduction against the defendant. The form of action is technical and conventional; in effect the lady, through her father, accuses the gentleman of being the father of her child. It is very hard to bring home to an Englishman the extraordinary standard of chastity that was in fact attained in Ireland in those days; virginal innocence was maintained by the vast bulk of the rural population, a section of the community comparatively unfamiliar to Mr. Justice Boyd. In the case in question the County Court Judge had quite properly assessed the lady's character and refused to believe a word she swore. She appealed; and the appeal came before Boyd. To him the very slatternly "victim" told her story; and to the young man's counsel she admitted to a general standard of life that was hardly consistent with rigid virtue. The young man in turn came into the box and told his version; he was a decent, quiet lad, of respectable family; and he denied the whole story, which reeked of improbability. Boyd looked at him. "You say you never had anything to do with this girl?" "Never, my Lord." "How old are you?" "I'm twenty-six, my Lord." "Have you ever had anything to do with any other girl?" "Never, my Lord." "Oh! my goodness! Twenty-six; and you never had anything to do with any girl! Do you expect me to believe that? Or anything else you say? I'll reverse this dismiss, and give a decree for £50 and costs!" And he swept the Court with a glance that proclaimed his own satisfaction that he had been able to detect a hypocrite in his fraud.

There was a sequel, either that Circuit or later; I think later. Boyd was the Judge; and at Tralee Assizes I was being led by Ned McElligott in a similar case, although our client did not appear to be quite as innocent as the Clareman. When we were discussing the case with him we told him of this earlier performance of

Boyd's and Ned said to him: "He may ask you also whether you ever had anything to do with any other girl." "Begor, that'll be a hard question," said the man. "It will not," said Ned. "Legally, he has no right to ask you that at all, so I don't mind telling you the proper answer. You just say to him: 'Ah, my Lord, is that a fair question? Sure, wasn't your Lordship young once yourself?'" "Oh, Misther McElligott, sure, I'd never dare to say that!" "Well, if you won't, you'll lose your case." And at last we screwed his courage to the sticking-place. Alas! vain are the wiles of counsel. There came out some new evidence about the alteration of a date on a letter which made it quite unnecessary to go into the general character of our client, who found himself doomed to pay for his frolic. And the anticipated question was never asked; and would have been forgotten, if Ned and I had not been dining with the Judge that night; and we told him the story. To our horror he burst out: "Oh! my goodness! McElligott, I'll never forgive you! Never!" "Oh, Judge," said Ned, "it was only a joke; I never thought you'd mind." "Mind? Mind? And you went to all that trouble, and then you never passed me up a note to tell me to ask the question? I'll never forgive you; never!" And he champed his teeth, and burst out into a hearty laugh, to our intense relief.

However, to return to the Mad Assize. Having set right the standard of morality in Clare, Boyd came on to Limerick, where it fell to his lot to try the crime in the county. He had told the High Sheriff of Clare that he was disappointed with the Clare list, as he had hoped to try a murder case (which, in fact, would have fallen to the lot of Cherry in Clare; the Judges alternated county by county between civil and criminal work). Limerick county now proceeded to oblige by sending before him a woman charged with the murder of her newly-born child; and, to do him justice, he tried the case very well, and did his best to persuade the jury that the proper verdict would be "Guilty of Concealment of Birth." Unfortunately, the jury suspected a trap of some sort; they insisted upon finding their verdict in the special form: "We find that the prisoner wilfully caused the death of her child by strangulation." "A most intelligent verdict," said Boyd; "where's my black cap?" Matt Kenny, who was defending, suggested that it was arguable that the verdict was not one of murder. "I'll hear you afterwards," said the Judge, "but I must sentence her first; give me my black cap." It then appeared that the black cap had been mislaid; so, most reluctantly, Boyd adjourned the case until the next morning. By that time the black cap had been found, and Matt Kenny had realised that the point which he had sought to take was a bad one; but he suggested that in a case of the kind it would be a farce to go through the ritual of sentencing the woman to death, when everybody knew that the worst that would happen to her would be a few months' imprisonment. "Oh, no, no," said Boyd. "You can't play ducks and drakes with the law like that. The statute makes it obligatory." He turned to the wretched woman in the dock. "Attend to me now," he said. "I'm going to sentence you to be hanged——." The woman gave a scream, and collapsed in the dock, to the great surprise and distress of the Judge, who was really a kindly man. "Don't mind, now; don't worry at all!" he cried; "nothing will happen to you at all, beyond a short imprisonment; but I have to go through this form, because the law says I must. So pay no attention at all to what I am going to say to you; it's the greatest nonsense, but I must do it; don't worry yourself at all." He turned to his crier. "Now give me my black cap." He assumed it and turned again to the fainting woman in the dock.[1] "Anne Malone," he said, "you have been found guilty of murder after a most careful trial by a jury of your fellow-countrymen. The little life that God sent you to be the prop and comfort of your old age you wickedly and maliciously destroyed. That crime was murder; and for murder the law prescribes only one punishment: the punishment of death. Expect no mercy here below; look to your God above for mercy, for the only sentence which the law allows me to pronounce is that you be taken from the place where you now stand to the prison where you last were confined, and thence to a place of lawful execution, and that there you be hanged by the neck until you are dead; and may the Lord have mercy on your soul!" He threw off the black cap and added excitedly: "Now, it's all the greatest nonsense; nothing will happen to you; take her away, and take care of her." And the prisoner, who fortunately had been unconscious during this vindication of the majesty of the law, was carried below. It is hardly necessary to add that she was reprieved a few days later, although some ten days after I heard the Judge uneasily wondering whether he had posted the letter to the authorities which was intended to invoke their clemency.

I have no memory of his court in Tralee on that occasion; but I dined with him there, and he told me a very amusing story. I have already said that he was appointed in very troubled times; and for many months he could not move without being conscious of the

[1] See page 9.

presence of a couple of detectives at his heels. This was very irksome to him, for he had not the remotest idea what fear meant, and he would have enjoyed a scrap with an assassin. At last the strain became too much for him, and he obtained leave of absence. He left no word of where he was going, got on board his yacht, sailed around the south coast of England for a few days, and then put into Falmouth or some other western port. It was long before the days of wireless; in fact, it was 1887, the Jubilee year, and Boyd intended to go to London for the celebrations. As he rowed ashore he became aware of two figures standing on the quay; there were the sleuths! How they had got there he never found out. He went to London; they were on the train, and he saw them outside his hotel the next morning. So he called them in. "Now, look here," he said. "This is London, not Dublin; can't you leave me alone?" They protested that they had to do their duty. "I know," said the Judge; "but don't you think it would be enough if you were to call around every morning to make sure that I was still alive?" The R.I.C. men grinned; they confessed that they had never been to London before, and that they thought they might make good use of their time. And so a bargain was struck; every morning they came to the hotel and got from the Judge a programme of the sights to see during the day, and, I have no doubt, privilege tickets to a number of places. At length the great day came when Boyd, amongst others, made his way to Westminster Abbey to take part in the Jubilee Thanksgiving Service. (It may have been Saint Paul's; I tell the tale as 'twas told to me.) The Judge had some difficulty in making his way to his place, which proved not to be of the best. As he looked round him he saw, perched in the centre of the front row of an excellent gallery of seats, his two detectives! When they turned up next morning, he asked them how they had managed to get such good places. "Secret Service, sir," was all they said.

After Tralee, Cork. Here indeed Boyd had a murder case to try; one of the most remarkable that I remember in the south of Ireland. A man named William Scanlan was accused of the murder of his young sister-in-law; she was found shot dead in a graveyard near Charleville in north Cork. The prisoner was a farmer of substance; I think he had made money in America. He had undoubtedly been carrying on an intrigue with the girl, and at the time of her death she was in a rather advanced state of pregnancy. If my memory serves me, she was decoyed to the churchyard by a pretence that the prisoner was going to meet her there and carry her off to America. No living soul heard the shot that killed her, although the place was not remote from traffic. On the morning of the crime Scanlan was seen riding furiously along the road towards a fair that took place many miles from Charleville. The evidence, although entirely circumstantial, left little room for doubt of the prisoner's guilt. The prosecution was conducted by Redmond Barry, then Attorney-General, who led Moriarty and Ronan for the Crown; the prisoner was defended by Ned McElligott and James Rearden.

Boyd had read the depositions on his way round the Circuit; to some interlocutor, rash enough to question him about the case, he remarked darkly and vehemently: "O-ho! The rope reins! The rope reins! 'Tis the rope reins that'll hang him!" Whether this meant that a rope reins on a horse was evidence that the rider must have saddled the horse in a sudden emergency—or whether it merely drew a parallel between the reins and the hangman's rope—or whether it had some occult meaning that never emerged from the Judge's mind, I do not know. But the trial was complicated by the fact that the witnesses included some who from one cause or another were unable to attend the trial; and in each of these cases the Attorney-General proposed to read the deposition, having first proved the necessary conditions. McElligott objected; and in his first objection made a really effective point, which, before the Lord Chief Baron, would certainly have excluded the deposition. Boyd listened to him with a look of bitter hatred. As McElligott sat down, before Redmond Barry could get up to reply, the Judge said: "Is that your point? Humph! I don't think much of it. R-read the deposition!" And each time the point was taken, Boyd waved McElligott down and said: "Let the deposition be read!" However, the climax came when Boyd charged the jury. At a particular point he said: "I will now read you the deposition of Bridget Foley." "With respect, you'll do no such thing, my Lord," said McElligott. "Bridget Foley gave evidence, and you cannot read her deposition." "I'm not going to read her deposition," said Boyd. "That was a slip of the tongue. Now listen to what Bridget Foley said." And he proceeded to read out from what was obviously a printed copy of the depositions what Bridget was supposed to have said. Now, a witness often says less in the witness-box than she had said in the laxer court where the deposition was taken, so that it is sometimes important to keep out the document. Boyd continued his reading; Ned McElligott, watching his own copy of the deposition, saw that, phrase for phrase and word for word, it was what the Judge was reading. So once again he protested. "I am *not* reading from the deposition," said the Judge. "Mr. McElligott, you have no right to interrupt my charge like this. Now I've lost my place. Where was I? 'The deposition of Bridget Foley, taken——' " "Well, my Lord," said Ned, "if your Lordship is not reading from the deposition, where do those words come from?" Boyd coloured, and looked very uncomfortable for a moment; then, with the candour of a schoolboy, he said: "Well, if I *am* reading from the deposition, it's only because the clear print is easier to read than my own badly-written notes. I'll now read from my notes, *and I'll be twice as hard on you!*" In the interests of justice it is perhaps just as well that the jury disagreed; for a conviction after such a trial could hardly have been allowed to stand. Whether error on the record could have been suggested I do not know; but at least the prerogative of mercy would have been invoked, and the entire punishment remitted. As it was, Scanlan was tried before the careful William Kenny at the following Assizes, and duly convicted and hanged.

I forget whether it was at that or a later Assize that Boyd tried another prisoner in somewhat unusual circumstances. The accused had been tried some seven or eight years before on a charge of rape; the Crown Counsel had not pressed the charge too hard, as it had seemed that the lady had not been very earnest in her resistance, and the jury had accordingly disagreed, with the result that the trial was adjourned to the following Assizes. In the interval the prisoner "levanted"; and for several years he wandered around the world, until one day, having taken the advice of a sea lawyer, he landed at Wexford; and hardly was his foot on the pier when a burly constable

H

of the Royal Irish Constabulary had him by the collar. "What do you want me for?" asked the accused. "For that rape you done eight years ago," replied the minion of the law. "Ha-ha," said the prisoner, "the Statute of Lamentations has run since then." "Begor, it has not," replied the constable. "Did ye never hear tell of the Statute of Nullum Tempus?" After this exchange of learning the prisoner was brought to the Cork Assizes and put on his trial before Boyd. He was defended by Michael Comyn. The Judge eyed the prisoner with marked disfavour; and when he came into the box to give evidence, sat back and fixed him with a basilisk look, and made no effort to take a note. Michael Comyn wound up an impressive re-examination by asking him: "Did you ever assault this girl on that day?" "No!" replied the prisoner. "Did you ever take any liberties with her on that day?" "No!" replied the accused. "Were you even in her company on that day?" "No!" said the prisoner; and Michael Comyn sat down. As the prisoner turned to leave the box, Boyd, whose glare had become more and more ferocious, and who by this time was breathing hard through his nose, said: "Tell me: did you throw stones at the old sow on that day?" Now, twenty-eight years have passed; but nobody has ever been able to discover what Boyd meant by this extraordinary query. The prisoner had no idea what it insinuated, and staggered back to the dock; counsel duly addressed the jury; and Boyd turned to sum up. "Gentlemen of the Jury," he began, "isn't it a nice state of affairs when decent girls like that can't go for a country walk without being attacked and ravished by fellows like that man in the dock?" After this impartial opening he settled down to deal with the evidence, and in the course of it he said: "A-ha! he can tell a lot of stories; but there was one lie he dared not tell; he had to admit he was in the girl's company on that day." "He never said that," said Michael Comyn. "What's that you're saying?" asked Boyd angrily. "If you've any objection to my charge, stand up and say it out like a man; don't be mutthering to yourself down there." Thus adjured, Michael Comyn stood up and said: "My Lord, your Lordship has just told the jury that my client admitted being in the girl's company on that day. My Lord, he never said any such thing." "OH-H-H! MY GOODNESS!" cried Boyd; then, leaning forward, and hissing out the words, he added: "FIFTY TIMES AT LEAST!" In the circumstances the second disagreement was not a surprise.

The sequel was a sad one. The prisoner came to be tried a third time before Mr. Justice Molony, as he then was, and was defended by another counsel, who somewhat unwisely brought out the fact that during the prisoner's absence from Ireland he had been engaged as servant to an Archbishop, which let in the unfortunate counterblast that he had been discharged from that employment because of a similar offence against the cook. So he was finally convicted, and got two years hard labour for a crime that in all probability he had never committed in those far-off days when he had been eight years younger.

In the meantime, Boyd had transferred his attention to the civil cases. There was a civil bill appeal about the value of a parcel which had disappeared during its intended journey from Miltown Malbay to Fermoy. In those days this involved beginning the journey on the West Clare Railway and changing to the Great Southern and Western system at Ennis. The owner of the parcel had sued the G.S. & W. Railway; but as he had been unable to prove that the parcel had ever been handed to a servant of that company, the County Court Judge had rightly dismissed his claim. On appeal his counsel called a witness who swore that a friend of his had been travelling by a later train that day and had heard the guard talking to a porter about having handed a parcel which was the same kind of parcel as this to the guard of the Great Southern train. "That's not evidence!" gasped the outraged counsel for the railway. "I don't want evidence; I want the truth!" said Boyd. It is not to be wondered at that in the circumstances he reversed the County Court Judge. "I'll give a decree for nine pounds in this case," he said. "The claim is only for five pounds," said Cecil Atkinson. "I'll amend it," said Boyd. "You can't— there's no machinery," cried Atkinson. "No machinery?" said Boyd. "Do you see that pen?" And he made the necessary alteration. "Any expenses?" "The plaintiff's railway fare is fifteen shillings," said his counsel. "It's only ten shillings," cried the agonising Atkinson. "I'll give him a pound!" thundered Boyd. By the way, the Chairman of the Great Southern and Western Company was Sir William Goulding, who also was the Chairman and principal shareholder in a big manure factory. I refrain from details of the case in which a passenger claimed that through the carelessness of the company's servants in charge of a part of a station, a pair of trousers of his had been ruined. The company's counsel suggested they were not irretrievably destroyed; they were still serviceable. "No, Mr. Atkinson," replied Boyd, " not even to the Chairman of the company!"

VIII

AT THE time that I actually joined the Munster Circuit, its oldest member, or "Father," was Stephen Ronan, K.C. I do not think I ever saw a greater contrast between two brothers than that between Stephen Ronan and his brother Walter. The latter was a solicitor practising in Cork; he was a tall, handsome man, genial and forthcoming, rather lazy in a pleasant way, and giving the impression that he enjoyed life—as indeed he well might, for he had a charming home and a delightful family and the means of providing for them; so what more could a reasonable man want? Stephen, on the other hand, was a bachelor; he was not more than about five feet four inches, and he recalled Falstaff's description of Mr. Justice Shallow, "a man made after supper of a cheese-paring." He had, nevertheless, been an active sportsman in his young days; he told me that he possessed the remarkable power of being able to catch a cricket-ball in full flight on the back of his hand! He weighed for years exactly nine stone. He wore a long beard of a whitening iron-grey when I knew him; he had a long nose, on the end of which perched a pair of steel-rimmed spectacles; and he smoked a pipe with a prodigiously long stem. He was cranky and irritable; he broke out into quarrels in Court upon the least provocation; he was afraid of nobody. He had seen the Bench manned by his juniors, until the Lord Chief Baron was his only senior on it; for some reason never appreciated by his colleagues, he was passed over again and again until just before the war he was appointed a Lord Justice of Appeal; and he promptly distinguished himself by becoming the most impossible judge we had ever known! "I declare to God," said a Kerry witness, emerging from Court after a brisk passage in the witness-box, "that new judge is like a bag of weasels!" And it was a fair comment.

I think that everyone agreed in esteeming Ronan the finest lawyer at the Irish Bar. A shrewd judge once told me that the three best lawyers in Ireland were Christopher Palles, Stephen Ronan, and Maurice Healy: I hasten to add that he referred to my father! Each of them was steeped in the waters of the common law, and looked upon statutory enactments as a bather might consider the limitations of his pool, or the dam that contained its waters. Before the Lord Chief Baron, Ronan never lost his respectful manner; he felt he was arguing with an equal. Before a judge of whom he did not approve, he took no pains to conceal his views. He hated Mr. Justice William O'Brien. At the end of a long argument one day, the Judge somewhat angrily said: "Misther Ronan, Misther Ronan, you forget yourself! You lay down the law, as though it were your province to do so; please remember that in this Court it is I who lay down the law!" Ronan looked at him; then he looked at the clock, and said: "And your Lordship will please to remember that I am here to teach you the law to lay down, so that, if possible, you may lay it down correctly!"

Ronan was not merely regardless of the polite phrase: he had the most eccentric habits in Court that I ever observed. When addressing a witness he invariably looked away from him and shook a pen at him. Once he was engaged in a Chancery action before the Master of the Rolls. The proceedings pursued their quiet and comparatively uninteresting way for most of the morning; the

Court crier, perched in a little pulpit at the back of the Court, gradually fell into a profound and peaceful slumber. Ronan stood up to cross-examine a witness, and his first few questions were asked and answered in conversational tones. Then Ronan turned his back on the witness, and, shaking his pen fiercely towards the crier's box, screamed: "Then where is the document, sir?" The unfortunate crier woke up with a start, gaped, and stammered: "I'm sure I don't know, Mr. Ronan!" The poor fellow was dismissed; but it is only fair to say that as soon as Ronan knew what had happened he immediately procured the reinstatement of this innocent victim of his eccentricity.

He was in the habit of punctuating his sentences with a curious nasal sound, something like a staccato bleat. As he grew excited, these noises were multiplied, and Stephen began to dance from one leg to another, to put one foot on the seat, to pull at his beard, and to do a number of other weird things of a gravity-removing nature. I shall never forget a case at the Cork Assizes in which he prosecuted a prisoner for the larceny of a large number of household articles, which the accused was alleged to have stolen from the house next door. The prisoner invoked the aid of the long arm of coincidence and said that all these things had been inherited by him from an aunt in another part of the country. I thought Stephen would explode with indignation: an indignation directed, not at the wickedness of a thief, but at the insult to the intelligence of the jury involved in the putting forward of such a defence. When he came to make his final speech, he addressed the first part to the dock behind him; he then turned to the Grand Jury box, which placed him with his back to the jury. By this time he had worked himself into a passion of rhetoric; he was prepared to accept coincidence in respect of one or two articles, "but, gentlemen, when we find that the missing goods comprise a chiming clock, a silver tray, a pair of candlesticks, a canteen of cutlery, a tea-urn, two silver dishes, and a snuffers"—he stooped under the table and began to pull out the articles—"and the very next day there are found in the prisoner's house a chiming clock" —he banged it on the table—"a silver tray"—down it crashed—"a pair of candlesticks"—thump! thump!— "a canteen of cutlery"—this took a little effort to pro- duce—"a tea-urn"—and he gave it a polish—"two silver dishes"—crash! crash!—"and a snuffers," and he held them up and attended to several imaginary wicks, "and the only explanation of their possession offered by the prisoner is that he inherited them from an aunt whom we have not seen——." There was a burst of laughter, and the Judge interposed: "You forget, Mr. Ronan, she is supposed to be dead." There was nobody left upon whom to turn his back, so Stephen looked at the ceiling and said: "Heh! Was she ever alive?"

There was a traditional story of the terrible revenge he once had taken on William O'Brien, when that Judge had been more than ordinarily offensive to him. Stephen had in some way enraged O'Brien, who took a malicious pleasure in jumping upon Ronan upon the least oppor- tunity. The most skilful and learned counsel will commit a series of peccadilloes every day, asking leading questions, or getting out a bit of unimportant hearsay evidence. Every time that Ronan offended he was pulled up by the Judge with a: "Misther Ronan! Misther Ronan! Where are we coming to now? You know you can't ask that!" And a series of observations about the duty of counsel and the peril of departure from the strict rule of law would follow. Stephen chafed; but as the Judge was taking great care to be correct, he could not successfully defend himself. The junior Bar grinned maliciously at the discomfiture of their leader; this did not prevent them from gathering round him in the Bar-room, at the luncheon adjournment, with hypocritical expressions of sympathy and regret. Stephen sat there in silence, puffing away at the long pipe. At last he rose, hobbled over to the fireplace, knocked out his ashes, and said as he stowed the pipe away: "If you young gentlemen would care for a little amusement, heh, just be in Court after the adjournment, heh. I promise you you will enjoy yourselves."

The Bar did not ignore this invitation; and it was in a very crowded Court that the hearing of the part-heard case was resumed. The Judge was even more overbearing than he had previously been; and there were many more passages at arms in which he appeared to score heavily over counsel. All of a sudden, Ronan interrupted his examination of a witness, and, looking very fixedly at the Judge, said to the witness: "Now, do not answer this question unless his Lordship permits it"; and he framed a very careful sentence which he put to the witness. There was an immediate explosion on the Bench. "Misther Ronan! Misther Ronan! Sure, you know very well that you can't ask that! Nobody who knew any law at all would ask such a question as that!" Stephen looked at him; an observer might have augured trouble from the light in his eyes. "I propose to argue it," he said tersely. And he framed an argument on first principles, without referring to any authority. The Judge broke in on him: "I never heard such nonsense; go on with your case, and ask some other question." "Oh, but I had not finished!" cried

Ronan; "I have authority here," and he dived under the table, and from a secret cache produced a volume of the Irish Law Times Reports. "It is a decision of Baron Dowse sitting where your Lordship is sitting now; and he was asked to disallow this very question; and, heh, he ruled it was admissible, heh! he allowed it!" He looked around at the assembled Bar, with the nearest approach to a wink that he would have permitted himself; and he waited for the Judge's answer.

William O'Brien was not in the least perturbed. "That is a Circuit decision," he said contemptuously, "it was probably given with one eye on the clock and one on the time-table. Besides, the learned Baron was more famous for his humour than for his law; and I'll not follow his ruling. Get on, now; waste no more time over this matter."

"Oh, but I haven't finished yet!" cried Stephen. "I have here a decision of the English Court of Appeal" (and he cited the case and volume of the reports), "and it turned on the very same point, and here is the decision of a very powerful Court that the question is admissible. Does your Lordship admit it now?" And he hopped along the counsel's row, chuckling to himself, and occasionally glancing around to see how the boys were enjoying it.

O'Brien's face clouded; too late he realised that he had been led into a trap; but he was a gallant fighter and he determined to go down with his colours flying. "Misther Ronan," he said, "you know well that there is only one transpontine court that is binding upon me, and that is the House of Lords." "Heh! Heh! And that's why I brought with me the decision of the House of Lords, confirming the Court of Appeal, heh!" And he boldly turned to his audience, to ensure that the Judge would realise how publicly he had been humiliated. "What does your Lordship say now?"

"Ask your question," said O'Brien, sulkily. Ronan looked at him sweetly. "The question seems to annoy your Lordship," he said; "and, as it is of no importance whatsoever, I will not ask it." He enjoyed an uninterrupted Assize after that.

I had one most unhappy experience with him. The late County Court Judge Hynes when still at the Bar once asked me to hold a brief for him in Mr. Justice Barton's Court. He explained to me that he represented the trustees of a fund, two of the beneficiaries under which had quarrelled, and were litigating their dispute by way of an originating summons. With the merits of that dispute the trustees had no concern; all I should have to do would be to stand up at the end and ask that my costs should be provided by the unsuccessful party. It sounded just the sort of case that I could do as well as any man at the Bar; and I made my way to Court with a serenity that was soon to receive a rude shock.

When I arrived in Court I found that Stephen Ronan was representing one of the litigants and Herbert Wilson, K.C., the other. Wilson was probably thirty years younger than Ronan; he was a handsome fellow, a learned Chancery lawyer, and the last man in the world that I should have expected to figure in a "scene in Court." The case had been fixed for two o'clock; and while waiting for the Judge to come in Stephen stood at the side of the Court, warming his back at the fire.

The ever-courteous Barton took his seat on the Bench; but Stephen made no move. The Judge coughed; the case was called on; still Ronan continued to stand apart like Saint Peter. After an awkward interval, he addressed the clouds: "My junior isn't here; my solicitor isn't here; my client isn't here; I haven't read my brief; still, I'll go on." And he assumed his proper place, and opened the case. After a few moments a brilliant extemporisation occurred to him. "My Lord," he said, "I will make this offer to my friend here and now. If I am prepared to guarantee the payment to my friend of the interest on these shares, will he accept that guarantee and withdraw these proceedings, or is he still determined that these shares must be sold? Will he accept that? Will he accept it? Come, I want an answer!"

"One moment, one moment," said Wilson, imperturbably. "Before I accept that, I think I might at least be told what this guarantee means. Is it the guarantee of my friend, Mr. Ronan, which I am prepared to accept for an unlimited amount, or is it the guarantee of his clients which isn't worth the paper it's written on?"

Ronan turned to him: "You're an impertinent young puppy!" he said in a voice appropriate to the mention of the time of day. "And you're a hectoring old man," replied Wilson; "but if you think you can come in here and bully me into neglecting my clients' interests you are making a mistake." Poor Barton nearly fainted; himself the politest of men, he could not bear a scene of this kind, which were rare on the Chancery side, though not so uncommon in the King's Bench Division. "Gentlemen, gentlemen," he cried piteously, "cannot some solution be found on lines other than these?" Fortunately, Ronan's junior had just come into Court, and had distracted his attention; a moment or two later, I heard him whisper across to Wilson, with an engaging grin that disarmed his opponent, "Herbert, I'm sorry." The clouds vanished; both counsel rose, and in complete unison demanded that my clients should provide their costs! When I recovered consciousness an order to this effect had been made; and I felt myself to be comparatively lucky inasmuch as my clients had not been ordered to pay the sum out of their own pockets.

I think that Ronan was unconscious of his own angularities. He certainly was kind to young men; he went out of his way to soften a rebuke, and he was glad to pay a compliment to a neophyte. But we were all afraid of him. It is an unwritten rule of the profession that all members of the Bar shall address one another by their respective surnames, unless sufficiently intimate to use a Christian name or a nickname. To us all, Ronan was "Mr. Ronan." Hailed by a somewhat impertinent junior as "Well, my dear Stephen!" he is reputed to have replied: "Well, my dear Wenceslas!" which did not encourage further familiarity.

He professed the most complete atheism during his life, which may have been one of the reasons of his late promotion. Under the Liberal administration, candidates for office were scrutinised with a view to soothing Nationalist susceptibilities; and it was assumed that Nationalists would not approve of any appointment likely to give offence to the Catholic hierarchy. Rumour has it that Stephen consulted Charles O'Connor, afterwards Master of the Rolls, as to what steps he should take to remove a possible veto. Charles O'Connor suggested that at least an outward conformity to the discipline of the Church into which he had been born might do no harm. Ronan thought for a while, and said: "I'll do it. Where do you attend service?" "Oh, I go to the 11.30 Mass at the University Church on the south side of Saint Stephen's Green," said O'Connor. Ronan made a careful note; O'Connor did not see him the following Sunday, but came to the conclusion that he must have attended another Mass. On Monday morning he chaffed Stephen upon his absence. "But I was there!" cried Ronan, adding, "the service seems to have changed a good deal since I was a boy." "What church did you go to?" asked O'Connor, anxiously. "The one you told me, the University Church, the one with the big pillars in Stephen's Green." Charlie O'Connor was horrified. "Good Heavens, man!" he cried; "that's the Presbyterian Church!" Ronan chuckled. "I *thought* the practice was different to what I had known as a boy," he said.

Stephen had a passion for music. Any dalliance with the gentler arts was unsuspected by most of his colleagues; but one night Joseph O'Connor met him in the neighbourhood of Fitzwilliam Square, and was immediately dragged in to hear Stephen perform a potpourri of *Carmen* on a pianola. Joseph insists that Stephen sang all the melodies; this may be taken with a grain of salt. By the way, my dear Joseph, I am not quite sure if it was you who told me this story; and if not, I make humble apology for suspecting you of having ever been capable of departing in the smallest detail from the accuracy of truth!

Stephen's atheism proved to be of the kind practised by Mr. Daredevil; in his last illness he was visited by Father Tom Finlay, S.J., and reconciled to the faith of his fathers. But his will was overlooked and remained unaltered; and when he died, it was found that most of his money was destined to further the unbeliefs he had tardily abjured.

His methods were well exemplified by a fable launched in the autumn of 1914; according to the tale, Stephen found himself in Paris at the outbreak of war, and hastened to offer his services. Questioned as to his capabilities, he replied: "I am the King's Advocate in Ireland, and have the right to lead in any matter appertaining to Admiralty jurisdiction." So the puzzled Staff sent him around to Antwerp to take command of a body of Marines. These soon found themselves in action; and presently an aide-de-camp galloped up, and said: "The general has sent me to give you the order to charge." "And where is it?" asked Stephen. "But I'm giving it to you," said the bewildered officer. "Do you mean to say there is no document?" asked Ronan, indignantly. "No, of course not." "Then I decline to charge. I decline to charge until you bring me a written order, signed by the party to be charged!"

He was a man who never spent money unnecessarily. His general retainer for the old Midland Railway Company (who owned the Belfast and Northern Counties Railway in Ireland) brought him the compliment of a pass over the system, which gave an alternative and more beautiful, although longer, route from Dublin, via Liverpool, to London. Once when he was arguing a case in the House of Lords he began to ornament his speech with a little improvisation; and he said: "My Lords, I could not help thinking, as my train drew into Euston this morning——" "St. Pancras, Mr. Ronan," said Lord Atkinson, who knew his Stephen.

There was a barrister named Breakey whose appearance bore some resemblance to that of Ronan; both were small men, grey-bearded and long-nosed; both wore forensic garb; and a small boy from the office of the *Freeman's Journal* is to be excused for having mistaken the one for the other. Breakey did not practise; he donned his wig and gown as a sure means of getting admission to any Court that might be crowded. He was not treated with too much courtesy by members of the staff of the *Freeman,* for which paper he used to report. And I suspect he must have occasionally been difficult about his "copy." Nothing of this was present to the mind of Stephen Ronan, when, one day, as he was addressing the Lord Chief Baron and another Judge, he found his gown being viciously plucked by a very determined small boy, who kept whispering the single word "Copy!" "Go away!" cried Stephen, indignantly. "Not without your copy," replied the small boy. "I have no copy," cried Ronan. "I was told that if you said that, I was to report you," said the youth. "Will you go away!" cried Stephen; "I have no papers of yours." "Mr. Gallagher told me I was to pay no attention to whatever you said," replied the boy; "he said you were always making excuses, and that he wasn't going to put up with it any longer." By this time the Chief Baron perceived that something unusual was up; he saw Ronan's irritation, and heard the recurrent word "Copy"; so he addressed the youth and said: "See, my young friend, that is not the way to get the copy of a document from learned counsel. If there is any document a copy of which you wish to see you must apply to Mr. Ronan's solicitor, and ask him to supply you." "But it isn't Mr. Ronan's copy, it's Mr. Breakey's copy I want," said the determined small boy. "Mr. Ronan," said the Chief Baron, when he had stopped laughing, "I think you had better protect your colleague from the fury of this young man by letting the *Freeman's Journal* know of the comedy of errors which we have enjoyed." And, to his credit be it said, Ronan called specially at the office of the newspaper to prevent any possible harm to poor Breakey.

When he became a Judge, Ronan also became impossible. He had the misfortune to take the place of Lord Justice Holmes, a strong and venerable Judge, who had managed to keep some check on the garrulity of the Lord Chancellor, Ignatius O'Brien. When Ronan supervened, chaos came again. It was hard to say which talked more, or more irrelevantly. One day, when Serjeant Matheson had stood silent before them for three quarters of an hour, while they snarled and squabbled, he said suavely: "If I might venture to interrupt your Lordships for a moment." And I remember a case just after the war had begun in which my uncle, Tim Healy, was appearing for the respondent in an appeal; the Court was against him, and I think rightly so, but I never heard an argument conducted in so impossible a fashion. At last (and I think he had probably said all that he had intended to say) Tim said sadly: "Of course, if your Lordships will not hear me——." "You mustn't say that, Mr. Healy," cried Ronan. "All day long," said Tim, "I have been trying to utter two consecutive sentences without interruption; and I have failed." "Mr. Healy——." "It's impossible to conduct an intelligent argument in this Court," and Tim, who had been tying up his papers, threw them on the table, and turned to walk out of Court. "Mr. Healy! Mr. Healy! I'll not say another word, if you'll come back." Tim turned. "I will not," he said; and he walked out.

This peculiar relationship between Bench and Bar must seem very odd to English readers; but it was not regrettable. At this time more than once deputations from the Bar approached the Court of Appeal and declared that the day was fast approaching when counsel would refuse to practise in that Court; and invariably penitence

I

was expressed and reforms were promised. The improvement would last about a week; then the babble would break out again. If it had not been for the patient Lord Justice Molony, as he was at that time, who carefully noted the facts and figures, and followed the argument as far as his colleagues would let him, no business at all would have been transacted. Nor was the Court of Appeal the only one held under correction by the Bar. When Mr. Justice Dodd once in Cork clumsily used some phrases which in their natural meaning were grossly offensive to a junior barrister, the Munster Circuit passed a resolution at the midday adjournment calling upon the Judge to apologise in open Court at its reassembly, under peril of finding no counsel prepared to appear before him. Dodd, who needed no compulsion to set right a wrong once it was pointed out to him, made full amends in a crowded Court. In an earlier age Mr. Justice Keogh had similarly offended, Pether O'Brien being the victim; and the Judge had directed that all the doors should be kept open so that the Court might be as crowded as possible when he made his apology. And perhaps I may be pardoned the vanity of chronicling the handsome conduct of the old Lord Chief Baron towards myself at Tralee Assizes about 1913.

At the previous Winter Assize in Cork I had appeared for one of three prisoners accused of highway robbery. Two had been convicted, but the jury had disagreed about my client, against whom the evidence was slight. He was, accordingly, remanded to stand his trial at the next Kerry Assizes, and there found himself arraigned before the Chief Baron and a Kerry jury—the latter a more favourable tribunal than that impanelled at a Cork Winter Assize. The Crown case was duly presented; I made it clear by my cross-examination that the defence would be an alibi, and when the Crown case closed I paused for a moment before I called my first witness, hoping to get some hint from the Bench that a submission might succeed. None came; so I put a witness in the box. The old Chief Baron glared at me: "You are not going to call evidence in this case, Mr. Healy?" he said. "Not if your Lordship is prepared to direct an acquittal," I replied. "I am NOT!" he thundered fiercely. "Then I must prove my case, my Lord," I said. He gave a snort, and bit savagely at his left ear; "Go on," he said. So I called my alibi evidence; and I am bound to say I could not detect the flaw in it; the witnesses had all the appearance of being superior and honourable people. I then addressed the jury and the Crown replied. Then the old man turned and lashed at the jury with every whip that scorn and indignation could put into his hand. And in the course of this fierce diatribe he used the phrase "When I was at the Bar, there were counsel strong enough, aye, and honourable enough to say 'I will not put such witnesses in the box to commit perjury!'" and he finished his charge by practically directing the jury to find my client "Not Guilty," which they promptly did.

I left the Court a little bewildered; but I had got my man off, and I was not conscious of having earned rebuke, so I was not worrying very much, knowing that the old man's bark was worse than his bite. Not so my colleague, Barney Roche, who went in to the Judges' room, and bearded Palles as he sat at lunch. "Chief," he said, "you were very unfair to young Maurice Healy in what you said about him." "What did I say that was unfair?" asked the Chief Baron. "You said that he had acted dishonourably in not keeping those alibi witnesses out of the box." "I did not!" said the old man, astonished that he could have done so. "You did indeed," said Barney, "I made a note of what you said; here it is. And I think you should put it right." "I will indeed," said Palles. "Tell Healy to be in Court when we resume after the adjournment." A few minutes later I received a message that I was wanted in the Lord Chief Baron's Court. I went down, not knowing what was afoot. In came the Judge, and took his seat. "Mr. Healy," he said, "I have been told that this morning when I was addressing the jury I used words which might be understood as imputing dishonourable conduct to you in your conduct of the case. As dishonour is a word that I am sure I could never properly associate with your name, I have sent for you to express my regret with the same publicity as attached to my error."

Do you wonder that we worshipped him?

IX

THE TIME has come to speak of one of the best-known members of the Munster Circuit, who gave rise to more good stories than perhaps any of his colleagues; almost all of them unconsciously. Patrick Daniel Fleming was the son of a farmer in the neighbourhood of a little town in south Limerick, the name of which is spelt Kilfinnane, but which he characteristically called "K'lfénnan." It must be stated at the outset that he spoke a language of his own; the sounds of 'th" and "dh" were entirely beyond his ken, except when they were inappropriate; the short "e" was frequently turned into a short "a," and an "i" into an "e." Certain good rustic words and phrases persisted in his vocabulary; but within those limitations he was a man of education. Indeed, it was one of the grievances of his later life that Doctor O'Dwyer, the Catholic Bishop of Limerick, had refused to assist him towards a scholarship. That prelate had reached the episcopal throne without ever having been a parish priest; and Paddy Fleming used always to speak of him as "dat bishop dey squz out of a curate." (I apologise if I have misspelt the word "squz," which is pronounced *skwuz*, although I have never met it in any other context.) As a result of this lack of episcopal patronage Paddy went to Dublin University, where he graduated with distinction, being awarded a gold medal in English Literature. Perhaps there was no oral examination. He then came to the Bar, where he built up a robust junior practice, and took silk somewhere about 1904. This was about the time when I first came to know him. He had already achieved a

certain portliness; his jolly, rubicund face shone with
well-being; his goggling eyes betrayed an eagerness for
controversy, which his tight-lipped mouth, garnished
with a brown moustache, kept in severe restraint. He
had inherited the Irish farmer's lofty contempt for the
labouring classes, whom he used always to describe as
"natives"; rustic Abigails in his mouth became "dem
serving-gerrls," and they and their kind were mere
hewers of wood and drawers of water, deserving of no
consideration. He also inherited from his forebears a
rigid sense of economy; and when once he was persuaded
to go on a Cook's tour at an inclusive price of £30, he
succeeded in returning to Ireland without having spent
a penny above the quoted figure, although absent for more
than three weeks. In vain was it suggested that there must
have been tips, drinks, laundry, various petty expenses;
no, de contract was for tirty pounds, and tirty pounds was
all he paid. But this careful frame of mind did not ever
cause Paddy to appear a mean man; indeed, I fancy he
was a generous man in a proper case. But we loved to
jest about his alleged closeness. Once, as he was driving
to the Judges' lodgings for dinner in company with James
Rearden, the car broke down, and another had to be
procured. (Paddy's account of the adventure next day
contained the sentence: "What wit de joltin of de car
and de couple of glasses of sherry dat he had before de
danner, poor Jim becem damned amusin.") Someone
asked Paddy had he paid anything to the driver of the car
that had broken down. Paddy goggled at him, his face
aglow with a triumphant smile. "I nearly did," he confessed, "but den I remembered dat it was an entire contract, and dat he couldn't plead a *quantum meruit!*"

Paddy rarely made a remark that was not shrewd.

"I love to see dem attorneys buying law-books," he said one day; "it's all for de good of trade!" Once, when he had been appointed to prosecute at the Winter Assize, the emoluments attaching to which task would depend on the number and importance of the cases dealt with, somebody asked him had he a big bag? "Fair, fair," replied Paddy; "but I see by de *Cork Examiner* dat dere's been a nice little murder in de County Kerry!"

Dick Hennessy was the proper foil to set off Paddy Fleming. Dick was an extraordinary little man, looking rather like one of Dicky Doyle's drawings. He was short and broad, with a very large head, and no neck at all; indeed, he used to have his shirts made with a collar attached that turned down from the neck-band and did not stand up even a quarter of an inch. His red hair extended into Victorian side-whiskers that partly covered his rosy cheeks; his high voice was continually raised in witty comment upon his colleagues. I believe he enjoyed a large junior practice before Pether O'Brien appointed him counsel to the Attorney-General. When Pether was raised to the Bench Dick took silk, and, like many a good man before and since, saw his practice vanish in a night. I never could understand why he was not appointed a County Court Judge; he would have discharged the duties of that office with an efficiency that would not have been impaired by his wit and humour. He preferred to remain amongst us at the Bar, doing a case here and a case there, and enlivening every Court with his irrepressible comments upon everybody from the Judge to the prisoner in the dock. He looked upon Paddy Fleming as his special property; a real affection existed between the two men, but it afforded Paddy no protection from the shafts of Dick.

Once during the course of Limerick Assizes they went for a walk together. Their way lay through a country churchyard, and they spent a few minutes examining the inscriptions on the tombstones. "Ah!" said Paddy, "I find dem tombstones very longwinded!" Dick looked at him. "Yes, my dear Pat," he said, "when you come to die we shall take care that no such fault shall sully your memorial. We shall make it epigrammatic in its brevity." He paused for a moment; then he added: "I think it will be sufficient if we put

> P.D.F.
>
> D.O.M.
>
> R.I.P."

For the benefit of the uninitiated it must be explained that in the Irish County Court the Judge could give a decree; or he could dismiss the case without prejudice, if there were some curable defect that the plaintiff might remove before suing again; or he might dismiss the case on its merits, which was final. These dismisses were usually spoken of by their initials D.W.P. and D.O.M.

Paddy must have been in the mood of a tourist that Assize, for I remember his telling me that he had visited the Limerick Cathedral, and that he had been greatly impressed by the mural tablets in the floor; and he also gave his approbation to a new walk that the Corporation had made, saying: "Gor, man, dey've turned it into a rreglar bouvelard!"

A week later in Tralee, he went for a walk with, I think, Matt Kenny. They climbed a hill outside the town and Paddy paused to wipe his brow just outside the gate of a prosperous-looking farm, the owner of which happened to be standing by. "Dat's a fine farm o' land you have," said Paddy. "Oh, 'tis not bad, Counsellor," replied the farmer, good-humouredly. "How many acres have you?" asked Paddy. "I have forty, Counsellor." "How many arable, and how many pasture?" The information was given readily; also how many cows he had, milch and dry, how many sheep, what family, and a host of other intimate details. Paddy paused for want of ammunition; and the farmer, thinking it was his turn to shew a polite interest, said: "They tell me, Counsellor, you're not doing too badly yourself beyond in the town?" Paddy looked at him, in silence. "Come on," said he to Matt Kenny. And without a word further he strode along the road. Fifty yards further on he stopped. "'Tis a ting," said he, "me fader offen tolt me: ye can never fondle a dog, but it'll lep on ye!"

It was at the same Limerick Assize that included the murder trial which I have described that I went into the Criminal Court where I found Paddy prosecuting a man for a bad stabbing offence. Dodd was the presiding Judge; he sat at the apex of a horseshoe-shaped Court with the jury on his left; defending counsel sat under the jury-box and were faced by prosecuting counsel. The young barrister who was defending the prisoner was a protégé of Paddy's; he was more agricultural than philosophical in his tastes, and his forensic methods were unfamiliar to a judge unaccustomed to the rural society of southern Ireland. When the time came for him to address the jury he arose, and, leaning familiarily against the edge of the jury-box, he addressed its contents as one of themselves, with frequent references to his daily meetings with them at various social and sporting functions. His Doric speech was entirely beyond the comprehension of the Judge, who waved the issue paper to the jury, saying:

"Now, gentlemen, what do you think?" The case being a plain one, the jury did not care to acquit the prisoner without going through the form of a retirement to consider their verdict; and as they vanished through the door of the jury-room, Paddy gripped my arm, and, nodding towards his young friend, said to me in an intense whisper: "I tolt dat fella's fader he'd a rright to send his son to Thrinity College, Dublin, de wan place dey larn ye to talk English properly!"

"In dis case, my Lord," he said in a case about water, "it would have been sufficient if de landlords had acqueeced in our taking dis water for t-wenty years; but, my Lord, dey have been acqueecing and acqueecing, and dey've never stopped acqueecing!" It was in the same case that he described a vain visit of his client to a watering-trough in search of water; "and, tanks to de conduct of de defendants, dere wasn't a thrinckle in the throck!"

"Is your client a widow, Mr. Fleming?" asked a Chancery judge, one day. "No, my Lord; quite de contrary," replied Paddy.

It will, I hope, be realised that I have only been recalling that part of Paddy Fleming's sayings and doings that made us laugh; if read alone, it might suggest that he was unlettered and even unintelligent. Nothing could be further from the truth. He knew his law through and through; his general reading was not wide, but he could make a good speech, vigorously delivered, and none the worse for the occasional bursts into Flemish. His opinion was very sound; his strategy was admirable. He had a thorough knowledge of the ways of his fellow-countrymen; I can still hear him suddenly punctuate a cross-examination with a triumphant "Ah! me fine fella!

dat won't pass mustard wit me!" And as he drew the
witness on nearer and nearer to the little trap he had
prepared for him, his eyes would goggle wider and wider,
and his lips would close in a tighter and tighter smile,
until at last the noose was jerked with a veritable roar of
triumph! He was admirable in consultations; he would
check the exuberant tactics of his junior, and explain how
he intended to lead the opposing witness along the slippery
slope until there was no returning; "and den I'll hand
him me nice little dockiment and shew him what a liar
he is!" Two of his idioms must be chronicled. Every
statement was likely to be prefaced by the phrase "Oh,
gor', man." Every speculation began with the words
"I wonder to say." And the word "twice" was always
pronounced "too-wice."

During the war he was appointed County Court Judge
for Meath. For several years he gave universal satisfaction
to all who entered his Court, and when he died he left
behind him a memory of sound judgment and sympathetic
administration of the law. And yet I think that the things
by which he would prefer to be remembered are those
that made his popularity amongst his colleagues, which I
have tried, I hope not unkindly, to reproduce in these
pages.

To raise a similar memorial to Dick Hennessy would
be impossible. Dick's wit had the effervescence of
champagne; it had vanished before the smile had come,
but new bubbles had by then arrived, and kept on
succeeding one another as long as he continued to speak.
He rarely allowed himself to be drawn into controversy
and thus has left no memory of witty retorts; casual and
irrepressible comment was his long suit. I remember
a day in Cork when he came into the Crown Court as we

were awaiting the return of the Judge. The Clerk of
the Crown and Peace, Henry T. Wright, was already in
his place under the Bench; his severe aspect was apt to
overawe those who only knew him superficially.   A
rustic juror had come forward and had made an application to be excused for some reason; Henry had listened
impassively and had replied: "You must make your
application to his Lordship when he takes his seat."   The
wretched juror was retiring in confusion, when Dick
Hennessy's voice was heard remarking in an impersonal
way: "No wonder the poor fellow thought the Court
was sitting!"

Once Dick was instructed to defend a prisoner; he
had associated with him a junior who felt that the presence
of a leader exonerated him from all responsibility, and
hardly deigned to undo the tape of his brief. To every
question that Dick asked him he gave the unvarying
answer, "I dunnaw!"   All the morning Dick toiled
unaided, and at last, just before the adjournment, he
raised a point of law which he argued with some vehe-
mence. "I appreciate your point, Mr. Hennessy," said
the Judge, "and I'll hear what Mr. Ronan has to say after
the adjournment."   And he rose. After the adjournment
Stephen Ronan stood up to reply, and in his usual way
looked everywhere but towards the Bench. "My Lord,"
he said, "heh! the answer to my friend's point, heh, is so
obvious, and the question has been so often decided
against him, heh! that I cannot do better than refer your
Lordship to the page in Archbold where the cases are
collected. Your Lordship will find them all on page—on
page ——. He paused; looked up; and said: "Heh!
It is most extraordinary! Before the adjournment, heh!
I had marked the page in Archbold; and now I find that

somebody has torn out the page, heh!" "Oh!" cried Dick at the top of his voice, "Thank God! My junior has done something at last!"

At the first trial of the highway robbery case to which I have referred, Dick was one of the counsel for the prosecution. In my speech to the jury I had dwelt upon the unsatisfactory nature of the identification of my client, and to illustrate the possibility of error in moments of intense excitement, I told the well-known story of the witnesses of the execution of Mary Queen of Scots, all of whom differed on every detail but one, on which they agreed, namely, that the Queen's head had been severed by a single blow. Yet, when the body came to be exhumed in modern times, the one thing clear was that it had taken three strokes of the axe to complete the sorry business. Dick moved not a muscle as I embroidered this theme; and his own speech seemed to be giving the matter the go-by, until he came to his peroration, when he suddenly said: "And as for Mary Queen of Scots, well, we all know that she was the Queen of Sorrows; but little did she think when she laid her head upon the block in Fotheringay Castle that three hundred and fifty years later she would be summoned from the tomb to provide an alibi for the highway robbers of Coolanellig Wood!"

During that Assizes Dick was the object of considerable attention on the part of Matt Kenny. Matt confided to me that he thought Dick was unwell. "Why, Matt?" "'Tis his appetite I'm worried about." "Isn't he eating well?" "Well, judge for yourself. He had a cup of tea and some biscuits before he got up; then he had his breakfast: porridge, fish, bacon, and eggs. At eleven o'clock he had a half a dozen poached eggs—did you ever see Dick Hennessy eat a poached egg? He ties a napkin round what's meant for his neck; then he takes his knife firmly in his right hand, and does a sort of niblick stroke; there's a noise like a flirrip, and the egg is gone. Well, there were six flirrips at eleven o'clock, which did not prevent Master Dick from taking soup, fish, joint, sweet and cheese at half-past one. At three he had two tins of Brand's extract of chicken; and now, at four o'clock, he has asked me to go out and get him some sandwiches!''

I remember a case at one Winter Assize when the present Sir Thomas Molony was the Judge and Dick nearly got into serious trouble by reason of his irrepressible levity. Those desiring to treat religion lightly would have been well advised to choose another Judge's Court. Dick, however, cared neither for God nor man when it was a question of a jest; and he seemed to have found a fruitful field when he began to prosecute a prisoner of some social standing, the nephew of an eminent ecclesiastic, for burglary. The accused was alleged to have entered the house of an eccentric old lady by night, made his way to her bedroom, and helped himself to some money and articles of value. Dick outlined the story, and called his principal witness into the witness-box, where she was sworn with some difficulty.

"What is your name?" began Dick.

"Bridget Murphy," replied the old lady.

"And how old are you?" asked Dick.

"I won't tell you," replied the witness.

"Oh!" cried Dick, "I assure you I have no matrimonial intentions!" The Judge then interfered, and suggested that perhaps the question was irrelevant to the point at issue, which indeed it seems to have been. Dick, therefore, proceeded to get from the old woman an account of how she had gone to bed, fallen asleep, and been awakened by the sound of footsteps ascending the stairs. "And what did you do?" asked Dick.

"I reached for the holy water, and blessed myself," said the witness.

"Very right and proper," said Dick; "but what else did you do?"

"I commended myself to the protection of Saint Patrick and Saint Bridget," replied Mrs. Murphy.

"Admirable, no doubt," said Dick; "but what practical steps did you take?"

"I got out of bed and took up the poker," said the witness.

"Ah!" said Dick; "and, armed with the poker and the holy water, and under the protection of Saint Patrick and Saint Bridget, what did you do then?"

But here the Judge felt it necessary to check the laughter that had arisen in Court, and to suggest that the religious beliefs of humble people ought not to be made the subject of jest. Nobody can properly disagree with that ruling; but, recalling *The Little Flowers of Saint Francis,* and other pious works of simple mirth, I cannot help regretting the lost humours of the examination that might have ensued but for the interruption.

Dick was without exception the best after-dinner speaker I ever heard. He had just the right touch, what a chef would call a genius for *soufflé.* The nearest approach to him in my experience was the late Sir Ryland Adkins. But Ryland had a somewhat pontifical style; reverence was the last quality to be associated with Dick. He knew his Horace very well, and had much of the lazy humour. But his wit was alive with a pleasant malice; it was all pepper and mustard, with hardly a trace of vinegar. He deemed it his right and duty to comment upon the other members of the Circuit as a chronicler of the time; he spared none, and asked no mercy. I remember a day when William Frederick Kenny, junior Crown Prosecutor for Cork City, failed to turn up for the opening of the City Commission, the business of which had to be transacted by his unaided leader. That afternoon, Dick, returning from one of his many excursions in search of casual food, began to hold forth upon the conduct of the absentee. "I suppose the wretched William Frederick," he began, "has now reached the time of life when twenty minutes more in bed is worth a bag full of briefs." A series of nods and winks failed to awaken his appreciation of the situation, and he went on: "He ought to resign, if he can't do the work"—at this stage he suddenly realised that William Frederick had arrived by a later train, and was sitting listening to him. "He's here now, I perceive," said Dick, quite unperturbed.

Perhaps I ought to add that it was all part of Circuit life that we spoke of one another as though we hated and despised one another. "The wretched So-and-so" was common form, and meant nothing. When sudden death once removed one of our less fortunate colleagues, before nightfall enough had been provided for the pressing needs of his family, and within a few days more permanent arrangements had been made for fosterage and care. I never heard more malice than in those old Circuit days; and I never made better friends or met kinder hearts.

X

MATT KENNY, of whom I have already spoken more than once, is to-day one of three survivors of the debates in Committee-Room 15, from which sprang the Parnellite Split. In those debates he made what was, in the opinion of my uncle and my father, the best speech in that agonised assembly. He was the last member for the Borough of Ennis, disfranchised in 1885; he afterwards sat for Mid-Tyrone, until his loyal friendship for my uncle caused him to be driven out of Parliament. His successor, however, cannot have given much satisfaction to those who procured his election in place of Matt Kenny, for he was a worthy gentleman named George Murnaghan, uncle of the present Mr. Justice Murnaghan, who refused to lend himself to internecine warfare, and served his country loyally for many years. Matt, released from attendance at the House of Commons, took kindly to the Bar, where his shrewd advice was highly valued, not merely by his clients, but also by his colleagues. He was a silent man, except upon occasion; when he did speak, it was usually to make a few cutting observations, that curled around his opponent like the lash of a whip. He ultimately became Circuit Judge for Cork, where his administration was so excellent that he obtained an extension of his period of office when he attained the age limit. At the time of writing he is enjoying the pleasures of his Sabine farm, perhaps unconscious of the warm hold he has upon the affections of all who knew him.

When I first met him in Limerick in 1910, he had the impassive dignity of a Red Indian, and something of that cast of countenance. He took kindly to me for the sake of the name, and it was not long before we were close friends. He made me the recipient of several of his comments upon his colleagues, all of which were shrewd and enlightening. In particular, there was one member of the Circuit, to whom I shall lend the name "Dooley," whom Matt regarded with the slightly contemptuous amusement of a schoolmaster watching an unsuspecting schoolboy attempting some breach of the rules. Dooley had come to the Bar late in life, and the code of the profession was not instinctively present to his mind; it had to be learned by experience. He possessed an amount of cleverness which Matt would always describe as "animal cunning"; he was a born intriguer, and it used to afford Matt great pleasure to follow out the tortuous workings of his schemes, and then quietly expose them by a phrase. "I have a great pity for the fellow," said Matt. "He came to me once to consult me about his health. He told me he had been to every doctor in Munster and to the best men in Dublin; he had even gone to London to see a Harley Street specialist. I felt very sorry for the poor fellow." "And what advice did you give him, Matt?" "I told him consult a vet.!" and Matt roared with laughter at his own jest.

At that time there was great speculation as to what sort of a Home Rule Bill Mr. Birrell would introduce; and much of the discussion in the Bar-room turned upon national finance. I am afraid that not a few were wondering about the salaries attached to the offices to which they hoped to attain, and the solvency of the fund upon which such salaries would be secured. Matt, who in those days had no reason to hope that he himself would ever enjoy a salaried office, used to listen to these discussions with the detached amusement of a former legislator. One day he intervened: "If I had my way," he said, "I'd have two Consolidated Funds. I'd have an Imperial Consolidated Fund, and I'd quarter my friends upon that; and I'd have an Irish Consolidated Fund, and I'd quarter my enemies upon that!" "And what would you do with Dooley?" asked somebody, who knew Matt's attitude to that member of our fraternity. "O-ho! I'd put Dooley on the Poor Rate!" cried Matt, with a roar of laughter, thereby with one stroke delineating the exact worth at which he assessed Dooley's value in the National councils.

In 1919, when I returned from the war, I found Matt in a mood of political complacency. The man who had driven him out of public life had been overwhelmed at the General Election, only one of his eighty-four members being returned, and he himself having been turned out of a seat he had held since 1885, and out of an assembly that had known him since 1880. John Dillon did not take kindly to defeat, and for a long time he assumed that this was a mere temporary reverse that the passage of a year or two would cure. He continued to receive his old associates in council, and from time to time would issue a pronunciamento that revealed his hope of what is, in modern slang, called a "come-back." One day his colleague, John Muldoon, K.C., came up to Matt in the Law Library to pass the time of day. "I was up with John Dillon last night," he said. "And how's the great man?" asked Matt grimly. "He's very sore," said John; "he complains that of all the people who used to throng to his house when he was in Parliament, there's hardly a soul who goes near him now." "Is it lonely he is?" said Matt. "Let him send a telegram to Monsieur

Venizelos, and ask him down for the week-end!'' At that time Venizelos was also having experience of the fickleness of public opinion; but the future was to be kinder to him than to John Dillon.

When Matt became a judge he saw no reason to bridle his tongue, which had always been the scourge of the unjust. A prisoner was tried before him on a charge of robbery with violence, and showed such skill in defending himself that Matt deemed it his duty to take a hand in the prosecution (as a judge must often do in the interests of justice), and he stopped many of the earths the skill of the prisoner had prepared for his escape. A conviction followed; the prisoner was asked whether he had anything to say why sentence should not be passed upon him. ''Ah, me Lord,'' he said, ''you never gave me a fair crack of the whip!'' (This is a popular phrase, meaning ''a fair chance.'') ''Didn't I?'' cried Matt. ''Well, I'll give it to you now. Seven years penal servitude, and twenty strokes of the cat!''

That sentence revealed something of the hardness of the Clareman. Padraic Colum, in his terrifying translation from the Irish, has caught it to perfection:

> O woman, shapely as the swan,
>   On your account I shall not die.
> The men you've slain—a trivial clan—
>   Were less than I.

Clare murders were implacable murders; Clare heroism, well exemplified when the Quilty fishermen rescued the crew of a French barque from the jaws of almost certain death, was a hard and ascetic heroism, unassociated with the softer emotions. It is significant that it has been

in Clare that the cold, pitiless logician that now leads
the Irish race has found his firmest support; it was in
Clare that Daniel O'Connell first raised the standard of
Catholic Emancipation.   And when the souls of the wild
geese flew homeward after some European battle in which
the fate of France or Austria had been decided by Irish
swords, it was, traditionally, the coast of Clare that they
sought for their last resting-place.

Clare had given another beloved brother to the Munster
Circuit at the time when I first knew it; to-day he is
Attorney-General to the Government of Éire.   If I had
ever been asked to cite an example of an honest man, I
think that the first name that would have come to my
lips would have been that of Paddy Lynch.   He was
indeed an Israelite without guile; in an assembly that
rather prided itself upon its outward cynicism and contempt for the finer feelings he was never ashamed of
decency.   In the better sense of that term, he was a simple
soul.   "Chrétiens ont droit et payens ont tort" is a
splendid creed, if you live up to it, and at the same time
temper it with a kindly charity for the failings of others
who lack the light to practise it.   Paddy was never so
splendid as when the fate of some humble person hung
upon his efforts.   He had mannerisms, some of which, I
believe, he shared with Maître Moro Giafferi of the
French Bar; he loved to lull his audience into comfort
with a succession of softly-spoken sentences, and then
suddenly to thunder out some impassioned phrase in
tones that caused everyone in court to jump.   To hear
Paddy lead a witness along the flowery path until every
suspicion had been allayed, and then shout a fierce and
fatal question, with a vicious "Answer me that!!!" was
an experience of the dramatic not to be equalled in any

theatre. He never had made a parade of his politics; always a moderate Nationalist, when the gallant Willie Redmond gave his life for his beliefs at Wytschaete Ridge, Paddy thought it would be an indecent thing if the seat of that paladin amongst Irishmen were to be abandoned without a struggle to those who had disagreed with his views. He opposed Mr. de Valera and was beaten; it is to the honour of both candidates that he should now be official legal adviser to his former opponent.

Paddy was well aware of the fact that his brethren took a good deal of pleasure in hearing his mannerisms mimicked and imitated by a younger colleague, Joseph O'Connor. Joseph, before he came to the Bar, had distinguished himself as a journalist, especially by a series of police-court sketches which he called "Studies in Blue." The craft he there learned gave him a quick eye for a humorous situation; he seized upon an ounce of fact, added a dash of fiction, and produced a pound of amusing pastiche. At first, I think Paddy was annoyed when he heard that Joseph was making a special study of his mannerisms; but after a while he used to invite the jester to say his piece, and used to listen with amused approval, until the malicious Joseph would make the mock Paddy say something offensive to the views of the real Paddy, when he would assume the correct "We are not amused" attitude, and withdraw.

He loved to enshroud himself with an air of mystery. He affected dramatic and coincidental knowledge about the most ordinary affairs of life; he would suddenly give you the pedigree of a Limerick vanhorse, or tell you some secret and completely unimportant piece of family history, apropos of a passing event. Joseph was his junior in a murder case, and ventured to say that he feared their client would hang. "He will not," said Paddy. "And shall I tell you why he won't? Because I've got a point." He looked around him mysteriously, and added: "Shall I tell you? I will. Come over here where they can't hear us." And then began a series of movements as frequent and varied as those of Hamlet and his oath-takers. "I don't want any of those shoeboys to be listening to us," said Paddy. At last, according to Joseph, from abundance of caution he postponed the communication of the point until after the case!

With all his mannerisms and his pleasant foibles, Paddy was a formidable opponent, and a helpful colleague. He was staunch and loyal to the core; and his rugged good sense was supported by a solid foundation in law, and made his advice invaluable. I have no doubt at all that justice under his administration is tempered with mercy; and I am equally sure that the hounds of Banba are kept hard on the trail of all wrong-doers. I am sure he would rejoice to know the satisfaction with which at least one old friend read of the crown at last set upon his labours in the cause of justice and right.

There was a third Clareman whom I must mention; for he was one of the "characters" of the Circuit. Michael MacNamara, known far and wide as "Counsellor Mack," was an original. He was not alone a barrister; he was also a mapper; he was parish match-maker to the parish of Kilshanny; but it is believed that his principal source of income was his skill at the game of "Forty-Five." He was also the Court interpreter in Irish. He professed to be a great etymologist; he wrote several learned pamphlets to prove that the Irish and Maori languages were inter-related (and who am I to suggest that he was wrong?); and when King George V came to the throne,

the Counsellor published a Coronation Ode, which
began:

> Britannia's fame enlarges;
> Yes, Heaven gives and charges
> The mightiest of the Georges
> To bless and guard her throne;

and it continued for several pages to the same effect.
His Majesty was graciously pleased to accept a copy of
the work, which was the next best thing to appointing
the Counsellor Poet Laureate; and he would hardly have
been worse than Alfred Austin.

On one occasion when the Counsellor was engaged
for a plaintiff in the County Court, he had a great dread
that the defendant would swear himself out of the debt
by barefaced perjury. The fact that he was counsel in
the case does not appear to have prevented him from
acting as interpreter; and when the defendant came to
take the oath, the Counsellor addressed him in Irish:
"Listen carefully now to the terms of the oath, and
repeat after me—'If I do not tell the truth in this
case——' "

" 'If I do not tell the truth in this case——' "

"May a murrain seize my cattle——"

"What's that, Counsellor? Sure that's not the
oath?"

"Go on and repeat your oath: 'May a murrain seize
my cattle——' "

"Oh! Glory be to God! 'May a murrain seize my
cattle——' "

"May all my sheep be cliffted——" (i.e. fall over the
cliff).

"Yerra, Counsellor, what oath is that your trying to

get me to take? Sure, I never heard an oath like that before!''

"Go on, sir; don't argue with me; repeat your oath: 'May all my sheep be cliffted——' ''

"Oh! God help us all! 'May all my sheep——' yerra, Counsellor, are you sure that's in the oath?''

"Go on, sir!''

"Oh! God! 'May all my sheep be cliffted!' ''

"May my children get the falling sickness——''

"Arrah, Counsellor, tell his Honour that I admit the debt, and I only want a little time to pay!''

Some months after this I met Counsellor Mack in the King's Inns Library, and, having heard this story, and believing it to be an invention, proceeded to repeat it in his presence before an audience. To my surprise, the Counsellor not merely admitted its truth, but took great pride in it. "Wasn't I right?'' he asked. "What is an oath? Isn't it a calling on God to punish you if you don't say what is true? And what was I doing but bringing home to him the perils he was running?''

The Clare Bar also gave us one of the only two English-men that ever came over to practise in Ireland. Ernest Phelps had, I think some property in County Clare, and probably came over first with the intention of looking after it. He was made welcome on the Circuit, and, although he confined his activities on Circuit to Limerick and Clare, he enjoyed the confidence of all, and built up a good practice. He had the breezy, hearty manner of an old-time naval officer, and combined a delightful candour with an adroit sense of tactics that made him a very formidable opponent. He was an amused spectator of all our merry wars, but took little part in them, and I can recall no stories about him. The other Englishman,

J. E. J. Julian, had the misfortune to inherit some property near Fenit in County Kerry; filled with the spirit of chivalry, he threw up his practice in England, came over to live amongst his tenants, and got called to the Irish Bar. He stood for Parliament as an Independent Nationalist in West Kerry against the popular Tom O'Donnell in 1900, and put up a very respectable fight. But it was felt that he was a Broadbent; he was regarded with affection, but never got the confidence of the people. His tenants took advantage of his good nature, and ruined him; solicitors took little notice of him. He ultimately set up a motor business in Tralee; and when the war broke out he went off to France to drive an ambulance, being by that time an old man. He settled abroad after the war, and I am sorry to say he died in poverty. He loved the Irish people, and made great sacrifices for their sake; and I am afraid they were not grateful, and treated him very badly. Poor J. J.! Although he developed into a club bore in his later days, he told me the three best stories I know—none of them capable of gracing the present pages!

The contrast between the fates of Ernest Phelps and J. J. Julian is instructive. Ernest Phelps carried more guns; his intellectual equipment was very much greater; but both men had enjoyed the usual education of a gentleman, both were of the land-owning class, neither professed the faith of the majority of those amongst whom they proposed to live and practise. But Ernest Phelps made no secret of the fact that he held Unionist views, although I don't think he ever took any active part in politics; J. J., on the other hand, was determined to be more Irish than the Irish themselves. The bulk of Phelps's practice at first probably came from clients of his own way of thinking; but at the time I joined the Circuit he had attracted a number of Nationalist solicitors, and was constantly appearing for what Paddy Fleming called "natives." I mean no reflection on poor J. J., when I venture to think that the people amongst whom he had chosen to live considered such a conversion as unnatural in a stable-minded man, and withheld their full confidence for that reason. Ernest Phelps earned their esteem by his manly avowal of his true views, and their affection by the tact with which he prevented those views from obtruding themselves in any offensive way.

The first time I heard Ernest Phelps in action was in Limerick, and his opponent was a tall, handsome dragoon of a fellow, named Laurence O'Brien Kelly. Larry always did his best to conceal a learning which had been sufficient to win him the Brooke Scholarship; he had a rich brogue and a cheerful disposition, and he rather encouraged jokes at his own expense. He liked the pleasures of the table and of the turf; there was usually a "little horrse" in the offing that was expected to do great things. But even if Larry had been inclined to excess in the one direction or the other, there was always in the background a mysterious deity, respectfully referred to as "Me Ant," an expectancy from whom was a powerful aid to good living.

Shortly before I joined the Circuit there had appeared in the Bar-room at Limerick a neophyte named Guillamore O'Grady, who was rash enough to dress for Limerick Assizes as though he had been intending to take part in Church Parade in Hyde Park. I think he even sported a monocle. That evening Larry Kelly remarked in an injured tone: "That fella, Guillamore O'Grady, is mighty touchy." "Why, Larry?" "Well, I only went up to him and said: 'Gor,' Gilly, old man, I declare to God, you're an effeminate-looking beggar!' and the fella won't speak to me now!''

The first time I went to Ennis there were seventeen of us gathered for Bar Mess in Carmody's Hotel, about eight having arrived without warning. After the soup there appeared on the table two dishes; when the covers were removed, one was seen to contain a smallish leg of mutton, the other a pair of roast chickens. Larry regarded the scene with a look of horror; then, with an air of self-abnegation, he remarked: "I say, Poole, old man, just give me half of one of the chickens, and I'll manage the rest on the mutton!" Fortunately, at this moment further supplies appeared, and all was well.

When I returned from the war I was just in time to attend the Spring Assizes of 1919, and joined the Circuit at Limerick. I arrived to find Larry in the course of putting through an earnest trunk call to George Cullinan, our Secretary. "George, old man; the cellar is in an awful state; no, the claret's all right; no, there's plenty of champagne; no, it's the whiskey, George; there are only two bottles; yes, two bottles; and I've had to give a drink out of one of them to Ernest Phelps!''

Larry was very far from being the greedy fellow that these stories might suggest; but he loved to express himself in this fashion, conscious I think that we would garner our laughter. He was well able to take care of himself in controversy, and many of his colleagues must have regretted some rash attack that led to a counter-check. My uncle, Serjeant Sullivan, did not suffer Larry gladly; forgetful of his own younger days, he was some-times very unkind in exposing the faults of others. He had been brought up in a hard school; I can remember as a small boy his bitter distress when a client of his named John Twiss was convicted at the Cork Assizes of murder, and subsequently hanged.   My uncle blamed himself, unjustly as most people thought, for some little slip in the defence; and after many years he still brooded on it.   Just before the war Larry Kelly attended Cork Assizes, and provoked the Serjeant's wrath and scorn by some performance of his in Court; and for twenty minutes the Bar-room rang with his vituperation of the unfortunate Larry.   The latter remained quite unperturbed, and at length removed himself out of range by setting out on a walk.   He remained absent for a long time, and indeed was late for dinner, which caused him to walk up to the Father and apologise.   "I went up to the gaol," he said, "and the Governor shewed me all over it."   He produced a little paper packet from his pocket.   "I brought you back a little keepsake, Serjeant."   "What is it?" asked the unsuspecting Serjeant.   "'Tis a little bit of moss from the grave of John Twiss," replied Larry, grimly.   All accounts were paid.

XI

KERRY AND CORK have always produced the best brains in Ireland (need I stress the point that I reckon myself a Corkman?), and for a keen appreciation of the points of litigation I am inclined to give the palm to Kerry. In my time they were lucky in their County Court Judge. The gentle Charles Dromgoole was the antithesis of the Northern Irishman of legend (the latter a libel upon the real man, by the way). I cannot picture his bearded, kindly face without a smile, or his eyes without a twinkle. Kerry had on the whole been lucky in its Judges; the tradition of Judge Shaw, afterwards Recorder of Belfast, still lingered, and the interregnum of D. F. Browne was at least scholarly, if not very practical. There was a popular song by Percy French in which the praises of Drumcollogher were set forth at length. A very short experience of the new Judge caused Kerry to be nicknamed "Dromgooliher," and a parody of the song set forth delights which were by no means imaginary. I do not think I have ever seen patient good humour put to better employment. The crabbed, crotchety Kerry peasants soon succumbed to the charm of this man from the north, who was so *very* hard to deceive. Wars that had contributed a battle to every session of the Court began to peter out; families that had waged a ceaseless vendetta for generations commenced to show each other mild civilities. Where Dromgoole's hand learned its cunning I cannot guess; his practice at the Bar had been almost entirely on the equity side, and his acquaintance with oral testimony must have been of the slightest. Yet he sized up a witness to perfection and seemed to know by instinct where the truth lay. He was a man of great culture; his interests ranged over a large number of subjects, and his leisure rarely found him without a book. There used to be a pleasant gathering every Christmas vacation in his Dublin house, when his talented young family would entertain the assembly by clever performances under his direction and stage management of plays in more than one language. This breadth of outlook upon life had its reflection on the Bench; he never took a small view of a case, and sought to ensure that his judgment would not merely decide the particular dispute between the parties, but would smooth the difficulties that had led to the quarrel in such a way as to enable them to live in peace thereafter. Laughter in Court was welcomed without being sought after. Most of the jests came from the Bench in a form that kept them the private amusement of the Judge and the Bar. He never liked to see a witness held up to ridicule; "we laugh to-day and forget it to-morrow," he would say; "but the echoes of that laugh of ours will make that man's life a misery for months." Only one subject provoked him to sudden outbursts of anger. I am sorry to say that the country people in Ireland are addicted to an abominable habit of spitting, and are no respecters of places. A grave argument upon an abstruse point of law would be interrupted by an angry cry from the Judge: "Officer! Put that man out of Court, and don't let him come in again!" The offender, who had allowed his mouth to water too liberally at the sight of the legal pabulum, had dropped a quiet spit upon the floor; the lynx eye of the Judge had not missed it, and out the offender went. The bad habit was not limited to uneducated people. A learned old schoolmaster in Cork was once described to me as a man who could spit in nine languages. And a certain solicitor who added much to our gaiety in those days was apt to consider the floor of the Bar-room as one vast cuspidor. Nor was the custom confined to Ireland; when my uncle first visited America he found himself in the window seat of a railway coach with a neighbour who with great regularity discharged his accumulated juices through the window. My uncle, feeling uncomfortable, offered to change places with him; but the American replied: "Don't you worry, stranger; I kin shoot!"

Drumgoole began his circuit at Listowel in the north of the county; then he went on to Killarney, always a heavy sessions. Kenmare and Caherciveen were not visited every time, nor was Dingle; we finished at Tralee; where there was usually a fortnight's work. At Killarney and Kenmare there were excellent hotels; at Cahirciveen we were able to cross to the island of Valentia, where there was a really delightful hotel, more like a country house than a commercial undertaking, and we always felt ourselves the guests of the owner, and only dared to pay our bills surreptitiously. At Dingle the hotel was primitive but not uncomfortable; my main recollection of Dingle is that the inhabitants drew their water from a stream which flowed through the graveyard and collected itself in a spout which discharged through the wall, ready to fill any vessel placed beneath it. The health of Dingle was remarkably good. In October, 1917, we occupied a little village in the Artois, the water supply of which was a deep well, which was duly examined by our medical staff, and pronounced fit for human consumption. The third day we were there some enterprising fellows fished out of the well the body of the servant of the previous

G.O.C., the poor fellow having been missing for six weeks. My recollection is that we found the health of that village very good, too. What the eye does not see, the heart doesn't grieve at.

If the hotel at Listowel was not first class, the welcome was hearty. The waiter was a handsome old man, the " dead spit," as the phrase goes, of Mr. Justice Gibson. There was no explanation ever offered. Was it not Louis XIV—but perhaps the topic is irrelevant. John looked on every visitor to the hotel as his own personal guest; when he really loved you he struck a boiled potato in the fire until the room stank; then, delicately moistening his thumb and first finger with his tongue, he picked the cinder out and set it on your plate. When you taxed your bill and found an overcharge, John grinned and said: "I only put it on, sir, to give you the pleasure of knocking it off!"

Listowel was fortunate in its lawyers. Matthew Byrne was a man of scholarly education, well versed in the literature of ancient Ireland as well as in the classics. He loved the remote fountains of the law, and you had to be ready for a little excursion into black-letter when you saw him coming into Court with a bag of books. "In this case, your Honour," he said once to Dan Browne, "I rely on the decision in Taltarum's case." The astonished Judge was heard to mutter in his beard: "Bloody high-class law!" But the convolutions of the old law of real property gave joy to Matt Byrne's heart; and John Doe and Richard Roe were the dearest children of his fancy. His gentle nature kept him aloof from politics until the outrages of the Black and Tan régime caused him to appear as a champion of popular rights. I still possess the brief he sent to my uncle on behalf of

L

a very decent bookseller named Flavin, whose little shop had been closed on the *ipse dixit* of an Inspector of Constabulary, without trial, without even inquiry, without any opportunity being given to the owner to protest. I am happy to say that the Dublin Courts made short work of this injustice, though not prepared to accept the argument of Matt Byrne in quite the words he adopted for the instruction of his counsel. Every paragraph of the first three pages of the brief concludes with the exhortation: "To your tents, O Israel!" The subject-matter has little to say to Mr. Flavin's particular grievance, and consists of quotations from the works of Montesquieu, Edmund Burke, Bacon, Sir Thomas More, and a number of other philosophers, the gist of the argument being the incapacity of a policeman to see good in anything, and the admonition being well expressed by the final "To your tents, O Israel!" Matt was a noble fellow, and his death deprived the young Irish Free State of a valuable counsellor.

In marked contrast to Matt Byrne stood John Moran, brother of my client James Moran, of Limerick, but a much more genial and forthcoming member of the family. To John life was one long jest, to be annotated and chronicled with boisterous good humour. Once in Judge Shaw's day John found himself appearing against an old lady who had no friendly opinion of him. She mounted the table, took her seat opposite the Judge, and turned down towards her own advocate, who quickly got from her the evidence he needed. John stood up to cross-examine, and, laying a friendly hand on her knee, began: "Turn round to me now, my good woman, and answer me a few questions." The old lady turned and looked down at him: "Yerra," said she, "and what are you but an ugly old man?" "Look up at his Honour and repeat that now!" cried John. The Judge led the laughter.

On another occasion he appeared for a young actor, a member of a travelling company, who had been pitched into a hedge by the breaking down of a car he had hired to carry him from one country town to another, with sad results to his clothing, the seat of his trousers having been all but ripped off. John lifted his impressive six foot four and began an oration in which he pictured the thoughts of the young Thespian as he drove along the country road on a pleasant spring morning with the birds singing in the bushes and the sun shining up above. "And, your Honour," said he, "it would not be unnatural to suppose that in such circumstances his dreams would turn to his own future, and he would start picturing to himself the day when he would be a great star in the London theatres, another Henry Irving or Lewis Waller, or, maybe, Forbes Robertson; and all of a sudden there was a crash; he went flying through the air; and when he picked himself up the only famous actor he resembled was Mr. Barebohm Tree!"

At Assizes John would meet solicitors from further south, amongst them a silent Ulsterman named Girvin, who practised in Killorglin. Girvin was as bald as an egg; but he endeavoured to conceal this by wearing a wig of auburn colour. Indeed, he had two wigs, one longer haired than the other, and he would elaborately talk of having to go and get his hair cut, and then reappear wearing the shorter wig. One day there had been some confusion in the Court where William Moore Johnson was sitting, and the Judge had given orders, that if anyone else opened a particular door and came into Court, he

was to be put out by the police.   Girvin, all innocent of
offence, happened to enter the Court by this door, and,
to his amazement, was promptly seized by a zealous policeman and almost hurled out of Court.   Not unnaturally
he fumed with indignation and proceeded to unburden
his soul to a group of which John Moran was one.   He
asked all and sundry what he ought to have done by way
of protest.   John looked at him and said: "Well, Girvin,
if the Judge had done that to me I'd have taken off my
wig and I'd have gone for him bald-headed!"

Girvin was a strange but not unfriendly fellow, and I
often wondered what cantrip of fortune sent him down to
Killorglin to dwell amongst people alien to him in creed
and political outlook.   A delightful nephew of his was a
brother-officer of mine in the Royal Dublin Fusiliers; and
at Killorglin, Girvin's labours were shared by his son
"Horr'ld," who also was a gallant soldier, and, I fear,
died.   Father and son used to wander from town to town
in a funny little car, trespass upon which Girvin prevented by always bringing the gear-lever into the Bar-
room with him, where one or other of us would affect to
mistake it for the poker, and be only just prevented from
poking the fire with it.   On one occasion its dual existence
must have effected its efficiency, for, as Girvin sought to
return from an excursion to Killorglin pier, he put the
car into reverse instead of forward gear, and the next
thing he knew car and Horr'ld and he were in the water.
Everything was rescued except his wig.   About a fortnight later a fisherwoman came up to him and from the
depths of her ample bosom produced the missing tresses.

We met Girvin more often at Killarney than elsewhere; there he waged implacable war against his *bête
noire*, Maurice McCartie.   Maurice was a Corkman who

had settled in Kerry; he was one of the ablest solicitors I ever knew. He looked like a particularly ascetic and benevolent parish priest; his bright blue eye was like a bird's, and its glance was so gracious that he appeared to be without guile. But one had to get up very early in the morning to be ahead of Maurice McCartie. He lived with his sisters and his brother Denis, who was a ruddier and somewhat rougher edition of himself, as indeed behoved him, for Denis was an engineer and surveyor. The "mapper," as he was often called, was a powerful person in the counsels of the peasant, and many a brief came my way because of a kind word from Denis, who always insisted that the first question I ever asked him was: "Mr. McCartie, aren't you the biggest liar in the County Kerry?"—a grave reflection upon my advocacy, and a very false expression of my opinion of Denis.

Maurice's style may well be exemplified by a single story. A client came in to him one day with the announcement that a long-fought battle must come to a disastrous end. For years his enemy had been trying to get him out of his land; and now this rival was boasting that he had discovered an old deed which put his title beyond question. The existence of such a document seemed unlikely to Maurice, who, however, had no grounds for his opinion at that stage. He bade his man go down fighting, and perhaps something would turn up. When the case was called on in court, Eugene Downing, one of the most conscientious of solicitors, explained the facts to the Judge, dwelling upon the discovery of this ancient document, which he then proceeded to prove. Maurice asked no questions, merely asking to have a look at the deed, and then handing it back. Eugene closed his case.

"Now, Mr. McCartie," said the Judge. "I ask your Honour for a dismiss," said Maurice quietly. "On what grounds?" "There's no case to answer," said Maurice. "But the deed?" "The deed's a forgery," said Maurice. "A forgery? That's a very grave charge; how do you propose to prove that?" cried the Judge. "I'm not going to prove it; it proves itself," said Maurice. The Judge took the document in his hand and examined it very carefully. It had all the appearance of a venerable parchment, brown and crinkled with age; a first glance revealed no suggestion of forgery. "Will your Honour look at the stamp?" asked Maurice. "Well; the stamp seems all right." "And appears to be the same age as the document itself?" "Yes, of course." Maurice sat back; he enjoyed a mystery, and he had now given the clues. Eugene Downing was chuckling, for a more genuine-looking document had never been produced in court. The Judge was nonplussed. "I really cannot understand your point, Mr. McCartie." Maurice smiled. "Only that every embossed stamp has its date stamped on it," he said, "and that stamp is dated last month!" The fact that stamps are so dated has been observed by few people; look at the stamps in your cheque-book, and you will see that the date is carefully embossed on them. As soon as Maurice had seen that, he had concluded, quite correctly, that the document had been carefully prepared, stamped, then ante-dated, and put up the chimney to mature. Nobody ever discovered who was responsible for the forgery.

Many years afterwards that story stood me in good stead. I found a gentleman producing a number of what purported to be old receipts to vouch his bona fides; they were all stamped with twopenny stamps, although purporting to be pre-war! Maurice McCartie ought to have had the credit I then was accorded for detecting the fraud.

A generation ahead of mine, Maurice and his brother were close friends of Redmond Barry, another Corkman, destined to become Lord Chancellor of Ireland, and to vacate that office with tragic suddenness. There was still, in my time, a tradition of the days he used to adventure in Kerry, and in particular of one sessions at Cahirciveen when he and his brother and the McCarties decided to walk back to Killarney. They first spent a pleasant morning boating, in the course of which somebody produced a pack of cards; and it was agreed between them that whoever drew the ace of hearts should walk up to the nearest house, knock at the door, and hand the card in silence to whomsoever might answer. The ace was "forced" upon Redmond Barry, who, true to his bond, walked up to a pleasant house near by, rang the bell and silently handed the card to a charming young lady who answered the door. Many years afterwards, and on the eve of her own sad early death, Mrs. James Shuel, the wife of a well-known solicitor in Cahirciveen, told me the story; it was she who had answered the door, and she could not understand what the handsome fair-haired young man could mean by this tender of his heart.

The pilgrims did not get far upon their road; they reached Glenbeigh late at night, and sought rest at the hotel then kept by Mrs. Shea, later by her son Jack, whose beautiful voice was stilled for ever just after the war. Few fishermen who have tried the Kerry waters will need an introduction to that hotel, of which I am sure their memories will be all associated with hospitality. But on this unlucky night the travellers were very late in their arrival; they vainly demanded admission in the ordinary way, and finally sought their own entry by a window luckily left ajar. They had gathered the materials for a picnic meal in the kitchen, when Mrs. Shea appeared in her night attire, and, seizing a broomstick, drove them forth in ignominy. Neither their protests nor their threats would move her; and they had to pass the night as best they might in the outhouses. Next Quarter Sessions at Caherciveen found a cause listed "Barry and others *v.* Shea," wherein the indignant travellers sought to vindicate the law relating to innkeepers. The Judge, however, insisted that all concerned should come into his room and shake hands all round; and thus ended the battle of Glenbeigh.

The Dingle Sessions produced a larger percentage of Irish-speaking litigants than any part of Kerry; and it is significant that perjury, which was rampant in all other parts of the county, was almost non-existent in Dingle. The Bishop of Kerry had made perjury a "reserved" sin: that is to say, he reserved to himself the right to give absolution to a person guilty of the offence. But the vice continued, a blot on the fame of a clever people; Dingle alone upheld the standard of truth. A Kerry alibi was a phrase, something like the Ruy Lopez game in chess; just as it did not call for an Iberian to play the one, so a Kerry alibi might be produced in another county. Its essence was that the story was true in every respect except one: the date. The events sworn as having happened on the Tuesday were all true; but they had happened on the Wednesday, or on the Monday. Now, people go to Mass on a Sunday; or the fair day in such a town is a Monday; or Thomas O'Flaherty's funeral took place on a Tuesday; the attending Mass or a fair or a funeral is a fact, and one rather apt to get mixed up the most carefully prepared story. So that wonderful body, the Royal Irish Constabulary, used to keep careful record of the exact dates and times of such functions as might well come into the story of an alibi witness; and Crown counsel were always able to show an uncanny acquaintance with the daily routine of the rural population. Once a Kerry alibi succeeded at the Cork Assizes in circumstances that enshrine a lesson. The prisoner was a car-driver, accused of an agrarian outrage which had been committed on, let us say, October 4th. Identification was weak; the culprit had been masked and disguised; Richard Adams, who defended, had greatly shaken the witnesses for the prosecution; but William O'Brien was the Judge, and he had no intention of letting the prisoner escape. "My Lord," said Adams, "I have only one witness for the defence—Mr. Townsend, the well-known land agent." "What!" cried the Judge; "Misther Adams, do you mean to say that you are in a position to call that respectable gentleman to assist your client? There must be some mistake in this case. Let Mr. Townsend be called." The witness was duly sworn, and Adams examined him. "Mr. Townsend, do you remember Tuesday, October 4th last?" "I do, very well." "Where were you that day?" "I had to drive out to the neighbourhood of Macroom; I was in that part of the country all day, from nine in the morning until about half-past six in the evening." "Who drove you?" "The accused." "Could he have been anywhere near Riverstown that day at two o'clock?" "Absolutely impossible." "Oh-h-h, oh-h-h!" cried the Judge, "Misther Adams, there must have been some mistake on the part of the police. Gentlemen of the Jury, you had better find this prisoner Not Guilty;

let him be discharged. When a respectable gentleman like Mr. Townsend comes here and swears to the absence of the prisoner from the scene of the crime he obviously cannot be mistaken. We're all very much obliged to you, Mr. Townsend, for preventing a miscarriage of justice."

Adams was puzzled, for he had his own views about the prisoner's guilt; and yet Townsend was a pillar of law and order, and quite incapable of lending himself to a conspiracy to defeat justice. But Adams suddenly remembered that his solicitor, not the most particular of mortals, had impressed upon him that his first question to Townsend must take the form: "Do you remember Tuesday, the 4th October last?" He got out his diary, and turned back to the date. October 4th was a Wednesday!

A Tipperary alibi was a more elaborate affair than the Kerry kind. When the Crown witnesses had told their story at petty sessions, a mass of evidence was prepared in respect of each one of them to prove that he, the Crown witness, was somewhere else than the place he had sworn to on the day of the crime. This was a more difficult alibi to break down, as it did not even hint its appearance until the case for the Crown was being presented before the jury, which left no time for investigation and contradiction. The elder Mr. Weller would have greatly approved of the strategy and tactics of the defence in Irish criminal cases.

Tralee used to give us a fortnight's hard work at the end of the County Court Circuit. Tralee is a much more agreeable town than it looks. It has a pleasant park; there is an excellent little club; it used to be the depot of the Royal Munster Fusiliers, and Major Charier, who

died gallantly in one of the first battles of the war, produced his band on every possible occasion for the agreeable
amusement of the public. The bandmaster was not
always happy in his choice of music; in one short week
he played the Lord Chief Baron and Mr. Justice Kenny
into Court to the strains of "Hang Out the Front Door
Key," and enlivened the second marriage of a local
hostess by the strains of "The Merry Widow." It was at
Tralee that Pether O'Brien once decided to attend Mass
in state; and Dick Hennessy reported that "he walked
up the aisle looking for all the world as though he had
called to leave a card on the Almighty." This recalls
an earlier occasion when Pether and the Chief Baron
were going Circuit together, and an escort of lancers
and police had been provided. The High Sheriff called
to know whether the Judges would like to drive with
their escort to Mass on the Sunday. Pether, who loved
show, was heard through the open door to say: "Ah,
very conthiderate and polite! What do you thay, my
dear Palleth?" "Well, Pether," replied the Chief
Baron, "you may make a fool of yourself if you like, but
I'm going to walk!"

Pether had been Palles's pupil; and Miss O'Brien tells
how when her father and the Chief Baron were sitting
together one day and had differed in their opinions, Palles
was heard to comment on a proposition of the Chief
Justice's: "O, Peter! Peter! You never learned that
law from me!"

My only County Court memory of Tralee is of a case
in which it seemed that every legal *persona* in the County
of Kerry was represented. Judge Dromgoole settled
down for a long day of it; he marshalled the teams, to
make sure that nobody was missed, and then settled the

order in which he would hear the parties, and generally on what lines the case would proceed. The hearing took two days; almost an unprecedented thing in the County Court. Every advocate had his say; the Judge listened patiently to them all, no doubt congratulating himself that practically no part was being taken by a pink-faced, chubby little solicitor named Doctor O'Connell, but popularly known as "the Phyte Bull," because of a congenital incapacity to pronounce the letters "wh" except as an "f," which had caused some difficulty in a case concerning a bull of snowy hue. At last the case seemed to have perished from sheer exhaustion; the Judge looked patiently along the line, and said: "Well, now, is there anybody who wants to say anything else?" The "Phyte Bull" stood up, and diffidently remarked: "Your Honour, I have a preliminary objection to your Honour's jurisdiction." I think that Charles Dromgoole was nearer to blasphemy on that occasion than on any other in his life.

As I write, I suddenly recall one other case, the story of which should have been told by Guy de Maupassant. It concerned the estate of a man, rich as people were reckoned in rural Kerry, who had made his money in America, and had come home to die in Ireland. He had quarrelled with his own people, and took up his abode with a small farmer and his wife; and here he lived the last seven or eight years of his life. He was well cared for by the farmer's wife, a calculating woman, whose one thought was the money that he would leave behind him; she had a dread that if he went to a solicitor to make his will, the solicitor might persuade him to leave it in whole or in part to the relatives with whom he had quarrelled. And so he came to his dying bed, still intestate. Her husband fetched the priest, and he was given the last rites of the Church; then the priest asked him had he made a will, and, finding that he had not, set about helping him to make it. The wife fretted and fussed; but the priest firmly turned her out of the room; then he completed the document, and called in the servant girl to join him in witnessing its due execution. The will duly made, he took his departure; and no sooner was he gone than the wife was back in the room, searching and seeking until she found the will. It was all that she had hoped for; it left everything to her husband and herself and the survivor. There it stood, witnessed by the priest and the girl; but she felt unsafe. She took pen and ink and wrote in her own name as a third witness; and thereby signed away the inheritance of herself and her husband to the relatives the testator had declined to benefit.[1]

---

[1] Perhaps I should explain for non-legal readers' benefit that neither a witness nor the spouse of a witness can receive anything under the will he or she attests.

XII

SHORTLY BEFORE my own call to the bar there occurred a most extraordinary incident in the legal history of Ireland, which fortunately ended without anybody being a penny the worse. Judicial appointments were looked upon as the patronage-fund of the Government of the day; and up to the passing of the Local Government Act of 1898 every salaried position in Ireland had been filled by authorities that were remote from popular control. The establishment of the county and district councils was followed by an outbreak of local jobbery that was very regrettable; but the country recovered its balance fairly quickly, and it was generally admitted that the business of the counties was on the whole more efficiently administered under the new local government than it had been under the old Grand Jury system. I have no doubt that there was jobbery in those days also. But now a new appetite set in amongst those who formerly had no hope of dipping into the public purse; and when a Liberal administration took charge of the country, a class of person began to hope for judicial appointments that had never turned his eyes in such a direction before. The Irish Party had pledged themselves to accept no office or honour for themselves; a quiet word would sometimes be spoken for this or that candidate, but on the whole they maintained their disinterested attitude remarkably well until the Liberals came back. They then allowed themselves to be harnessed to the Liberal chariot on condition that their wishes were consulted about Crown appointments in Ireland.

My maternal uncle, the present Serjeant Sullivan, had pursued a somewhat unusual course in politics, which I have no doubt he understood himself, but which puzzled his relatives a good deal. Up to 1900 he had been a firm supporter of my other uncle; and, in the General Election of that year, had spoken for my father until some enthusiastic opponent had landed a considerable-sized rock in his eye. A newly-married man, he allowed himself to be persuaded to abandon politics; but his temperament was unequal to abstention. In the mean-time, all of our candidates had been wiped out except Tim himself, who told the House that there were two united Irish parties, of which he was one. The other boasting a somewhat larger personnel (eighty-four, if my memory serves me), was supported throughout the country by an organisation that had been founded some years before by Mr. William O'Brien, then strongly opposed to us; it was called the United Irish League. To the surprise of his relatives, A. M. Sullivan suddenly joined a branch of the United Irish League, giving as his reason a desire to keep vigilant watch over the purity of Irish administration. And when the Liberals came in he uttered a warning fulmination against any attempt to fill judicial vacancies upon any principle other than that of appointing the best-qualified candidate.

At this time the *Freeman's Journal* was the official organ of the Nationalist Party. Those of us who least agreed with its politics paid ready tribute to the ability with which it was conducted, and especially to what might be called the cultural side of its character. Much of this literary excellence was due to its principal leader-writer, Matthias McDonnell Bodkin, one of the most charm-ing and genial of men, of wide general culture, and particularly well qualified as a critic of current literature and the drama. These, however, were the qualities in least demand in his office; and where in his friendly and kindly nature he secreted the admirable political malice with which he inspired his leading articles every day was always a puzzle to me. He had been called to the Irish Bar while a member of the *Freeman* staff; and although he took a very active part in defending political prisoners in the days of the Land War, journalism remained his first love, and at the time of which I now speak he had all but ceased to appear in the Law Library. Occasional briefs, some of them of weight and importance, still were sent to him; but he was not holding himself out for practice at the Bar. On the other hand, he had sacrificed comfort and income to fight and win a Parliamentary seat in 1892, which he resigned in 1895. He had been a valuable supporter of the Party; he was personally extremely popular; and a hint went round that the triumph of the Liberals would enable the Nationalist leaders to procure for him a County Court Judgeship. Sullivan threw out a definite challenge to the Lord Chancellor to make such an appointment, and threatened to bring it to naught if made.

The statute governing such matters prescribed that the appointee must have been a practising barrister during the ten next preceding years. Bodkin's "practice" during that period had pursued him to his home, and had only necessitated an occasional robed visit to the Law Library. However, Sir Samuel Walker, the Lord Chancellor, was a loyal friend and a man of courage; and, when the County Court Judge of Clare died, he defied the lightning, and appointed Bodkin to the vacancy. Bodkin took the necessary oath and his seat; all the fulminations appeared to have vanished in smoke.

And then one day the Four Courts were startled to hear Sullivan applying for a conditional order of Quo Warranto, calling upon Judge Bodkin to show cause why he should adjudicate upon a claim by a tradesman named Griffin against a labourer named Stephen Markham. There was a very elaborate affidavit by Markham, which suggested that the statute governing such appointments had been disregarded, and that Mr. Bodkin had retired from the Bar more than ten years before his appointment.

The Court granted the conditional order, and a day was appointed for Mr. Bodkin to show cause why it should not be made absolute.

Here was a pretty kettle of fish! And misfortune dogged the Crown; for when the case came on for argument it soon became evident that the Court, composed of three Unionist Judges, were inclined to think the application well founded, and were not sorry to have a chance of "a crack at the Government." The Irish practice differs from the English in such matters, and I think the advantage lies across the water; for the Court that hears the cause shown against the rule over here may not have heard the original application; in Ireland the applicant began again and fully stated his reasons. Sullivan thus had an opportunity to explain step by step the implications of his argument; and before the end of the day it was evident from the interpolations from the Bench that the Court were in full sympathy with the view for which he was contending. Up to this point the only *legitimus contradictor* had been Mr. Bodkin; but at the adjournment it was felt that something desperate must be attempted if the case were to be saved. So the Attorney-General was approached, and the direful tidings conveyed to him.

M

The Attorney-General was Richard Cherry, of whom we have spoken already; his own appointment had seemed to Sullivan almost as bad as Bodkin's. But, like many men occupying a position beyond their average capacity, he suffered from what is now called an inferiority complex; and he determined that he was not going to allow *his* administration to be made a laughing-stock. So he hastened into Court the next morning, and demanded to be heard. Pether O'Brien, who was presiding, suggested that he should wait until Sullivan had finished his argument. Cherry protested that this would be a waste of time, as his argument would be based upon the doctrine that the King could do no wrong. Sullivan made a pleasant contribution to the effect that even the titular head of the profession ought not to talk nonsense like this, which did not calm the indignant Cherry. He next protested that the writ of Quo Warranto was a prerogative writ and could not issue without his consent, which had not been obtained. Pether then began some very naughty cherry-picking, in the course of which he said: "You are the titular head of the profethion." Cherry leaped to his feet: "My Lord," he cried, "that phrase has been applied to me by junior counsel with the object of insulting me. Of him I took no notice; but of your Lordship I must and will take notice. And if your Lordship insists upon insulting me——." "Yeth?" asked Pether, in a tone of eager interest. Cherry fumed; his colleagues whispered to him, and Pether, quite unabashed, said: "Now, Mither Attorney-General, go on with your great conthtituthional argument." Cherry then spent the morning putting forward doctrines that would have rejoiced the heart of James I or James II, but which found little sympathy upon the Bench. In the afternoon

Redmond Barry, the Solicitor-General, took up the argument, and, with a skill that might have saved Napoleon at Moscow, retreated from every position that Cherry had taken up, and based him upon the firmer ground that there was no definition of what was meant by a "practising" barrister. He was followed by Serjeant O'Connor and the present Sir Thomas Molony for Mr. Bodkin, and the argument was carried over until the next morning.

It was evident that the Court had not been impressed by the cause shown against the conditional order; and on the last morning everybody assembled in Court expecting to see poor Mattie Bodkin expelled from the judicial bench he had so lately ascended. But there are more ways of killing a dog than to choke it with a pound of butter. As soon as the Court sat, it was learned that Mr. Stephen Markham had filed a second affidavit. In the course of it he stated that he had been horrified to learn that his name had been used for the purpose of challenging the jurisdiction of Judge Bodkin; he had only sworn an affidavit to resist the rapacious claim of Mr. Griffin, and had never authorised the present proceedings at all. Mr. Birrell told the House of Commons that a pint of porter had persuaded the deponent to make his first affidavit; it never appeared what inducement procured the second and I am sure it did not come from Mr. Bodkin. Of course, as soon as this affidavit was filed, the motion fell to the ground; and Judge Bodkin served Clare for many years as County Court Judge. At first he was not a conspicuous success; but his good nature and common sense took charge of his Court, and when he retired he was universally regretted. His period of office covered that evil chapter of history associated with the name of the Black and Tans. The Most Reverend Dr. Fogarty, the bishop of the diocese that covered Judge Bodkin's territorial jurisdiction, had to fly secretly from his home to avoid being murdered; but in this atmosphere of terrorism, Judge Bodkin refused to be silenced, and at the imminent risk of his life continued to denounce the infamies that were being perpetrated by these notorious servants of the Crown. It was in a large part due to his efforts that blackguardism was at last checked; and many a Clare household can thank Judge Bodkin for having been spared from arson and loot.

His distinguished son, Professor Thomas Bodkin, is also a member of the Bar, but has directed his talents towards a wider and a more important world. However, my heart leaps up when I behold in the centre page of *The Times* some fierce paragraph to show that he has not yet learned to suffer fools gladly, and can castigate them in a style not wholly emancipated from the invective of the Irish Bar.

The Law Library, always rich in ballads and pasquinades, produced an account of the Bodkin case which became very popular. A copy of it was given to me by the late William Byrne, who told me that he believed the author to have been J. M. Lowry, a colleague of ours with a gift for light verse which enriched every Dublin pantomime. I am sure he will, if still alive, bear me no ill-will for reproducing, and perhaps misquoting his ballad: I feel certain that he finished it off with better polish than this version shows.

QUO WARRANTO

Come, all true-hearted patriots, and listen to my tale;
'Tis all about a County Court where Justice doth prevail,
Likewise concerning Mattie B. (from truth I will not budge),
And how bould Markham tried to drive from Clare her County
    Judge.

Says Markham: "To my simple mind it certainly appears
Matt hasn't on the hazard stood for ten preceding years;
Then how he came to get the job is what I'd like to know."
Says Sullivan: "We'll find that out by a Quo Warranto."

To try the case the Judges sat; in number they were three—
In order to obtain, of course, a clear majority:
The Lord Chief Justice of renown in story and in song,
Mr. Justice Madden, and Judge Wright who's never wrong.

Then Cherry rose.   In wrath he spake: "I am the great A.-G.,
And no one dares to move this writ without the leave of me.
Quo Warranto can never go unless I'm in the swing,
For I'm Attorney-General and represent the King."

" My friend," the Lord Chief Justice said, " if what you thay
    be true
The Bill of Rightth ith buthted up, and Habeath Corputh too,
And all our Conthtituthion'th gone of which we thtand in need,
And all the time the Baronth thpent with John at Runnymede."

Says Cherry, complimental-like: "A legal mind you've got,
And, just like 'Homocea,' you're always on the spot;
All them ould things is shwept away, and anyone with brains
Knows that the King's Prerogative is all that now remains."

"Suppose," said Madden, J., "the King, a guest in Dublin
    town,
Broke ev'ry pane of window-glass while walking up and down,
And thus were brought before the Court, what would your
    action be?"
Said Cherry: "Faith, I'd enter then a Nolle Prosequi."

"Well, then," the Lord Chief Justice said, "the Crown mutht
    lothe thith thuit,
For in thith cathe the Court mutht make thith order abtholute;
And though not for one moment would I my Thovereign
    bluff,
Thtill, in thith cathe Prerogative'th not worth a pinch of
    thnuff."

And when the dark and direful news a messenger did bring
To Windsor's Royal residence and broke it to the King,
Says he: "My bold Prerogative, a Monarch's proudest boast,
Lies with the other Castle Jew'ls, and is for ever lost."

There was a less reverent version which made His
Majesty remark:

"If that be so," replied the King, "'tis plain beyond a doubt
My bloody Royal Prerogative is fairly up the spout."

But the adjective, no doubt, referred to Prerogative
in Tudor days.

Having commenced to transcribe verse, let me go on.
In 1911, Mr. John Masefield, already known to the
cognoscenti, blazed into general popularity by publishing
"The Everlasting Mercy," which sent the *English Review*
into goodness knows how many editions. Everybody
remembers how the sinner in the poem chronicles his
life by decades, and how the foulest language is inter-
spersed with the most delicate phrases. It appeared at a
stage in the career of John Francis Moriarty when he had
already won back a prominent place at the Irish Bar; he
had been appointed Serjeant, and was moving heaven
and earth to procure the succession to the next vacant
Law Officership. It was at this time that the following
lines were circulated in the Law Library; and I am driven
to rely on my memory to recall them, for I have had no
copy now for more than twenty years.

THE EVERLASTING MERCENARY

BY

JOHN F. MASEFIELD

From '79 to '81
I had no politics—not one.
The Rule of Rome and Rule of Three
Meant very much the same to me,
And anyone could make me feel
Quite bored by mentioning Repeal.
I cared but little for the State—
I was a shocking reprobate!

In '81 I can aver
My conscience first began to stir.
We lost the Member for our Borough,
Of which I had a knowledge thorough.
I knew the side to turn my coat:
I knew the price of every vote:
I knew the candidate to bleed,
And bled him too—I did, indeed;
And with his money in my hand
Decided that I would not stand.
Perhaps you'll say I sold the cause—
That was the sort of chap I was!

From '81 to '84
A Liberal was Chancellor.
'Twas then I first became a suitor
To be appointed prosecutor.
I got the job, and got the Light—
I was a Liberal all right.

From '84 to '86
That Party played such funny tricks
I grew uneasy in my soul;
My anger I could scarce control,

At length their quarrels grew so heated
They sought the polls—and were defeated.
I read with pain their sordid story—
'Twas then I first became a Tory.

But during those first years of error
I had been called the Holy Terror;
I went to Mass, I went to Church;
I left the Devil in the lurch.
In vain for me Eve ate the apple;
I went to Church and went to Chapel.
In vain did Smiling Sin come greeting;
I went to Chapel and to Meeting.
I lunched off holy oil and chrism:
I learned the Shorter Catechism.
The creeds were sometimes not the same,
But I could swallow all that came.

Such was my state before I turned;
But now the fire that ever burned
Blazed forth in all its majesty:
I found that I was conscience-free.
I took to visiting the races:
I rather fancied pretty faces:
I paid, whene'er I chose to dine,
Five pounds, exclusive of the wine.
For years my bliss was unalloyed—
    And then came Mr. Justice Boyd!

O comrades!   'Tis a bitter thing
To leave the paddock and the ring:
To leave the women and the wine:
At half-crown table-d'hôte to dine!
I cursed my luck: I cursed my fate:
I cursed the men whose food I ate:
I cursed each jockey and his gee:
But most I cursed Lord Salisbury.

O world of lips! O world of laughter!
O cruel harpies following after!
O bitter vultures, overblown
With money that was not my own!
They beat me fiercely to the ground:
I offered sixpence in the pound—
While poor old Gladstone, like a fool,
Tried, without me, to pass Home Rule!

One thing, and one alone, was plain:
I'd have to go to work again.
I dodged the dirty breed of Silke
And lived in quiet, like poor Dilke.
'Tis strange, but as a matter of fact 'tis
Thence that I trace my present practice.
My conduct was beyond all blame;
I played the—well, I played *my* game,
Until at length, in 1903,
A gown of silk was given to me.

From 1903 we soon arrive
Down to November, 1905.
'Twas then the Tories got the sack;
Next year the Liberals came back.
My heart leaped up when I beheld
The size to which their numbers swelled.
I said: "Don't lose your civil manner, man,
But write, congratulating Bannerman;
And he has friends to face his task with,
So drop another line to Asquith;
And, though it goes against the gorge,
You'd best be civil to Lloyd George."
I wrote in quite a pleasant style:
They said; "You'd better wait a while."
I quickly answered: "Right you are, gents!"
And soon was put amongst the Serjeants.

We thus come down to 1910;
The Liberals were returned again,
No longer as a party free,
But with a small majority.
I heard a politician shout:
"John Redmond now can turn them out!"
And, ere the echoes quite had whist,
I had become a Nationalist!

O Erin! Country of my heart!
For many years we've lived apart.
I never knew your ancient wrongs—
I never was much good at songs,
And thus I never learned to weep
To hear George sing "The West's Asleep."
But now I'll warble like the mavis
The wildest strains of Thomas Davis,
Or Wolfe Tone, or King Brian Boru—
There's nothing that I will not do!
I'll sing, with all the force of Hedmondt,
The peerless glories of John Redmond.

When o'er the mountains wandering
You come a-walking in the Spring
Your feet are bare on the young shoots,
Or else I'd gladly lick your boots.

Yes, Erin! And 'tis all for love.
Yet swear to me by Heaven above—
One boon I crave—one boon you'll grant
To me, your faithful sycophant;
When next from off the path he trod
And treads, a Judge is called to God,
And poor Ignatius takes his place,
And Tom Molony with ill grace
Becomes Attorney-General,
O! grant, dear Mother, that I shall

Not seek in vain the Castle door,
But shall be made Solicitor!
And kick with all the force you can
The wretched Alex Sullivan;
And do not let your foot be light
When saying "No!" to Dudley White.
I do not care, upon my honour,
What hurt you do to James O'Connor,
Provided first you slit the gorge
Of foul, fat, self-besotted George.
Then, Erin, will I sing your praise
On all appointed holidays,
And be your servant—till the hour
The Tories next return to power.

I am, save that I'm turning sallow,
Exactly what I was at Mallow.

There are needed a few notes to the above piece of history. It was in 1883, and not in 1881, that William Moore Johnson became a judge and precipitated the contest at Mallow. I wonder if Hedmondt, the tenor, has many surviving admirers now. The "George" twice mentioned was Serjeant George MacSweeney, another journalist who had come to the Bar and was receiving considerable support from a section of the Irish Party. He regarded himself both as an oracle and a musician, and I think that on the whole I preferred his singing, as the first person singular did not occur so often in it. He was a special protégé of Ignatius O'Brien, another Cork journalist who by political influence became Serjeant, Law Officer, and Lord Chancellor. O'Brien was suppressed in favour of James Campbell during the war, and as he received the consolation of a peerage, the wits of Dublin suggested he should take his title from the little village of Stepaside, near his own residence. He

preferred the more euphonious title of Lord Shandon.
James O'Connor and Dudley White were two other
candidates for office at that time, the latter *pour rire*.
He was, however, a clever mimic. James O'Connor
was a man of real ability, but absolutely without a sense
of tradition. He would have been a brilliant success in
America. In Ireland he was a failure as a Law Officer,
but a good Chancery Judge, and a better Lord Justice of
Appeal. He came to the English Bar after the establishment of the Irish Free State, but after a few notable
appearances grew tired of it, and returned to Ireland,
where he successfully petitioned to be allowed to resume
the profession at which he had began, and was once more
admitted a solicitor. He died, still a young man, and
hundreds went hungry.

Ignatius O'Brien, above mentioned, was by no means
the least creditable appointment made by the Liberals.
He had enjoyed a fairly good practice, most of it in
Bankruptcy; he had been standing counsel to the *Freeman's
Journal*, but this was his only connection with politics.
His appearance was most truculent, and earned him the
sobriquet "Pugnacious O'Brien"; his real nature was
kindly, and he spent his considerable means with unosten-
tatious generosity. But when he became Lord Chancellor,
the fable of the inflated frog came true. Never was a
judge so pompous, or, for that very reason, so inefficient.
At first the presence of Lord Justice Holmes kept some
sense of tradition in the Court of Appeal; and Cherry,
as a Lord Justice, had at least the merit of holding his
tongue. But, when Holmes went, the disintegration
set in; when Cherry became Lord Chief Justice, disaster
was completed by the appointment to the vacancy in the
Court of Appeal of Stephen Ronan. O'Brien maundered;

Ronan frankly interrupted. O'Brien insisted upon informing counsel of the way his mind was operating. Serjeant Sullivan once interrupted such a soliloquy by sweetly suggesting that the operation of what his Lordship was pleased to call his mind, would become relevant if his Lordship would first listen to the facts of the case. Quite a lot of progress was made during the remainder of that day. Usually, however, both he and Ronan were insuppressible, and counsel were unable to make the simplest statement without interruption. Billeted where the railway crosses the road a mile west of Ypres, I received in February, 1918, from my friend T. C. Tobias an account that had appeared in the Dublin papers of a particularly bad episode in which the late W. M. Jellett, K.C., had found himself unable to get a word in edgeways in the disputes between the Lord Chancellor and Lord Justice Ronan. With these he sent me some verses of his own, a parody of the "Walrus and the Carpenter," in which he neatly hit off the situation; if I had not lost them I would certainly take the liberty of reproducing them. I, in reply, sent him the following two squibs, the second being a parody of a charming little poem by Mrs. Charles Masterman:

(I)

I'll tell thee all, and then some more:
   'Twere pity to be short;
I saw a learned Counsellor
   Who practised in our Court.
He looked a carven bit of steel:
His manner was abrupt:
Said he: "My Lord, in this Appeal——"
   Said I: "Don't interrupt."

It seemed a national disgrace
  Besides a private grief
That in what looked a lengthy case
  MacSweeney held no brief.
Said I: "You cannot recompense
  Us for his learning's store,
Although you're (in another sense)
  A lengthy Counsellor."

Said he: "My Lord, in this Appeal
  I am with Mr. Brown——"
My hand constrained in grip of steel
  Lord Justice Ronan's gown.
"I hope," said I, "they're going to talk
  Of treason and attainders;
Last week I purchased, on a walk,
  'Fearne on Contingent Remainders.' "

But he was thinking of a plan,
  Quite different from me,
Of interrupting every man
  From two to half-past three.
" 'Tis plain," said he, "that Jellett's here,
  For he has just sat down,
But I should like it made more clear
  As to *which* Mr. Brown——"

I heard him then, for I had found
  In my subconscious state
An absolutely virgin ground
  Whereon to ruminate:
Was Barry's resignation good,
  And was I well appointed?
"Come! earn," I cried, "your livelihood,
  Though times may be disjointed."

"My Lord," said he, "in this Appeal——··
  "You've said all that before;
We're only waiting here to reel
  Off cases by the score.
Have you considered Pearce *v.* Brookes?
  And don't deal in a stale way
With that immortal case of Cooke's
  v. the Midland Great Western Railway."

"In this Appeal, my Lord," said he,
  "I'm hoping to be short——"
"But, Mr. Jellett, that can't be
  If you disturb the Court.
You've tried four different times to-day
  To argue, without waiting
To understand the wondrous way
  My mind was operating."

A sound came from my left-hand side—
  'Twas like a leafy rune
Fluttered by some old law-book in
  A busy month of June.
"Perhaps," said this absurd L.J.,
  (He makes me very nettled)
"Counsel has only come to say
  That this Appeal is settled."

"My Lord," said Jellett, "that's correct;
  And, after all I've heard,
I wish that I might now collect
  A penny for each word.
My generous fee I'd gladly trade
  For nobler recompense—
Unless, indeed, they only paid
  On every word of sense."

And now, when Wilson feels his fob,
  Or Sullivan guffaws,
When "Thank-you-Kindly" seeks a job,
  Or Bartley seeks for flaws,
Or lengthy-winded counsel plead,
  And talk in double Dutch,
I memorise this little screed,
Reflecting that my sorrow's meed
Is greater than all these indeed;
For, though our places are well feed
Beyond our wildest dreams of greed
(Not that we ever were in need),
I still must tell my rosary-bead,
And frequent prayers to Heaven speed
For one relief to intercede:
—Ronan and I are both agreed:
  Molony talks too much!

(II)

"What is the Sound that fills the Hall beneath the mighty
    Dome
Where Themis runs an apple-stall, and idle counsel roam?"
" 'Obiter Dicta' is its name, and yonder is its home,
    Where two old judges babble on, babble on, babble on,
And trace the law from Babylon right down to Kingdom
    Come."

"The men that walked in Babylon were goodly men and tall
Who climbed upon the battlements and rhymed upon the wall
About Prince Humpty Dumpty, and what time he had a fall—
    'For that's the point,' they babble on, babble on, babble on,
'Unless 'twas "In the course of" he got no award at all.' "

"But who is Number Three who sits with beneficent glance
And never interrupts at all (he never gets the chance)?"
"Ah! he imports into the court the element, Romance,
    For while the others babble on, babble on, babble on,
He takes the facts and figures in, and work can thus advance."

"But this is as it used to be before the war began,
When I used sometimes hold a brief with Serjeant Sullivan."
"You must expect consistency at least from such a man;
    And thus the twain will babble on, babble on, babble on,
Tracing the way from Babylon O'Brien's easement ran."

I may add that there stands upon my mantelpiece a
sketch by the late Norman Kough,[1] my countenance
adorning the body of a bird perched upon *Walker's
Rhyming Dictionary*, the label being "The Jackdaw of
Rhymes." The work is a libel, for I have never used the
book in question; but I have allowed the Statute of
Limitations to run without taking action; and poor
Noıman is now, alas! beyond the jurisdiction.

---

[1] Reproduced as a frontispiece.

N

XIII

I WONDER WHETHER Hughie Irvine is still alive? It
was once my privilege to appear for him before the
Lord Chief Baron in a Civil Bill Appeal that concerned
the sale of a horse to a Miss Healy of Bandon. Miss Healy
was one of five very beautiful sisters, the daughters of a
prosperous Bandon merchant whose name was the same
as my own; I was once asked by an exile in Montreal
whether I was a son of Maurice Healy of Bandon, and I
blushed with pride to think I was looking so handsome.
This particular Miss Healy had bought a horse from young
Irvine; and the animal had not proved satisfactory. So
she had brought her action for breach of warranty, and
the County Court Judge had pronounced a decree in her
favour. At the hearing of the appeal she had given her
evidence clearly and well, but it left a possibility that the
warranty had not been as complete as she had thought.
The old Lord Chief Baron was not incapable of admiring
female charm; and we felt we were fighting a losing battle
when Hughie went into the box.

To say that I examined him would misrepresent the
facts. He took a long breath, turned to the Judge and
began: "Now, me Lord, the way of it was this: . . ."
and he then poured forth a story which seemed to be
uninterrupted even by his breathing, and into which it
was impossible for me to introduce a question. On it
went, and on; dramatic gesture lent its aid, and an
occasional expletive made an unwonted appearance in the
witness-box. The effect of it was that no man sold a
horse in Bandon fair without first striking a few chords
in honour of Apollo; to say that such poetic phrases were
mere puffing would do scant justice to the poet, but the

jargon of the law is hateful to Euterpé. "The real truth, me Lord," said Hughie, "was this:" and there followed a history of the animal in question which would have prophesied to any intending purchaser the deterioration the horse subsequently suffered. I could see the old Chief Baron simmering; soon he began to breathe hard through his nose, and, kicking the desk as violently as he could, he thundered: "See, sir! That is not what you told Miss Healy at Bandon Fair!" "Ah, no; but I'm on me oath now, me Lord!" replied Hughie, in the most natural way in the world. And he won his case.

Many people believe that Hugh Irvine was the original Flurry Knox. I think that Miss Somerville and her charming partner were wont to make their characters composite; but Hughie was well known to them, and had many of Flurry's characteristics. He had a fond mother who doted on him; she encouraged all his sporting proclivities, and more than once came to his rescue when prosaic creditors were taking too practical a view of life. But at last she felt that she was being imposed upon. A dealer named Barrett brought an action against her for the price of some horses he had purchased on her son's instructions, for which the latter had either neglected or refused to pay. Barrett claimed that Mrs. Irvine, by her conduct, had held out Hugh as her general agent for the purchase of horses. The action afforded Pether O'Brien an opportunity to enshrine in the Law Reports an excellent example of his style. He presided in Dublin when an application for a new trial was made, and this is the commencement of his judgment:

"If this case is deemed worthy of a place in our law books, or is made the subject of a story in any metropolitan or local magazine, it may be well intituled 'The Enfant Gâté of Roscarberry.' A fond mother paid some money—the price of horses which her son, a spoilt boy, had bought, and it is argued that she thereby held him out to the world as, and constituted him, her general agent to buy horses on her credit to any extent his juvenile fancy might suggest. That, in fact, if another Waterloo was to be fought in defence of the liberties of Europe, this impulsive youth might horse, at her expense, a Brigade of the Greys, Inniskillings and 1st Royals, to add another page to the history of chivalry. If the law permits this, the man in the street, to whom I have so often referred as the embodiment of common sense, may well regard Mr. Bumble's famous dictum not merely as historical, but true.''

He then proceeded to examine the facts of the case, and proceeded:

''The defendant was referred to as if she kept a fashionable pack of hounds in elaborate kennels. The Roscarberry pack was certainly interesting by reason of its diversified character. Variety has a charm of its own. What is unique is always attractive. The pack was composed of all sorts and conditions of hunting dogs—uniform neither in size nor pace nor breeding— and although it was styled 'The Roscarberry Foxhounds,' it could boast of only one pure-bred foxhound —*lucus a non lucendo*. The proclivities of the pack were as diversified as its composition; it pursued with equal ardour every description of quadruped, whatever the nature of the scent. I am not sure that the feathered tribe was altogether without some measure of attention. However, though the menage at Roscarberry was not quite up to Leicestershire standard, I feel quite certain that the heart of the young Master was, so far as related to physical courage, in the right place, and that he often afforded good sport, and that the followers of the pack had not infrequently, to use an expression amongst hunting men, 'a clinking run.' The mother's heart was proud, and the field was at once gratified and grateful. This was all very interesting and picturesque, but it did not at all involve that the mother held out her son as her general agent to buy horses.''

For those whose appetite has been whetted sufficiently I may add that the above quotations are from the report of the case in the Irish Reports, the citation being (1907) 2 I.R. 462.

My reference to the susceptibility of the Lord Chief Baron has stirred another pool of memory, probably going back to about 1905. The old man had developed a liking for ocean travel; and it was his custom to cross to America during the Long Vacation, his companion very frequently being Matt Bourke, of whose old-world courtliness I have already spoken. On the occasion of which I speak they had crossed from Dublin to Liverpool and taken passage for New York in, I think, the *Adriatic*. Those were the pre-Runciman days, when all the first-class mail steamers called at Queenstown; and it happened that a party of us were going aboard at Queenstown to bid farewell to some American friends. On the tender we ran into Standish O'Grady, Clerk of the Crown and Peace for the County of Cork; he had deemed it his duty to call on the Lord Chief Baron as he passed the harbour.

Standish was, I think, the fattest man I have ever seen; an aunt of mine once gazed at him in amazement and murmured in awe-struck tones: "To think that that's all one man!" His size, however, had not prevented him from shaking a fairly lively leg all his life; and (in appropriate surroundings) he liked still to be considered "one of the lads."

As we emerged on the promenade deck we ran into the Chief Baron and Matt Bourke, and they kindly stopped me and held me in conversation for a few minutes. Thus I happened to be there when Standish arrived, and began to pay his addresses. But at the same moment as he reached the side of the Chief Baron he was recognised by Miss Delia Darling, under which name I disguise one of the most charming and least strait-laced of musical-comedy stars, who positively screamed: "Why! If it isn't dear old Standish O'Grady! Stan, my angel, do come and have a drink!" Now, I am perfectly sure that Standish would gladly have accepted that invitation in almost any other conceivable circumstances; but for the moment he did his best to pretend that he had not heard it, while with his hand behind his back he made violent signals to the lady to go away and be a good girl. But she was not to be put off: "Stan!" she cried, "introduce your friends!" Standish by this time was dissolving into a pool of perspiration; but the Chief Baron, with a very mischievous smile, said: "Come on, Mr. O'Grady: present me to the lady; and if you will not accept her invitation, I certainly will!" I believe that Matt Bourke acted as the perfect chaperon during the trip across the Atlantic; but I am not certain that he entirely approved.

The Cork Assizes once contributed a leading case to the law relating to the sale of goods: Wallis v. Russell.

It was tried before Pether O'Brien, who greatly enjoyed himself. Mrs. Wallis had brought her action against Messieurs Russell, who were well-known merchants in Cork, in respect of a crab which had been purchased for her supper, and which made her seriously ill. In those days such actions were not common; but Mrs. Wallis happened to be the mother of one of the most original and courageous solicitors in Cork, who at a later date distinguished himself by having his office premises and their garden, situated in the main street of the town of Midleton, declared to be a holding that was partly agricultural or pastoral, and thus entitled to the benefits of the Irish Land Acts. To a mind of such daring an action about a diseased crab would be a trifle. And so the case was launched. There was no doubt about Mrs. Wallis's illness, or about its cause. The whole point was, whether the salesman had warranted the crab to be fit for human consumption. There is a section of the Sale of Goods Act which deals with the matter; and a young lady went into the box to describe her purchase of the crab.

"I am a companion to Mrs. Wallis," she said. "I went out to buy her some little tasty thing that she might fancy for her tea; and I suddenly thought of a crab. I knew that Russell's had cooked crabs; so I went in there, and asked the shopman for a nice cooked crab, telling him I wanted it for Mrs. Wallis's supper, so as to make known to him the purpose for which it was to be used." Pether pricked up his ears. "You thaid that?" he asked. "Yes, my Lord." "In thothe very wordth?" "Yes, my Lord." Pether reflected a moment. "Remarkable the thtrideth education ith taking," he commented. "Go on." The young lady took up her tale. "Well, then, when I had told him that, he looked at the crabs, and he selected one and gave it to me. So I, relying on his skill and judgment, took it——." "Thtop, thtop!" cried Pether. "You uthed thothe wordth altho?" "Yes, my Lord." "Where were you educated?" "At the Ursuline Convent, Blackrock, my Lord." "And thinth when have the Urthuline Thithters included Thection Fourteen of the Thale of Goodth Act in their curriculum?" "I don't know, my Lord; I did not get beyond domestic economy." "Ah-h! That'th where it ith; they teach you to buy food?" "Yes, my Lord." "And they tell you, 'Never buy anything without telling the shopman what it ith for, tho that you can thay you have relied on his thkill and judgment'?" "Yes, my Lord." "What admirable nunth!" said Pether. "Go on!" But his sarcasm went for naught; the young lady's story was implicitly accepted by the jury; and Mrs. Wallis received such comfort as the law could afford her, and set a head-line for the example of other persons unfortunate enough to poison themselves with unfit food.

There must have been an extraordinary facial resemblance between Lord Herschell and Pether O'Brien. I have seen, not merely photographs, but caricatures, in which the English Lord Chancellor might well be mistaken for the Irish Lord Chief Justice. The latter was full of mannerisms, of which his lisp was the least notable, being a sibilance, rather than a lisp. He hated a wig, and, five minutes after coming into Court, he would have taken it off and put it on the table in front of him, from time to time playing a tattoo upon his massive bald pate. He had enormous lips, with which he made slightly sarcastic suctional noises. He nearly always knew where the truth lay; sometimes he was too lazy to make sure it had reached the jury. "Thith cathe mutht be thettled," was a common phrase in his mouth. And yet, at the Bar, he had been noted for his courage; and Ajax never defied the lightning with greater imperturbability. Once he was associated with John Naish in a prosecution in Cork; Naish was a person of very delicate susceptibilities, and did not at all care for the somewhat unscrupulous methods then in vogue in Crown practice. A consultation was held on the night before the trial; Pether threw himself on a sofa and appeared to be taking no interest in the proceedings. Naish was greatly worried by the fact that the Crown case rested almost entirely upon the evidence of an informer, who, ostensibly for his own protection, had been kept during the remand in a sort of Police Home outside Dublin, where he had lived like a fighting-cock. Naish knew that this fact was well known to the defence; but what was his horror to learn that the police, in order to keep their man well on their hands, had also given their hospitality to his mistress! "Good Heavens!" cried Naish; "do you hear that, O'Brien?" "Yeth," replied Pether lazily. "But—but—what are you going to do when that comes out in Court to-morrow?" "What I shall do then will make stir enough to be heard from here to Dublin," replied Pether (the remark is not quite accurately transcribed); and he declined to give John Naish any further comfort. But Pether knew the man with whom he would have to deal. The prisoner was being defended by a completely useless but entirely lady-like member of the Circuit, who may remain nameless. The moment came next day when, having elicited the fact that the informer had been the guest of the constabulary, he began somewhat gingerly to approach the suggestion that another guest had shared his quarters. Pether was on his feet in a moment, with a deprecatory hand outstretched. "My Lord," he said, "your Lordship knowth me; your Lordship knowth my friend; never hath the honour of the Bar been entruthted to thafer handth than hith. My Lord, hith latht quethtion thuggethted that he wath about to enter upon an inquiry that might compromithe a lady'th honour; my Lord, I know that I have only to appeal to hith thenth of chivalry, and I shall not appeal in vain." And, as the wily Pether had anticipated, his opponent blushed a fiery red and steered away from the perilous topic!

Oddly enough, the case in which Pether took the greatest pride was the matrimonial petition entitled Ussher v. Ussher, in which he presided over the Court that heard the application for a new trial. His judgment is a careful one, and shows a greater degree of erudition than was usually evident in the reasons for his decisions; but the case itself was a remarkable one, and attracted much attention at the time. William Arnold Ussher was a landed proprietor, living at a country house called Eastwell, in the County Galway. He had been born and brought up in the Protestant religion; but one would gather than the teachings of his Church had sat lightly on him, and had little effect in discouraging him from gratifying his desires. There came to be engaged as housemaid in the house a young girl named Mary Caulfield, of great beauty, and of remarkable character. I once had the privilege of reading some letters that Mrs. Caulfield wrote to Mr. Ussher in connection with this unhappy affair; they were worthy, in substance, of a Roman matron and in style, of Doctor Johnson. The girl was her mother's daughter; and when her master began to turn amorous eyes in her direction she quickly made him realise that here was to be met no light-o'-love, but a modest and virtuous young woman.

Attracted by the difficulty, Ussher only became more assiduous in his attentions; he protested that his desires were honourable, and so far prevailed upon the girl as to make her believe that he was prepared to offer her marriage. But, true to her religion as to herself, she drew his attention to the impossibility of a mixed marriage in Ireland (for dispensations for such are seldom, if ever, granted there). He, ready to be hanged for a sheep as for a lamb, offered to become a Catholic to marry her. But he explained that on his mother's account the whole matter must remain secret for the present.

Mary Caulfield did what any sensible Catholic girl would do; she consulted her priest; and well for her if the parish had been administered by a wise and well-instructed ecclesiastic. Unhappily, the parish priest was a Father Fahy, who appears to have been a very simple and unlearned man; no doubt he was dazzled by the thought of the great land-owner becoming a convert to his faith, and he had the intention of making everything easy for Mr. Ussher. At any rate, he appears to have taken no advice; although he obtained from the Bishop, Doctor Gilmartin, a faculty for the celebration of the marriage in the house and not in a church, he does not appear to have asked any questions which would have opened the Bishop's eyes to the plot, for such it was, for the seduction of this innocent girl. Accordingly, on April 24th, 1910, Father Fahy was secretly admitted to the house; an unused bedroom served as a chapel both for the baptism of Mr. Ussher and for his marriage to Mary Caulfield. The only other person present was Agnes Kavanagh, the cook in the house; and for this reason the marriage, lacking a second witness, was invalid according to the discipline of the Roman Catholic Church. Indeed, according to the decrees of the Council of Trent, such a marriage is not merely invalid; it is null and void.

But the marriage was quite good enough for Mr. Ussher's purpose; and for some time he enjoyed the pleasures of matrimony with a girl who truly loved him, and gave willingly all that she had to give. To her it was a grievous shock to find that the fierce blaze of his affection burned itself out in a few short months; and a matter of horror to discover that, through the blunder of Father Fahy, they were not properly married at all. A marriage so imperfect in the eyes of the Church can be validated afterwards; but Mr. Ussher was now tired of his wife, repented of his "wedding," and not only refused to validate the ceremony, but seized upon this means of getting rid of his responsibilities. The opinion of counsel was taken; five of the most eminent names that daily echoed in the Law Library were signed to a petition of jactitation of marriage; and the frightened girl was told that she might as well let judgment go by default.

She, however, was not lacking in courage; Johnnie Moriarty was instructed on her behalf, and right well he conducted her defence when the action came to be tried before Mr. Justice Kenny. Kenny was himself a Catholic, but would have been the last person to suggest that he was a theologian, or had made any special study of theological matters. And it was amusing to watch Johnnie airing his hastily scrabbled-up knowledge of the laws of the Catholic Church, pretending that all this was native to him. I remember how, when addressing the Judge, he gave a long disquisition upon the ritual of the reception of a non-Catholic into the Catholic Church, winding up with the phrase: "And then, my Lord, the priest administers the sacrament of baptism, *sub conditionem*." Kenny paid no attention to the phrase; so Johnnie made a long detour, came back to the same spot, and again used the words "baptism *sub conditionem*." Again Kenny let them pass without observation; and once more the chagrined Johnnie ran around the course, and for a third time used the same phrase. "You mean," said Kenny, "the priest baptises him?" "No! my Lord," said Johnnie triumphantly; "let me explain it to your Lordship. Baptism is a sacrament that can only be once administered, once and for all; but it can be administered to and by persons who are not Catholics. So, when an adult, who may have thus been baptised before, comes to be received into the Catholic Church, he only receives the sacrament of baptism *sub conditionem*, that is to say, on condition that he has not already received it in his youth." Kenny made a note; but I could see that he was annoyed at having allowed himself to be dragged at Johnnie's chariot-wheel like this.

I am glad to say that in both Courts the marriage was pronounced a legal and binding marriage. What became of the parties I never heard. If, indeed, Mrs. Ussher is still alive, she might be pleased to know how her courage and constancy had won the admiration of the Junior Bar, and had given her a crown more lasting than the beauty which had worked her so much hurt.

The first time that I can remember seeing Pether O'Brien was also the first occasion I was present at a murder trial. It took place at the Cork Assizes, and must have been somewhere about 1905. The prisoner was an ex-Head Constable of the Royal Irish Constabulary, named Foster; the victim was a little pensioner of the

American Army who had returned to Ireland and taken up his abode in Cork. He was a harmless little man, well liked by all who knew him, and known by sight to most people in Cork. One of the most conspicuous things about him was the watch and chain he wore with innocent ostentation, the chain being adorned with some very distinctive medals. Foster was a frequent companion of his, and they were often to be seen together taking a drink in one or other of their favourite houses of call. About six o'clock one winter evening they were thus seen in a bar, which they left in one another's company. At about a quarter to seven Foster returned to the same bar, and it was observed that he was wearing the pensioner's watch and chain. He said he had bought them. The pensioner was never seen alive again; but at about a quarter past six that evening somebody walking along the Mardyke had heard a scream from the direction of the river. About ten days later the pensioner's body was discovered a little lower down the stream, being kept under water by a layer of stones. At the back of the skull was a savage wound, such as might have been caused by a violent blow with a blunt, wedge-shaped instrument. Not far from the body was found the heater of a domestic box-iron, just such an implement as might have occasioned the blow; it had blood upon it, and near it was found a crumpled fragment of wall-paper, roughly torn off from the piece, with marks that suggested that the heater had been wrapped in it; in pattern and shape the paper corresponded with the wall-paper in Foster's room, from which such a piece was missing, and his landlady identified the heater as one that she had vainly sought since the night when the pensioner disappeared. If Foster had been trying to make things easy for the Force to which he had belonged, he could hardly have done more; and yet there was a great dread amongst the advisers of the Crown that he would escape conviction. For once Cork Court-house saw the Crown Solicitor "standing by" every juror that in a case tinged with politics would have been counted "safe." But there was no ground for their apprehensions; the prisoner was convicted after a very short retirement of the jury. I had been standing outside the Court with a school-friend, and was a little dismayed to see my father approaching, thinking that he would not approve of such morbid curiosity. To my surprise, he beckoned us over and brought us into Court, getting us quite good seats, which we reached as James Campbell, then Solicitor-General, concluded his final speech for the Crown. I learned afterwards that he had left the House of Commons at eight o'clock the night before the case began, not having opened his brief; he read and mastered it before his trip across on the night mail, which reached Cork at ten thirty-five next morning; and at eleven o'clock he began a masterly statement of the case to the jury. Admittedly it was an easy case; but few counsel would to-day treat a prosecution for murder so cavalierly.

Pether came out on the Bench to receive the verdict of the jury; but on hearing the fatal word he immediately got up and went into his retiring room again. The wretched Foster sat there like a trapped animal, conscious of every eye that was turned upon him; Henry Wright, the Clerk of the Crown and Peace, directed the warders to take him below. In a few minutes Pether returned; he had only retired to write out a little allocution, warning the prisoner that his fate was sealed, and exhorting him to address himself to the Divine clemency, reminding him that "The wideness of God's mercy is the wideness of the sea." He then sentenced him to death.

In that story the whole of Pether O'Brien is seen. With all his careless ways, he was founded and grounded in his religion; yet an exhortation of this kind would not come naturally to his lips, and he felt he must retire and invoke the assistance of Father Faber. It probably never occurred to him that he was doing a cruel thing in keeping the miserable man before the crowded Court while he polished his phrases; nor, indeed, would he be likely to be moved by any pity for so wicked a murderer. I remember my father's comment that he might well have spoken *extempore*; and Pether had a good command of language when he liked, although Dick Adams once said that his vocabulary was limited to five words! But he feared accidental incongruity on a solemn occasion; and he preferred to trust to his pen than to his tongue.

When the wretched prisoner came to be hanged, Cork was flooded with copies of a broadsheet ballad, of which I only remember the first verse:

> The dreadful hour has come at last—
>   The day when I must die ;
> O ! What a shock, at eight o'clock
>   To meet my God on high !

In a perverse way, the precision of that rendezvous always reminds me of Robert Louis Stevenson's "By punctual eve the stars were lit."

I only once met Pether outside Court; but with the assured impudence of youth I then told him a story which gave him a malicious pleasure. I was dining with him during Cork Assizes in 1912, and his kindness and obvious pleasure in the society and conversation of the younger members of his old Circuit emboldened me to ask him if he had heard a story about another Judge ("whom," said I, "I shall not name,") who had during a recent Assize at Limerick been a guest at a public banquet in that city, at which he had replied to the toast of "His Majesty's Judges." In the course of his speech he had said that he could not refrain from expressing his gratification at finding so great a respect for the administration of the law in Limerick; for, whenever he went abroad, not merely as the Great Red Judge, but even when walking the streets as an ordinary citizen, he had found the people taking their hats off as he passed. Unfortunately, the next toast was "The Armed Forces of the Crown," to which a General, possessed of a sense of humour, replied. He said that when he first came to Limerick, he also had been impressed by the respect of the people for the armed forces, because, whenever he went abroad, not merely when riding in state, but even when walking out to buy an ounce of tobacco, he found all the passers-by taking of their hats. At first he had assumed that this was a compliment to himself; but a closer acquaintance with the city had made him aware that about every second house in the principal street was a Roman Catholic chapel!

Pether listened to the end with an amused smile; but an affectionate hand had gripped my arm at an early stage in the story, and sympathetic pressures testified to his enjoyment. Only at the end did he say, with delight: "Thith wath Dodd!" And of course it was.

Pether only just missed being a great man. He lacked the independence of the Chief Baron; and it would have been difficult to imagine him leading an unpopular movement unless there were obvious compensations. But he

o

was kind and he was deservedly popular. In his book, *Letters and Leaders of my Day*, my uncle has told the delightful story how Pether crossed specially to London and secured the personal intervention of the Prime Minister to save a little country postmistress from dismissal. And I am sure that there were many other kindnesses of the same nature. His name sounds musical in the ears of the Irish people, not because Lord O'Brien of Kilfenora is the loveliest title ever heard in the House of Lords, but because Pether O'Brien never allowed the dignity of his office to disguise a genuine and typical Irishman.

XIV

TRIAL BY JURY is essentially an English institution; and the law relating to jurors and the procedure for empanelling them and making them a part of the administration of justice has filled at least one very large, learned, and entertaining book. It was written by a blind Irish barrister named Huband; and ten copies were sold of the first edition. Nothing daunted, the author produced a second. A more delightful book to open for half an hour's entertaining reading I cannot imagine: at any rate, in a lawyer's library. And yet, with all this learning upon the subject, one never sees any legal argument about the jury in England. I have only once heard a juror challenged in an English Court. On circuit the Clerk of Assize will lend a ready ear to any private suggestion from counsel that it might be as well if John Smith of Pounderby Lodge, Muggleton, did not sit in the case of R. *v.* Stiggins, as there was a rumour that Mr. Smith had been heard to say that he was glad to see that bounder Stiggins caught out at last and he hoped he might get seven years. In practice, this is sensible and admirable; but it means that the jury is not being selected according to law. In Ireland no such soft methods were adopted; the prisoner had twenty peremptory challenges if accused of felony, and six if charged with a misdemeanour. In a civil action each party had six peremptory challenges. In addition, in any case it was possible to challenge for cause any juror against whom cause or partiality could be shown. In England challenges are made by counsel; in Ireland they were the province of the solicitor. A good solicitor always armed himself with a copy of the jury-panel well in advance; sometimes he was able to prove that the panel had not been constituted according to law, in that the jurors thereon had been arbitrarily or unfairly selected. In such a case he would instruct his counsel to move to quash the panel, and, if successful, would thereby paralyse the business of the Assizes until another panel could be formed.   On the assumption that the panel had been well struck, his next duty would be to inform himself of the personal character and outlook of as many members as possible, and to mark his list with emblems of a descending scale, discriminating the most dangerous from the merely dangerous, the doubtful, the possibly favourable, the good friend, and the ferocious partisan.   The presence of a single one of the last variety would ensure that the worst that could happen to his client would be a disagreement of the jury.   But when the names came to be called in Court it necessitated all the skill of the expert gambler to put one's challenges to the best advantage.   With only one left, it might be the wiser course to let a doubtful man go unchallenged and reserve the last for the possibility of a dangerous man being called.   The Crown had no right of challenge; they could order a juror to "stand by," but if the list ran out without a jury being completed, the Crown had then to go back on their "stand-byes," and the presence of one of these on the jury was not calculated to improve the chances of a conviction.

Perhaps the most amusing story about a jury is one in which my uncle figured a great many years ago: probably about 1902.   I tell the tale as it was told by the late Barry Galvin, one of the ablest and most popular of the Cork solicitors, and in the case in question he was acting on behalf of the plaintiff.   The *Irish Times*, usually a sensible and moderate paper, the mouthpiece of respectable Protestantism in Ireland, had for once allowed itself to be lured from the path of prudence, and had published a statement that Canon MacInerney, a highly esteemed Parish Priest in north Cork, had allowed a member of his flock to die like a dog without the consolations of religion. A more terrible libel on a Catholic Priest can hardly be imagined; the indignant Canon issued a writ immediately, and in due course the action was listed for hearing at the Cork Assizes. Inasmuch as there had been absolutely no foundation for the charge, one marvels that the action should ever have been allowed to go to trial; but those were days of ferocious political and religious feeling, and it was assumed on both sides that the jurors would pay no attention to the evidence, but would vote on party lines. The chances of a verdict were thus rendered remote. Let me say in parentheses that only in a case where party feeling was unusually high would I ever have doubted the opinion of a City of Cork Special Jury; both in the city and the county, jury work was admirably done, and I doubt if there was ever a better tribunal in the world than a County Cork Special Jury. But the issues in this case seemed to call for party loyalty to an unusual degree; and it was with a very long face that Barry Galvin met my uncle in consultation on the eve of the trial. "We're beaten, Mr. Healy," he said. "There are four Protestants to one Catholic on the panel." In a special jury, this was not surprising; for, although the proportion of Catholics to Protestants in the whole population would probably have been ten to one, most of the Protestants were moneyed people, and would thus be more likely to be qualified as special jurors.

My uncle appeared to be quite undismayed, but said nothing on this topic; and in due course the case was called on before Mr. Justice Johnson the next day. The first juror called was Mr. Alexander McOstrich, a well-known stockbroker, and a Presbyterian. "Challenge for cause!" cried Tim. Now, when a juror is challenged for cause, the next two jurors on the list are immediately sworn without right of challenge, and they hear evidence and decide whether the cause shewn is good. The jurors having been sworn, "Now, Mr. Healy," said the Judge, "what evidence do you call?" "Alexander McOstrich," replied my uncle. The surprised Mr. McOstrich made his way to the witness-box and was sworn. "Mr. McOstrich," said Tim, "how many shares in the *Irish Times* company do you hold?"

"None!" replied the astonished witness.

"What!" cried my uncle. "Do you swear you have no interest in the company?"

"I do, Mr. Healy," said McOstrich.

Tim looked nonplussed for a moment; then he asked: "When did you get rid of your shares?"

"I never had any, Mr. Healy."

"Does your wife hold any, or did she ever?"

"I am a widower, Mr. Healy, and have been for many years. I do not believe my wife ever had any such interest."

Tim seemed puzzled; suddenly he said, softly: "Have you got your bank-book with you?"

"No, Mr. Healy, but I can shew it to you in ten minutes, if his Lordship will allow me to fetch it."

"My Lord," said my uncle, "I respectfully ask that your Lordship should adjourn for a quarter of an hour to enable Mr. McOstrich to fetch his bank-book."

"Certainly, certainly," said Billy Johnson; "I will grant leave for the fullest investigation." And the Court emptied for a short time.

When it opened again, Mr. McOstrich was there with, not one, but several bank pass-books, and appeared to be anxious for their thorough examination. But Tim addressed him. "Mr. McOstrich," he said, "during the adjournment I have been instructed as to your reputation and integrity, and I erred in my suspicions a little while ago. I admit I cannot shew cause against your serving as a juror, but I will challenge you peremptorily instead, and thus, perhaps, relieve you of a duty you might have found unpleasant."

McOstrich withdrew, probably rather pleased than otherwise to have escaped service; the calling of the panel continued. Not a Protestant answered. Few people care to have their bank accounts examined in open Court. The Catholic jurors, however, had no dread that anyone would ask to see their bank accounts; and twelve good Papists were sworn to try the issues in the cause. No sooner had they taken their seats than the defence, seeing their hope of a disagreement gone, surrendered, apologised, and paid damages. But Canon MacInerney was broken in health by the attack that had been made upon him ; and I do not think he long survived.

Let me add two comments. Immediately afterwards there set in a *rapprochement* between Protestants and Catholics in Cork, and, thank God, the tide never turned, even in the worst of the bad days. When Doctor Meade, the Protestant Bishop, died, he had the longest funeral ever seen in Cork; and it was observed that nearly every mourner took off his hat when passing the Catholic churches on the way. I should also like to bear tribute to the moderation and good feeling which animated the *Irish Times* during all my acquaintance with it, which must have begun very shortly after Canon MacInerney's case, and lasted until after the war.

Some purists have suggested that my uncle's tactics were hardly legitimate. It is true that he had no knowledge of any particular transaction in *Irish Times* shares on the part of Mr. McOstrich; but the latter was a very likely shareholder, and chicanery of all sorts (with which, of course, Mr. McOstrich must not be associated) was rampant in such circumstances, and my uncle's motto was always "À corsair, corsair et demi." Whether he foresaw the extent of the success his tactics would attain I do not know; he was a mystic, and a sure instinct frequently led him to success along paths where others would plunge to disaster. At any rate, justice was helped and not hindered in the case in question.

It must be admitted that there were some very bad juries in Ireland, and I have seen some very bad ones in this country as well. But the Irish juries, even when bad, had sometimes the mitigating grace that they added to the gaiety of the Court. There was the very rural jury in Listowel that once was assisting Judge Shaw to try a case of rape: the jurisdiction of Quarter-Sessions was wider in Ireland than over here. The prosecutrix gave her evidence with a complete absence of embarrassment, and with such a readiness to go into detail that the Judge turned in disgust to the jury and said: "Ah! gentlemen, you daren't hang a dog upon evidence like this! Just put your heads together and see if you want to go any further before acquitting the prisoner." The jury collogued; then the foreman said: "Your Honour, we're unanimously of opinion that the boy didn't do it; but should your Honour be wishful to hear any more evidence, we wouldn't be stopping you!"

Then there was the Limerick jury that, in spite of the most earnest appeals of Richard Adams, then County Court Judge, acquitted a prisoner of a bad charge of stabbing, in the teeth of the clearest evidence of his guilt. Adams addressed the accused: "Patrick Murphy, you have been acquitted by these twelve jurors of the crime of which you were charged. Take a good look at them, Pat; study their faces well; for I give you my solemn promise that if ever you are found guilty before me of doing to any one of them what you did to the prosecutor in this case, you won't get a day's imprisonment for doing it!"

It was perhaps that prisoner, or another in similar circumstances, that Adams dismissed with the words "You have been acquitted by a Limerick jury, and you may now leave the dock without any other stain upon your character."

Perhaps the limit of inconsistency was attained by a Tralee jury in a case of larceny. A young fellow sold some cattle at Kenmare, and at once became the object of much endearment on the part of a somewhat disreputable lady of the town, who made him take her into a public-house and give her several drinks. She adopted the tactics of Jack the Giant Killer, and when he had gone half-seas over she got hold of his bundle of notes and made off. He, however, missed his money at once, and informed the police; they pursued the lady to her home, where they found her seated in front of the fire. As they came in, she jolted her lap so as to throw its contents into the fire; but the police were quick enough to grab what fell, and it proved to be a bundle of notes, which were identified by the purchaser of the young man's cattle, as the notes he had handed over. On that evidence the jury acquitted the woman of larceny. Her solicitor was swift in pursuit of the spoils of victory; he asked that the notes should be handed back to his client. "Yes," said the Judge, curtly. At this the jury shewed every sign of astonishment and dismay. After a hasty consultation, the foreman said: "Your Honour, it was the intention of the jury that the girl should go free, but that the boy should have his money back!"

An accidental inclusion of a particular tradesman or expert on a jury may sometimes seal the fate of a prisoner. The combination of this and another fortuitous event convicted a man named Patrick Ryan at the Cork Winter Assizes of 1911; and those associated with him, for one of whom I appeared, were convicted the following year of conspiracy. I wonder whether at this distance of time I can remember the story.

It began with the will of a Father Foley of Tarbert. He was the parish priest, and he had put by a moderate fortune, a considerable portion of which he desired to go to his nephew, another Father Foley, after his death. There was a probate action in which some disappointed members of the family sought to establish that the old man was not in full possession of his faculties when he made the will; the case was tried by Pether O'Brien, who at first leaned against the validity of the will, but was converted when he heard how the dying priest was able to take a keen interest in how his dogs had run on the day that he died. The will once established, the younger Father Foley entered into enjoyment of his heritage, but, being himself a priest on the Scotch mission, he put his brother Michael and some other members of his family into residence at a farm called Plover Hill, situated between Tralee and the little port of Fenit, which place formed part of his new estate. He himself used to come over from Scotland for his holidays; and, unfortunately, he found things not going as he would have wished at Plover Hill. Disputes ensued; ultimately he turned out his brother and sisters, and thereby labelled Plover Hill as an evicted farm. To deal with anyone working an evicted farm was a serious matter under the Irish code of conduct; the purchaser of crops became a marked man liable to reprisals. Now, although it never came out at either trial, rumour had it that the real offender against the "code" was a big army contractor in Tralee, known as "Ponther Connor"; he had concluded some very big deal with those working the farm of Father Foley, which supplied the sinews of life to an enterprise that must otherwise have failed; and Ponther was marked for vengeance.

Unfortunately, a poor little man named Cournane had also bought a load of turnips from Plover Hill; and one day in March he met Michael Foley, the evicted brother, in the streets of Tralee. Foley said to him: "I'll see you for those turnips from Plover Hill"; not a very violent threat, and probably if the truth were known not intended as more than a warning not to do it again. In the light of what happened a few days later, it assumed a far more sinister meaning.

Michael Foley had a sister who was married to one Patrick Daly, known to everybody as "Bob." Their home was at Fieries. Travellers by rail to Tralee, as they approach Farranfore Junction, may observe in the plain to their left a sinister-looking Druidic grove, with

a church spire appearing above the trees. This is Fieries.
It was not far from here that occurred the terrible murder
of the Curtins that so roused the splendid indignation of
Robert Louis Stevenson. Murder broods in the air. I
never set eyes on the grove of Fieries without feeling
what the French call *la frousse*.

But if Fieries looks horrible and sinister, Patrick Bob
Daly was of a very different appearance. There are
people whose very faults are the result of their virtues;
any harm Bob Daly did sprang, I am sure, from his
sympathy and friendship for his brother-in-law. Even
when he stood in the dock, his handsome smiling face
suggested nothing but good-humour and kindliness. I
always felt sorry for him, for I think he was led astray.

At this time he had working for him a remarkable
fellow named Patrick Ryan. Ryan had been a soldier,
and had greatly distinguished himself in the South African
War. On the occasion when Lord Roberts's son lost his
life, Ryan had swum the Tugela under fire, picked up his
wounded company commander, and swum back to the
British side with him. I forget how many bullet wounds
there were in the officer's body when he reached land;
he was dead, but his death took nothing from the gallantry
of Ryan's action. After the war the soldier settled down
in Fieries, where if one quality more than another distinguished him, it was his love of children and the trouble
he would take to keep them amused. He was kind, good-
humoured, generous; and he valued a human life as
nothing, where a question of friendship or loyalty was
concerned.

There was a cattle fair at Castlemaine, a town some
twelve miles from Fieries. Either it took place on
March 25th, or else March 25th was the date of the

conversation I am about to relate. That March a little girl had been engaged to work in Bob Daly's house; and a night or two before Castlemaine Fair the little girl's mother happened to be passing the forge at Fieries when she noticed a group of men talking. They were five in number: Bob Daly, Michael Foley, Patrick Ryan, Michael Clifford, a labourer of Bob Daly's, and another man with a name not common in those parts which I forget. The old lady swore to hearing each of them say one sentence; the rest she forgot. Each one, however, conveniently said in her hearing enough to show that he was plotting vengeance against somebody who had been dealing with Plover Hill Farm. She explained her ability to overhear so much, by saying that she had pretended to have got a thorn in her foot, which she affected to be taking out. But they caught sight of her, stopped their conversation and told her to be off.

On the morning of the fair-day, the little girl heard Bob Daly wake Clifford, and saw the latter start off towards Castlemaine with a couple of beasts. The road he took was at the south side of the River Maine; at the north side of it, at three fields distance from the stream, and climbing along the side of a hill was the road from Castlemaine to Tralee. One could get back to Bob Daly's farm at Fieries by that road, too, but it was a roundabout way to go.

Ponther Connor had been expected at Castlemaine Fair that day, whence he would have returned later on to Tralee. Some angel visited him in his sleep, and he did not go. Clifford, not finding Ponther Connor, made no effort to sell his beasts, and drove them back, not the way he had come, but by the Tralee road. Legend has it that when he told Ryan and the fifth man, whom he found by the side of the road at the point nearest to Bob Daly's farm, that there was no sign of Ponther, one of the two wanted to go home, but the other was for firing off his gun; and it was then that mention may have been made of the unhappy Cournane, who at that moment was driving peacefully home to Tralee, a mile or two behind Clifford.

As Cournane approached the spot where Ryan and the other man were in hiding, there was a report; Cournane fell back, wounded in the arm. A casual acquaintance to whom he had given a lift was nearly blinded with small shot; Cournane's son was unhurt, and was able to run for assistance. The fifth man, whose name I have forgotten, and who had been with Ryan, has never been seen from that day to this. Whether Ryan had been recognised by Cournane or either of his companions, I cannot now recall. It must be remembered that the Maine, a fierce and fairly deep stream at that spot, ran between the scene of the outrage and Bob Daly's farm; to get from the one place to the other by road would take a couple of hours, or at any rate a very considerable time. But Michael Foley had been seen to go down towards the Maine that day with a long rope; and the belief was that he threw the end across the river, and hauled Ryan home to establish a good alibi. That afternoon it happened that the useful old lady was going up to Bob Daly's house to see her daughter. As she passed up the causeway, she saw Ryan in a ditch, washing a pair of trousers. "Keep your eyes to yourself," said he, as she passed.

The police were represented in that area by a young District-Inspector of the Royal Irish Constabulary named O'Beirne; he had an able lieutenant in the person of

Sergeant O'Rorke of Farranfore. The police have suspicious minds, and always have a shrewd idea as to who is responsible for a particular crime, even when they have no evidence. Mr. O'Beirne and Sergeant O'Rorke cannot have had a scrap of evidence that night when they decided to arrest Ryan. The Sergeant called at Bob Daly's house at about ten o'clock; he asked to see Ryan, and was told he was in bed. He asked to be shown where Ryan was sleeping, and went straight up and arrested him. Now remember, in the eyes of Sergeant O'Rorke as he saw things at that moment, Ryan was a desperate man who had attempted to murder one man that day, and would not trouble much about an extra policeman. I have always thought that the Sergeant showed the highest bravery on that occasion, quite equal to that of a soldier leading the "forlorn hope."

Ryan had undressed himself; he was told to get up and dress. He possessed two pairs of boots; both were by the side of his bed. Both were country made, and had hammered into their soles by hand little shamrock-shaped groups of hobnails, which, in the case of machine-made boots, would have been absolutely regular, but, having been done by hand, shewed some little distinctive peculiarities. And Ryan, being quite at liberty to put on his other pair of boots, had the ill-luck to choose those he had worn during the day. It was an unfortunate choice, from his point of view.

Mr. O'Beirne, meantime, had been struck by the relative positions of the scene of the crime and the bounds of Bob Daly's farm; he drew a line on the map, and set a number of his men to look for footprints. Three were found; and from these casts were taken. Every little peculiar feature of Ryan's boots appeared.

and later a second accident showed that Ryan's luck had left him. The jury that tried him contained a shoemaker; and when the others were inclined to take the view that one pair of boots was very like another, it was the shoemaker who demonstrated to them the unlikelihood of such a fortuitous coincidence in all the *minutiæ* of the pattern as here appeared; and it was this that caused them to convict the prisoner. He was sentenced to seven years' penal servitude. At the following Assizes, Daly, Foley, and Clifford were tried and convicted of conspiracy; whether to murder or to do grievous bodily harm I cannot now remember. Clifford got off with a light sentence, which enabled him to pass the forge of Fieries once more on March 25th, two years after the conspiracy. And that night as he reached the grim spot he dropped dead.

I can remember two stories about that case. When Ryan was to be tried for attempted murder, the Crown employed George Hickson of Tralee to make a plan of the *locus in quo*. It will be appreciated that this covered a great deal of country: the triangular route to and from Castlemaine, the road to Tralee, and the road out to Plover Hill. George did the entire job well and truly, until at last he came to Fieries which he had left to the end. Just as he was approaching the village he heard the whistle of a train, and, looking at his watch, realised that it was much later than he expected, and that, if he did not catch the train which was approaching, he would be stuck in Fieries for four hours. All he had to do was to "plot in" the little village, showing the various places mentioned; that could be done from the 25-inch Ordnance sheet, which was quite modern. So he ran for his train and finished his plan in his office.

Maurice McCartie was defending Ryan, and had instructed his brother Denis to make a plan also. On the eve of the trial Denis met George Hickson in the Imperial Hotel, Cork, and said: "Hickson, may I have a look at your plan and compare it with mine?" "Certainly," said Hickson, and produced it. "Oh-h! My-y God!" cried Denis. "What's wrong?" asked George anxiously. "Nothing," said Denis, "except that you've put the forge at Fieries at the wrong side of the road!" "I did not!" said George indignantly, "I took it off the Ordnance Sheet." "Yes," said Denis, "but the forge was burned down the year before last; and they put up the new one at the other side of the road!"

The disaster was greater than it sounds, for I remember that there was one very large plan, about ten feet by eight feet, and there were about twenty copies of a smaller edition, all of which had to be corrected before the next morning. Denis loyally sat up all night correcting George's plans; a good turn that I am sure the good-natured George Hickson repaid before very long. But what hard luck!

The second story has to do with the trial for conspiracy. Johnnie Moriarty was at that time Attorney-General, and had come down to prosecute; I was defending at least one of the prisoners, and I cannot remember that there was any other counsel for the defence. The trial took place before Mr. Justice Molony, as he then was, and I have already drawn attention to the fact that he was a firm and fervent son of the Church. A police witness was in the box, and with a long pointer was explaining the large map to the jury. "Number 9 spot represents the fair at Castlemaine; number 10 spot is

P

the gate near which the shots were fired; number 11 spot is where the witness lived who was fetched by young Cournane." "And what is number 12 spot?" asked Johnnie. "Oh, that's the hut where Missioner Sullivan lives," said the constable. The Judge looked up; "Missioner" is not a very pleasant nickname in Ireland, having frequently been applied to those over-zealous people who, for some time after the Famine, endeavoured to redeem the Papist peasantry from the errors of their ways by the cogent arguments of a soup-kitchen. Johnnie saw a danger signal; here was one of his witnesses being discredited in advance by an unlucky sobriquet. "Ah! my Lord," he said, "it isn't what your Lordship thinks at all. This poor old man is called 'Missioner' Sullivan, because he follows the holy missioners around when they are conducting retreats and missions; and while they preach the word of God inside the church, he stands outside and sells rosary-beads and scapulars to the members of the congregation as they come out." "Yes, my Lord," said I, disgusted by this unctuous hypocrisy, "and when this case is over he is going to give the Attorney a rosary-bead." "Ah! I've got my rosary-bead!" cried Johnnie angrily, taking one out of his pocket, and dashing it on the table!

XV

I WONDER WHETHER the story of the "Que Estate"
would interest even legal readers? I tell it because it
once enjoyed a popularity on the old Munster Circuit;
and it is not without a moral, which I decline to underline.
It has several stages, or chapters, of which the first goes
back to the time when I was a student. I am afraid I was
rather an idler that year, and more intent on writing
oddments of light verse than upon seeking the remoter
fountains of the law. In marked contrast was a young
friend of mine, now an ornament to the Bench, and for
the purposes of this tale conveniently called Blank.
During the working year all forms of dissipation were
abhorrent to him; he slept with his books, and the oil
companies paid an increased dividend as a result of the
midnight hours he spent upon his studies. About law
we all believed him to know everything; and even if he
seemed for the moment to have lost his sense of humour,
we knew that it was only temporarily submerged. That
he would gain the Victoria Prize was an assumed fact;
I refrain from saying whether he did or not, lest I should
destroy his anonymity. The rest of us were not very
uneasy about that portion of the examinations which would
deal with the law covered by our lectures; but there
were one or two extra subjects in respect of which we
were left to our own reading, concerning which we had
grave doubts of the success of our unaided studies. That
Blank should have any such doubts would never have
occurred to us. He was omniverous, and his diligence
would have covered everything. One of the extra

subjects that year was the Law of Easements; and I may add that it shewed a lack of sense of proportion that those responsible for our education should not have prescribed lectures upon this branch of the law, which, at that time, governed about fifty per cent of the cases in the Irish County Court. It is an interesting study; and in the County of Kerry it called for a familiarity with a special table of values in connection with actions for over-stint. Rights of common of pasture were very frequent; attached to a particular holding would be the right to graze so many animals upon a common grazing. The unit by which this right was measured was a *collop*; I am told that this is a corruption of the Irish word *colpach*, meaning a two-year-old heifer. Obviously, one animal will eat more, one less, than another; the table began with a hen and went up to a horse. A cow reckoned two collop; a horse was a collop and a half; four sheep went to the collop; there were I forget how many hens, but only two geese, because the goose is a bird that fouls the land. The cunning trespasser would alter the nature of his collop from day to day, taking it in sheep one day and in cows another, and so forth. To keep track on him required accounts kept in several denominations; every action for over-stint drove Bench and Bar to despair, and I never remember one that was not settled.

All this is, by the way, to give a glimpse of the picturesque possibilities lurking in the law relating to easements and *profits-à-pendre*, concerning which we felt we knew so little and Blank knew everything. Our fears were allayed when we learned that the examiner would be the present Mr. Justice Murnaghan, then, as now, a mild and kindly person, not likely to set traps for us. And, sure enough, two out of the three questions that he set upon this part of the examination were simple, and I have no doubt that he meant the third to be as easy. It read: "What is a *que estate*?"

I finished my paper, or as much of it as I could; and I waited in the lobby for someone with whom to compare notes. One of the last to leave the hall was Blank; he had a worried and distracted air, and looked ill. I on the other hand was light-hearted and gay, and just in the mood for a jest. So when Blank asked me anxiously: "Did you know what was a *que* estate?" I replied in affected amazement: "My dear fellow, surely you knew that! Why, that refers to the Theatres Act, 1900, under which anybody occupying a place in a queue outside the theatre for a certain period acquires a sort of squatter's title to the spot." He looked at me vacantly, and went away, saying sadly: "No, I didn't know that." And he had repeated my bogus explanation to somebody else before he realised that I had been joking.

Perhaps I ought here to pass on for the benefit of the uninitiated the knowledge that I subsequently acquired upon this matter. You can only claim an easement by virtue of an estate in land. The easement attaches to the land, and therefore is the right of the freeholder. But the freeholder may temporarily part with his land; and it would be an obvious hardship if the temporary occupant could not secure the benefit of the easement. When, however, he sought to assert his right in Court he had to lay his claim through the estate of the freeholder, which estate he had, and through which (*per quem*) he claimed. This estate through which he claimed was called the *que* estate.

Whether it was quite as fair a question to set to second year law-students as Mr. Murnaghan thought it was may be judged from the subsequent chapters of the story. For at the Kanturk Sessions in the spring of 1911 I found myself appearing for the owner of a farm over which his neighbour had a private right of way. In the autumn floods the way had become flooded, and the neighbour, in pretended exercise of his right, had deviated through an adjacent field, to which he had done considerable damage. The owner of the damaged field sued him; but the County Court Judge dismissed the claim, holding erroneously that the existence of the flood had given the neighbour the right to a way of necessity. My client appealed; and the appeal came to be heard at the Spring Assizes at Cork before the Lord Chief Baron. I had looked up the authorities in the meantime, and had found an express decision in my favour, the name of the case being Bullard *v.* Harrison, reported in the fourth volume of Maule and Selwyn's Reports at page 387. These reports were not available in Cork, and I had to rely on the head-note, although, having subsequently looked up the judgment, I greatly regret I could not have cited it to the Chief Baron, because Lord Ellenborough begins by saying: "This record is full of a vast number of prurient novelties in pleading." However, all I had was the head-note in Mew's Digest, which reads: "A person who prescribes in a *que* estate for a private way cannot justify going out of it on the adjoining land because the way is impassable." And, armed with this, I sat waiting in Court while the case before mine dragged along to its close.

Suddenly I realised that here was my old friend the *que* estate, and I had not troubled to find out what it was. I hastily turned to my cousin, Timothy Sullivan, the present Chief Justice of the Supreme Court in Ireland, but then a junior barrister. "Tim," said I, "what is a *que* estate?" He read the passage, and said frankly: "I don't know, Maurice, but I'll go and look it up for you." "Ah, don't bother, Tim," said I; but he gravely rebuked me, and said that the Lord Chief Baron was a dangerous judge to approach with an authority not properly understood, and, so saying, vanished to the Bar-room to look it up for me.

After an absence of some little time, he reappeared. "Maurice," said he, " I'll make you laugh, now. I went into the Bar-room, and I looked up Gale on Easements, and Goddard on Easements, Carson's Real Property, and every other book I could think of; and I could find nothing. So I turned to Arthur Clery, and I said: 'Arthur, you're a professor; what's a *que* estate?' Arthur rubbed his hands and thought; then he confessed he didn't know. So I asked Paddy Fleming. 'I tink—I tink,' said Paddy; 'gor, Tim, I wonder would it be something about an easement?' So I told him I knew that much myself; and Johnnie Moriarty came into the room, and I asked him. 'My dear Tim,' said he, 'I don't know; but I'll find it for you.' And he began pulling out all the books I had been trying. So, just as I was about to come back to you, I saw Stephen Ronan come in; and I asked him. He pulled his beard, and puffed through his nose; then he smiled and said: 'Upon my word, Tim, I don't know!' So, if the Chief Baron catches you up on it, you can tell him there's not a man on the Circuit who can tell you what it is!"

I thanked him profusely, and just then my case was called on. I stood up and opened the facts, and then I said that, out of respect to the learned County Court Judge who had decided the case against me, I had thought it right to produce some authority; "and, my Lord," I added, "I have the good fortune to hold here the head-note of a case precisely in point and in my favour; it is Bullard and Harrison, and the head-note reads: 'A person who prescribes in a *que* estate——' ''

"A what?" asked the old man, rather crossly.

"A *que* estate, my Lord; I hope I am pronouncing it right; I never know whether to call it a 'ke' estate or a 'kew' estate——'' and I paused for guidance.

There was an appreciable silence; by this time many of the Bar had heard about the impending joke, and had gathered to see what the Chief Baron would say. But he looked at me very hard, and said: "Go on!" However, he gave me judgment, in which he made no mention of the *que* estate!

Two or three years after, I was dining one night with Mr. Justice Dodd. It was an intimate party; there were only four of us present; and I, knowing that Dodd liked to look upon himself as Palles's understudy in all that appertained to old law, told him this story. He listened with amused interest, and when I had finished said: "And do you now know what is a *que* estate?" But I was too old to be caught in that way; I should not have told the story if I had not looked it up; and I gave the explanation I have given above. Dodd looked hard at me: "Yes," he said, "that's right." And I am perfectly certain that he had no idea whether it was right or wrong.

Ten or twelve years later, I wrote to congratulate him on his eightieth birthday, and received in reply a kindly, intimate letter written in the hand of a man of forty, and full of warm and cordial feelings. But there was a postscript: "Have you yet discovered what a *que* estate is?"

Now, *was* it a fair question to ask in the examination of second-year students?

The Lord Chief Baron comes into an extraordinarily large proportion of my memories. It was he who presided at the Cork Assizes, I think in the summer of 1908, over the first trial of the action which the Honourable Alexis Roche brought against Sir Timothy O'Brien for slander spoken in the hunting-field. I believe that Alexis Roche is dead; those who know the genial and mellow Sir Timothy of recent years may be surprised to learn that he once had a bit of temper, and did not always weigh his words. He was probably the most distinguished cricketer Ireland ever contributed to the game, although the names of Tommy Ross, Willie Harrington, poor F. H. Browning (who lost his life in the 1916 Rebellion), R. H. and Seppie Lambert, and A. D. Comyn, all spring to mind as challengers of that period. When I was at school, Lord Cadogan, as Viceroy, sent over a team of the Gentlemen of Ireland under the captaincy of Sir T. C. O'Brien, which gave a very good account of itself in England. We used to be told the tale of its glories by Father Tim Fegan at Clongowes, and there was one story which sticks in my memory, and which, in spite of its irrelevancy, I shall make bold to repeat. One of the matches of the tour was against a team captained by W. G. Grace, who paid his opponents the compliment of playing a wary innings himself, stonewalling for over after over, until the pall of boredom descended on the game. At last a ball struck W.G.'s pads; and the entire Irish eleven, including even Dan Comyn away in the outfield, raised a shout of "How's that?" The umpire signalled "Out"; W.G. appeared surprised, queried it, had it confirmed, and left; but before he went he muttered, a little surlily, that the umpire had been "terrorised"— a remark I am sure he regretted the moment he had made it, and he certainly had entirely recovered his good temper when the teams met at a dinner that night. Various members of the eleven contributed to a smoking concert afterwards, amongst others, one (was it Jack Treacy?), who gave a rendering of Percy French's song "Drumcollogher," to which he added a special verse, which went as follows:

> Then I joined the Eleven from Ireland
>   That was run by Sir T. C. O'Brien;
> He had leave from His Ex. to sign all the cheques,
>   Including the Bollinger wine.
> We played up at Lords on a Thursday
>   With a doctor called W.G.;
> Says he: "I suppose you gentlemen knows
>   You can't try no dodges with me?"
>
> Says I: "Have you been to Drumcollogher?
>   You haven't? Well! now, I declare
> You really should come to Drumcollogher,
>   And see the quare dodges we've there.
> We've only one dodge in Drumcollogher—
>   We all shout: 'How's that, Referee?'
> If he doesn't say 'Out!' we hits him a clout—
>   Oh! Drum is the place for me!"

It was the genial skipper of those days that, when hunting with the Duhallow hounds, accused Alexis Roche, the brother of Lord Fermoy, of being a horse-coper and a cheat.

Cork Court-house can never have presented a more fashionable aspect than when the action came on for hearing before the Lord Chief Baron and a Special Jury of the City of Cork. On the day that the words had been spoken there had been present many personalities of the

English hunting world; they and their friends were mustered in force, and the special reporters required about ten times the accommodation usually allotted to the press. Redmond Barry, then Solicitor-General, and (I think) Stephen Ronan, led for the plaintiff; James Campbell came specially to lead Johnnie Moriarty for the defence. I, squeezing into Court by some device, was surprised to see sitting on the jury a member of the Cork Club named Frank Morrogh, whom I had always supposed to be a close personal friend of Sir Timothy's. That night Redmond Barry dined at our house, and I expressed my surprise that Morrogh had not been challenged. Redmond Barry was gravely perturbed by my news; he seemed to think the chances of his succeeding had been imperilled.

Next morning as I made my way into Court a little before half-past ten, I was surprised to meet Frank Morrogh on the steps of the Court. I said good morning to him and passed on; when I got into Court all the other jurors were there. Soon counsel appeared; but the Judge remained absent. Suddenly the leaders on both sides were called into his room; after a little time they returned to Court, and shortly afterwards the Judge came in. Addressing counsel, he said that he had received a communication from a juryman which he thought ought to be made the subject of evidence. Frank Morrogh was called into the box, and stated on oath that during the adjournment he had been rung up by the secretary of the Cork Club who had told him that Sir Timothy would prefer a verdict against him for a farthing to a disagreement of the jury. The secretary was called and admitted that this was so; that he had passed on this information, as he believed, at the request of Sir Timothy, and without appreciating that he was thereby interfering with the course of justice. The Lord Chief Baron shewed great, but restrained, indignation; he dismissed the jury, adjourned the trial, and gave Sir Timothy an opportunity to shew cause before a Divisional Court in Dublin why he should not be punished for contempt of Court. The penalty proved to be a severe one; a £300 fine besides being ordered to pay all the costs thrown away. The second trial took place in Dublin before Mr. Justice Kenny and a Special Jury; the plaintiff was given a verdict for £5, which, however, carried his costs. It was a sad price to pay for a moment of thoughtlessness.

And thoughtlessness, or forgetfulness, can affect the most careful and prudent of men. I do not suppose that there was ever a solicitor who took so much trouble with his cases as did my father; and yet I remember him telling me a story about an action at the trial of which I was present. There was a merchant in Youghal named Richard Farrell, who found it worth his while occasionally to own small coasting vessels for the purpose of his business. One of these vessels came into collision with another craft, and Mr. Farrell was sued for damage. By his defence he pleaded, amongst other allegations, that he was not the owner of the vessel at any material time. The pleadings were closed; the usual interlocutory proceedings followed, including an application by the plaintiff for an order of discovery of documents, which was granted. The non-legal reader may have heard that it is possible to find out in this way what relevant documents are in the possession of one's opponent. It is the duty of the solicitor to prepare the affidavit of documents, and to set forth in the appropriate schedules all documents his client has which bear on the case, although he can claim privilege for a lot of them. He must also say what documents have been but are no longer in his possession, and say how possession of them ceased. My father prepared his affidavit and had it sworn by Mr. Farrell; and the trial of the action came on at the Cork Assizes. I can remember that Seymour Bushe and Matt Bourke were for the plaintiff; my grand-uncle, D. B. Sullivan, K.C., and the present Serjeant Sullivan, then a junior, were for the defendant.

There could be no doubt upon the plaintiff's evidence that the vessel supposed to be Mr. Farrell's was to blame; but at the conclusion of the plaintiff's case my father was called into the box, and produced a deed, whereby Mr. Farrell, before the date of the collision, had, for good consideration, transferred the ship in question to some-body else, who was not before the Court. I can recall Bushe standing up to cross-examine, and my father repelling what he thought to be a suggestion that this was not a *bona fide* transaction; and Bushe most handsomely said that my father would never be suspected of any bad faith. And thereupon there was judgment for Mr. Farrell with costs.

The next morning, on his way down to his office, my father suddenly stood still, and nearly collapsed. He had just realised that he had not included this deed in his affidavit of documents! Had he done so, the plaintiff would have had notice of the true state of affairs, and could have discontinued his action against Mr. Farrell before suing the right person. By this omission the plaintiff had been allowed to follow a false trail, and was now saddled with the costs of an unsuccessful action. When he woke up to this he would surely make application to the Court, and ultimately my father would be liable to pay these wasted costs, a formidable matter for him. He spent several weeks of grave anxiety; but apparently not even after their defeat did the advisers of the plaintiff notice the blunder, and he never heard anything more about it!

That must have been about the last time that Seymour Bushe appeared upon the Munster Circuit, although he continued for many years to prosecute at Green Street, the Dublin equivalent of the Old Bailey. He was the greatest orator of our time, a worthy descendant of his incorruptible great-grandfather, Charles Kendall Bushe, called "the Silver-Tongued." Unfortunately, in days more censorious than our own, there was a domestic tragedy, and Bushe thought it wiser to confine his practice to the Parliamentary Bar in London. I only heard him speak a half a dozen times; but he was most impressive. I remember one incident, which I mentioned to his cousin, Sir Plunket Barton, who put it in his little book about my uncle; but it will stand a second telling. Tim had gone up to Green Street to defend a prisoner, and sat waiting in court while the previous case proceeded. After a while it became necessary to swear a witness; search was made for the Testament, but it could not be discovered. At last somebody happened to turn towards my uncle, and beheld him deep in a perusal of the missing volume, entirely unconscious of the search. "Don't disturb him, my Lord," said Bushe, "he thinks it is a new publication!"

Another tale that I told Sir Plunket had reference to an action for breach of promise of marriage brought by a lady of close upon fifty against an old gentleman of over seventy, named Chevalier Bergin. The plaintiff was represented by Johnnie Moriarty; she came into court, dressed in a fashion not unusual in the early days of motoring, a flat cap on her head, to which was attached a long double veil, which she had swathed round and round her countenance. Johnnie, accepting the lady's own figure, introduced her as a damsel of twenty-eight years of age; unfortunately her birth certificate added nearly twenty more to the years that she admitted. When my uncle stood up to cross-examine her, he began by saying: "Madam, will you remove the *yashmak*!" "I don't understand you, sir," came a voice from the depths of the veil. Tim fixed his pince-nez: "Discocoon yourself, madam!" he said. After that, the case dissolved in laughter, although I believe the lady did get a small verdict.

The tale about himself in which my uncle took the greatest pleasure, related to an application for a liquor licence which he defeated by a happy interjection. The late Sir Frederick Falconer, Recorder of Dublin, was the licensing authority for the city, and rather averse to increasing the already enormous number of licensed houses in his jurisdiction. In those days there used to be an unlicensed hotel about half-way between Nelson Pillar and Amiens Street Station; it stood back some twenty feet from the building line and had a little bit of grass in front of it. The owner of this house was most anxious to obtain a licence; and he briefed Thomas Lopdell O'Shaughnessy, destined to be Falconer's successor, to make the application. Tim was instructed to oppose. Tommy pulled out the softest and sweetest stops of the organ, and became lyrical about the charms of his house. "It isn't an ordinary kind of city house at all, my Lord," he said, "it stands back from the road, and has in front of it a pretty little lawn——" "Yes, my Lord," said Tim, "and my friend now wants to turn it into a cruiskeen lawn."

Everybody has heard the tale of his comment upon his opponent, James Campbell, in the divorce case of Bishop *v.* Bishop. Campbell, in stating the case to the jury had affected to burst into tears; Tim, in opening the defendant's case, sought to put matters in their proper perspective, and complained of the exaggerated fashion in which Campbell had painted the husband's alleged grievances. "My friend," he said, "was actually moved to tears by the wrongs of his client—the greatest miracle since Moses struck the rock!" An unrestrainable roar of laughter went up in the court, where James Campbell was well known as about as tough-skinned a man as ever wore wig and gown. Nobody seemed more surprised at the success of his comment than my uncle, who had to pause for some moments before he could proceed. And then he did genuinely draw tears from more than one eye in court by his picture of the husband saying family prayers with his wife and daughter on the eve of starting for his solicitor's office to instruct him to file a petition for divorce. My uncle had one of the loveliest speaking voices I have ever heard, with great dramatic possibilities; and he well knew how to use it.

In 1900 he had accepted an invitation of his opponents to attend a meeting of theirs in North Louth; his arrival spread confusion if not consternation amongst his enemies, who had not expected him to accept. He forced his way into the waggonette from which they proposed to address the crowd; and while they hurriedly consulted as to their plan of campaign, he stood up and addressed the meeting himself. Five successive speakers on the other side tried to shout him down, and failed; one of them, the late A. J. Kettle, father of poor Tom Kettle who died so gallantly at Ginchy in 1916, lost his voice in the middle of his oration, whereupon Tim remarked: "Go down, Kettle; your spout is broken." It was some time after this Cyrano-like adventure that he found himself in bitter forensic controversy with an opponent who had the name of being rather bibulous. "Mr. Healy," said this ornament of the Bar, "please remember that you are not now on a brake in Dundalk." "It's better to be on a brake in Dundalk than on a bend in Rathmines," replied the impenitent Tim.

Once another opponent, a very vulgar man, annoyed him by some tactic in a case. Tim was on his feet in a moment; it was a disgrace to the Court—an abuse of the process of the Court—an attempt to deceive the Court—! His opponent wilted under the attack, and in his defence said: "Sure, 'tis a common thing in this Court." "It isn't the only common thing in this Court," retorted my uncle, with meaning.

Once a retort of his got into the Law Reports. There was a certain solicitor who believed in the principle "Always put off till to-morrow what need not be done to-day." There are postponements and postponements; for example, it was always a recognised practice to call the motion-list twice, and any solicitor whose counsel was not then available would rise in his place and say: "Second calling, if your Lordship pleases," and the case would automatically go over. But this solicitor was not so venial an offender. "Manāna," was the watchword of his life. And he might have continued this pleasant existence without interference, if he had not had the folly to accept some office which involved duties under the supervision of the Local Government Board. This was fatal; the wretched Board would keep pestering him, expecting him to stay in his office and work on a day

Q

when the river simply shouted for the attention of a rod. Izaak Walton triumphed; the Board was bidden wait. So at last the Board, unable to get anything done itself, determined to see what the King's Bench Division could do, and applied for a writ of *mandamus*. Then at last did the solicitor arouse himself; he briefed my uncle to appear for him; and Tim went into a court composed of the Lord Chief Baron and Mr. Justice Dodd (I forget who was the third Judge) and tried to explain the dilatory conduct of his client. For a long time he appeared to be doing no good; but his persistent harping on the human side of the case caused the Chief Baron at last to say: "What sort of man *is* this solicitor?" Tim looked up at him: "The sort of man, my Lord," he said, "that, when the last trumpet sounds, will stand up in his place, and say: 'Second calling, if your Lordship pleases!'" The solicitor escaped by the skin of his teeth. And Mr. Justice Dodd enshrined the story in the Irish Reports by telling it in his judgment.

Having told so many anecdotes of one uncle, let me conclude this chapter by a tale about another. When James Campbell became Lord Chancellor, he was inclined to be a little fretful when presiding over the Court of Appeal. In a certain case which Serjeant Sullivan was arguing before him, he took a strong view in favour of the other side, and made this clear by a series of interruptions. The Serjeant stuck to him, and continued to hammer away. In the course of his argument he referred to one item in the evidence. Campbell pounced in triumph. "Serjeant," said he, "doesn't that confirm the suggestion I was putting to you a few minutes ago?" The Serjeant looked at him gravely. "My Lord," said he, "everything is confirmatory of a prejudice!"

XVI

THE RETURN from Circuit usually marked the end of
term; a few busy days, and the Courts rose for the Easter,
Long or Christmas Vacation. But the Library buzzed for
those few days, as the Circuit stories were exchanged,
the few non-Circuiteers listening with cynical amusement,
and occasionally contributing some jest of their own.
Of the Dublin quidnuncs the most notable was one who
had better assume in these pages the name of Tommy
Tucker. Certainly it might have been said of him when
he died just after the war: "We could have better spared
a better man." Tommy came to the Bar rather late in
life, and had few of the usual qualifications. *Ruffs' Guide
to the Turf* was more familiar to him than any legal textbook; and his opinion upon a horse or a prize-fighter
would have commanded more respect than any view he
might express upon contract or tort. The first time I
saw him in the Four Courts he was angrily emerging from
Court 2 of the King's Bench Division, with a remonstra-
tive little solicitor trying to catch hold of the tail of his
gown; Tommy was saying, indignantly: "G—— blast it,
do you think I can win every b——y case?"—an opinion
that few who really knew him would have dared to hold.
Why Tommy Tucker was so popular I never could discover; but we all loved him, and would do anything to
get him out of a hole. Witness the fate of Robert Doyle,
afterwards Recorder of Galway, generous and princely
in his manner, and the most punctilious of men in the
matter of his obligations.

To Robert Doyle came Tommy one day in the smoking-room of the Library, with a very long face and a generally woebegone expression. "Robert," said he, "you're a gentleman; you'd never let a pal down." "What form of extortion is this?" asked Robert, who knew Tommy well. "Ah, now, if you're going to talk like that, I'll leave you alone and go to somebody else," said Tommy, who had a high opinion of the value set upon his friendship by those who did good turns for him. "Come on, Tommy; what is it?" The good-natured Robert was always ready to be drawn. Tommy grew confidential. "I have three dead certs for Punchestown that simply can't lose; and my b——y bookmaker won't give me any credit for a bet." "Well, what do you want me to do about it?" Tommy's mouth began to water; the possibilities were better than he had hoped. "Well, Robert," he said, "I was wondering would you authorise me to make a few bets in your name with your book-maker?" Robert stared at him, amazed by the audacity of the proposal; for Tommy was expected to conduct most of his affairs on a cash basis. He had a comfortable home; but those responsible for its amenities did not approve of his sporting adventures, and declined to finance them. Robert Doyle was inclined to think they were right, and began to shake his head. "Ah! Robert, you wouldn't let me down!" cried Tommy. "Sure, it's throwing money away; I had the tips straight from the stable." And he continued to plead, until Robert, his resistance undermined, said: "Well, Tommy, only this once; and it must be strictly limited to three bets, and each bet must be limited to a fiver." "Oh! Robert, I'll never forget this for you; I can't tell you how grateful am!" And Tommy was away.

At the end of the month Robert received his account from his bookmaker; there were all the entries he expected, and in addition a long series of items, all liabilities and all marked "per Mr. Thomas Tucker," amounting in all to some seventy pounds. The enraged Robert went in search of Tommy as soon as he reached the Library. "What on earth is the meaning of this?" he asked, angrily. "Ah, Robert, I had the devil's own luck; one of those three horses I told you of caught cold on the eve of Punchestown; another got kicked in the paddock; and the third needed softer going." "Yes, but I told you only to make three bets of not more than a fiver, and——" "Yes, I know, old boy; but I was trying to get back my losses; I felt my luck couldn't be out in every race, but it was." Robert fumed. "And what, may I ask, am I to do with this account for seventy-odd pounds?" he asked. Tommy glanced at it, as though surprised that Robert should take it so seriously; "Ah, pitch the beggar to hell, and plead the Gaming Act!" he said, easily.

I may add that I was a bit of a prig in those days; and, although I had been introduced to Tommy when he came down to visit his stepson at school, I had chosen to overlook this, and always declined to recognise Tommy in the Library, until his *bravura* defeated even my austerity. This must have been in 1913, for Jonathan Pim was Solicitor-General at the time; which means that I had been deliberately cutting Tommy Tucker every day for three years. Nevertheless, he came into our bay to ask somebody to take a half-crown ticket in a sweepstake on some race; and, having pouched one coin, he turned to me and said, as though we had been bosom friends: "Maurice, won't you try your luck?" I was so flabbergasted that I produced the necessary money; and a few hours later he came back to me to tell me I had drawn a b——y good horse, and he was prepared to give me three half-crowns for my chance. I, however, decided to stand on my luck.

The prizes were £7 10s. 0d., £5, and £2 10s. 0d.; and what was my surprise when Tommy came into my bay the next morning and handed me fifty shillings. He then paid a colleague of mine, named Sainsbury, five pounds. Sainsbury and I were amazed; such conduct on the part of Tommy was unprecedented. We went up to the smoking-room to discover who had won the first prize, and found that it was Jonathan Pim. Now, Jonathan was a highly respected member of an old Quaker family, and we had an idea that no Quaker would really approve of anything that had to do with horse-racing. So we went in search of Jonathan, and told him that we were sure that this money would be a burden on his conscience, and that we as the winners of the second and third prizes were quite prepared to relieve him of his ill-gotten gains and divide them between us. But Jonathan, who never went near the smoking-room, did not know what we were talking about. "Why," said he, "Tommy Tucker told me I hadn't drawn a horse at all!"

Poor Tommy! With all his faults he was a most amusing fellow; and he never bore any malice in respect of anything he had done. When he lay dying, the host of enquirers was an embarrassment; and Tommy kept sending bulletins to the Library, generally couched in the language of the turf. "Tell them my lungs are all right, if only my b——y old heart would give them a chance," is one which sticks in my memory. But the b——y old heart refused to give them a chance; it had been overworked in the past, and decided to take a rest at this critical moment. ''I've had to return all my briefs,'' Tommy gasped, the day before he died. It cannot have been a difficult task; nor would he have been remembered through them as he is for his own strange sake.

The hallucination that one is engaged in a huge practice is one that affects a surprising number of people. There was one poor man on the Munster Circuit, whom I can remember only once seeing in Court; but if you met him on the way down to the Four Courts in the morning, and fell into step with him, he would always complain of the vast pile of work that was engaging his attention: there was that important Admiralty suit (there were practically no Admiralty suits in Ireland, important or unimportant), and two heavy libel actions in the special jury list, and a very difficult case of contract, and an appeal in a will suit— the list went on as long as you would listen to him. And he believed it all firmly; I suppose there must have been vague conversations about the possibility of such cases materialising. But the poor fellow didn't make two hundred a year at the Bar.

Incomes at the Irish Bar were so small that the salary of a Judge, whether County Court or High Court, was a great attraction; the appointment did not, as in England, mean a loss of income; men gained by their promotion. Patronage in these appointments tempted would-be candidates to be good little Liberals or Tories as the case might be; and, when the Irish Party took to canvassing for their friends, the announcement of a new appointment, when it appeared in the *Freeman's Journal*, was sure to conclude with the statement that the appointee had been a regular subscriber to the Irish Party Fund. John Donaldson, a shrewd and kindly member of the

North-Eastern Circuit, used to say that it reminded him of an advertisement that used to appear at the foot of every report of a fire : ''Insure with David Drimmie and Sons.''

It was a strange thing that the North-Eastern Circuit, which included Belfast, did not make at all a proportionate contribution to the outstanding men at the Bar. James Chambers, for a short time Solicitor-General, tall, handsome, and good-humoured, was probably the pick of the bunch in my time, although the present Father of the Ulster Bar, John McGonigle,[1] was a very formidable opponent.   And if his young brother-in-law, Ambrose Davoren, had not perished in France in 1915, I have no doubt that he would have been in every respect an ornament to the profession.   Ambrose might well have been christened the Chatterton of the law.   He cannot have been much more than twenty-three when he died; but he was the close friend of the old Lord Chief Baron, who talked to him as an equal.   He treated law as Yehudi Menuhin treats the violin; he compelled it.   I had the benefit of his assistance when trying to write a law-book in 1914; and I never knew at which to marvel the more: the extent of his erudition or the modesty with which he displayed it.   Nor did he forget his secular learning in the thickets of the law.   There was appearing at that time *A History of the War*, by John Buchan, in an early part of which the distinguished editor had thus translated the speech of King Peter of Serbia on the eve of the Battle of the Ridges:

''Heroes,'' he said, ''you have taken two oaths —one to me, your king, and the other to your country.

[1] Just appointed a County Court judge.

I am an old, broken man, on the edge of the grave, and I release you from your oath to me. From your other oath no one can release you. If you feel you cannot go on, go to your homes, and I pledge you my word that after the war, if we come out of it, nothing shall happen to you. But I and my sons stay here.''

I can remember reading aloud that magnificent thing, which I have known by heart ever since; and Ambrose Davoren crying in delight: "I would love to translate it into Greek.'' A few months later we travelled over to Kent together, and I left him with his unit of the gunners near Sevenoaks. A couple of months later he was dead; and it is I who remain here. God rest him.

It was the Munster Circuit that gave the largest proportion of its members to the armed forces of the Crown; and some of those who had been the most eager of Sir Edward Carson's gallopers shewed a strange lack of enthusiasm when the chance of fighting became real. But let me be honest and admit that a large proportion of our Circuit contribution came from the Southern Unionists. I have always thought that insufficient justice has been done to that section of the population. In creed and in politics they held to their honest convictions; but they were Irishmen all, and their patriotism was none the less Irish because it included loyalty to the King. Not that the King was ever personally unpopular amongst the Nationalists; but his name and insignia had been stolen by the extremists on the other side and had been dragged into party warfare. I can remember a most amusing fantasy written by the late William Dawson, in which a dethroned King Edward VII was made to take refuge from the Ulstermen in Kerry; and the general comment was that he'd get a warm welcome, anyway. But perhaps the phrase was ambiguous.

When I was recruiting in Ireland in 1915, one of the most whole-hearted of our supporters was a member of the Munster Circuit named J. E. S. Condon. He was a Doctor of Laws; popular rumour said that the initials of his name stood for Jessel Erskine St. Leonards. But he was a simple man, with great faith in the value of the spoken word; and he had certain stock phrases with which he always filled up any threatened hiatus in his speech. "In the matther," was one of these; it appeared in the most unexpected circumstances. Malice invented a story of an appearance of his before Mr. Justice Barton. The *Evening Herald* had offered a prize for a walking-race; some objection had been lodged against Doctor Condon's client, who sought an injunction to restrain the newspaper from awarding the cup to anybody else. Stephen Ronan took a preliminary objection that no such application would lie; "and," said he, "I desire to know, heh, on what doctrine of equity my friend relies, heh, on what doctrine?" "Yerra, my Lord," replied the Doctor, entirely unmoved, "I apply to your Lordship, in the matther." "Yes, Doctor Condon, but Mr. Ronan is entitled to know on what doctrine you rely; and I confess it would enlighten my mind also." "Well, my Lord, I rely on the doctrine of springing and shifting uses." "Springing and shifting uses? But pray, Doctor Condon, how do you apply that doctrine to the facts of the present case?" "Well, my Lord, my client is an athlete, and a competitor, in the matther; and if he didn't spring, and he didn't shift, yerra, what use would he be at all!"

This sprang from the imagination of Joseph O'Connor; but I myself noted the exact words of the Doctor when one night he was delivering an impassioned oration from the top of a tram-car in the vicinity of Guinness's Brewery. The wrongs of Belgium had moved him to more than ordinary eloquence, and he suddenly cried: "Unfortunate Belgium, that for the last three hundred years has been plundered and ravaged, if not otherwise!"

One of those who loved to draw the Doctor out was Richard Littledale, K.C., tall, portly, and looking for all the world like a member of the Sanhedrin, although I do not think he was of Jewish origin. The Irish sometimes look very Jewish; my grandfather was quite rabbinical in his appearance, and many people said the same about my uncle in his later days. And, when I first began to appear, any reporter who was told that my name was Maurice Healy took one look at my nose and wrote down the first name, "Morris." But Dick Littledale had a majestic benevolence of mien with which none of us could compete. He was one of Dublin's leading musicians; and he could do what few musicians can do: he could whistle sweetly and accurately, almost like a flautist. He whistled at his work in the Library; one could frequently hear the strains of *Tristan* or some other Wagnerian opera, as Littledale and Ignatius O'Brien compared notes. I once suggested that they should each have a *leitmotiv* to herald their appearance in Court. But, oddly enough, Dick Littledale remains in the memory of my affection, not for his delightful chaff, nor yet for his musical performances, but for one of the most charming stories about children, which he once told me.

He was one of the band of snuff-takers that survived in the Library, which is not without its bearing on the tale. For, one morning, his three small children set forth, each with a shilling tightly clutched in one hand, to buy a birthday-present for father. Various suggestions had been made; but a red bandana handkerchief had been considered the most appropriate choice. There was a certain shop, known to the children, which dealt in such things, and it was thither that they directed their steps. Sure enough, displayed in the window was just such a handkerchief as they were seeking; but the price attached to it suggested a formidable difficulty; it was marked 2/11. And thirty-five pennies cannot be divided by three. However, the eldest boy went in, and asked to be shewn a bandana handkerchief; the shopman produced the one from the window, but the would-be purchaser affected not to have seen the price-ticket, and asked "How much?" "Two-and-eleven, sir," replied the assistant. The case seemed hopeless; but at last the boy turned to the shopman with a complete solution: "Make it three shillings, and we'll take it," said he.

The purchaser of that handkerchief became my brother-officer in the Royal Dublin Fusiliers, but I lost sight of him after the war. His father became Registrar in Chancery, a post he held until his death some ten years ago.

It will be appreciated that much of what has been told in these pages was hearsay, although, in most cases, I confined my chronicle to stories of men I subsequently knew personally. But the man who was responsible for more good stories than any other Irish lawyer never swam into my ken. Richard Adams was apparently the salt of the Library from the late 'seventies, until he was appointed County Court Judge of Limerick. He had an unbridled tongue, and the jest was out before he could tell whether it was good or bad, or even fit for publication. Women had not been admitted to the Bar in those days; the Library was a club of men, and many of the jests, well enough in an intimate male circle, would hardly bear repetition. The wittiest of Adams's jokes cannot go into print, harmless as they were in the company in which they were spoken. And he could sometimes deal with an indelicate subject in a manner to raise a smile, without straying beyond the bounds of propriety. Witness the commencement of his judgment in a certain case brought against a Limerick publican on the ground of nuisance. The publican considered that his duty ceased when he supplied liquor for his customers, and the architectural plans that are shewn to licensing justices in this country would have had about as much relevance to his business as those for the building of the Great Pyramid. The result was that a narrow passage between his house and his neighbour's assumed functions it was never intended to fulfil, to the great annoyance of adjoining householders, the nearest of whom brought his action for nuisance. Adams opened his judgment in something like the following terms: "It is a principle of the Common Law, of Roman Law, and the Law of Nations—a principle recognised in the Pandects, in the Code Napoleon, in the American Constitution, and in the teachings of Confucius, that a man should sneeze where he buys his snuff!" And he gave judgment for the plaintiff. The judgment was affirmed by the Judge of Assize, but not for the same reasons.

His daughter married the late Alan Laurie, the Deputy-Chairman of London Sessions, who told me a typical Adams' story, not so well known as some of the others. When Adams came to London he was in the habit of staying at a certain club, where he would make a fourth at bridge in the card-room. One night he found himself playing at a table where his neighbour was a most unpleasant person, whose not over-cleanly habits were tolerated more easily than his incurable habit of holding a lengthy inquest on every hand, in the course of which he lectured his companions from a very lofty standpoint. One evening when he left the room for a moment the others broke out into angry complaint about him. "I cannot stand his lectures," said one. "Yes," said another, "his speeches are as long as his finger-nails." "Ah! but not so much in them!" said Adams.

On one occasion Mr. Justice William O'Brien desired to give two of his nieces an opportunity of seeing what a Court was like. Adams was in charge of the prosecutions; and the Judge sent for him, and asked him so to marshal his list that nothing might occur calculated to bring the blush of shame to the cheek of modesty. Adams promised to take the greatest care; and when the young ladies appeared they saw before them in the dock a young man charged with the larceny of a pair of boots from a sailor in a common lodging-house. Nothing more unlikely to shock maidenly reserve could be imagined; and all went well, until the prisoner, who was defending himself, stood up to cross-examine. From his first question it appeared that a suggestion was being made that the code of conduct amongst those using the common lodging-house was not that usually accepted by respectable people. O'Brien looked up in alarm. The second question, which particularised the generalities of the first, was one which could not be tolerated in respectable female company; the Judge roared out: "Adams! Adams! You r-ruffian, Adams!" and swept his relatives off the

Bench; nor would he ever believe that Adams had not deliberately played a particularly offensive trick upon him.

I think it would be an impertinence on my part to repeat any of the better-known stories about Francis McDonagh, Q.C., who must have died before I was born. But my father told me two stories about him that I have not seen in print, so that I may be forgiven for setting them down. McDonagh was a survivor of another world; he always wore white kid gloves in Court, and he preserved the magnificence of manner of a Regency dandy, always speaking in a superlatively courteous phraseology, which a sneering delivery could at times make terribly offensive. His vanity was colossal, and was equalled by his disloyalty to his juniors. Nor were his lay clients safe when his own reputation was at stake. Those who happened to have listened to Mr. Denis Johnston's clever presentation of *Death at Newtown-Stuart* on the wireless, will need no reminder that McDonagh was brought " special" to defend Inspector Montgomery of the Royal Irish Constabulary, charged with the murder of his friend, a bank manager named Glasse. The jury disagreed on the first two trials; McDonagh, who had been very generously paid on each occasion, declined to come again unless his fees were secured to him. He was technically within his rights; but Palles, who was Attorney-General, was so indignant that he insisted that the Crown should guarantee the fees, rather than a man should be deprived of the services of the advocate he had chosen.

McDonagh then appeared; and, having twice succeeding in dividing the jury, there was no reason why he should not hope to do so again, even if he failed to secure the acquittal of his client. Unfortunately, Montgomery, whose duty it had been to prepare prosecutions in many cases, had a high opinion of his own powers as a lawyer; and he kept passing notes to McDonagh, suggesting questions to him. An advocate is frequently thus embarrassed by his client; the wise man knows when to ignore such advice, and when to follow it, but if he does follow it, he thereby takes the responsibility himself, and if he gets an unfavourable reply it is his own fault. And in the event of receiving such a reply, it is, of course, his duty to betray no emotion and to do all he can to cover up the effect of the answer. However, Montgomery was very pertinacious; and the moment came when he passed a note, suggesting a particular question. McDonagh took the note in full view of the jury, asked the question, and received a deadly answer. Immediately he turned towards Montgomery and threw up his hands in horror! Many people thought that this episode caused the conviction of his client.

My father said he only met McDonagh once. It was during the Cork Assizes, and he was walking down the South Mall with a barrister who had been junior to McDonagh in an action in which they had been successful the previous day. McDonagh stopped them, and in the most gracious tones he addressed the junior: "Ah, my young friend, I must again congratulate you upon the way you steered that case to victory yesterday!" "Oh, Mr. McDonagh, you are too kind; it was your skill, and yours alone, that secured our success." "Say not so, my young friend; modesty, an admirable quality, on this occasion betrays you; the victory was yours and yours alone." "But Mr. McDonagh, I only examined one witness." "My friend, you did a great deal more; do do not belittle your genius. By one Napoleonic move you secured our victory. I have just visited the attorney in his office, and he showed me the letter in which you made the recommendation that I should be retained to lead you!"

And having admittedly gone back to hearsay, let me tell one story of those days, told to me by Doctor O'Connor of Kirby Muxloe, near Leicester. It concerns a Metropolitan Magistrate who used to sit in Dublin in those days; and Mr. O'Donnell's Court was the scene of many a witty exchange between Bench and Bar. There was a form of proceeding which was very common in Ireland, which Stephen Ronan used to call a "Habeas Animam" application. One of the parties to a mixed marriage would die, an immediate battle for the children would break out, often resulting in kidnapping, which would be met by an application for a writ of Habeas Corpus. Not infrequently the kidnapper, strong in his or her religious beliefs, would defy the Court and go to prison. And this was the fate of a certain Miss A., who had hidden the infant child of her deceased brother or sister, I forget which, and, in spite of much grave and kindly adjuration on the part of the Judges of the Queen's Bench Division, point-blank refused to surrender the child or to disclose its whereabouts. So she was committed to prison for contempt of Court, the sentence being six months without hard labour. By a slip, the warrant directed that she should be confined in Mountjoy Prison, Mountjoy being the men's prison in Dublin. Alas! it has since attained tragic celebrity; and its grim portal, with the legend "Cease to do Evil; Learn to do Good," has opened and shut upon a host of political martyrs since the night when the sheriff's officer vainly sought to pass Miss. A. through its doors. The Governor

R

was obdurate; the warrant might specify Mountjoy, but it was an obvious blunder. And the Governor of the female prison was equally unreceptive; there was no warrant addressed to him, and he would not accept a prisoner without a warrant. So the poor lady had to spend the night as best she could on a couple of chairs before the fire in the sheriff's office.

The next morning, this episode quickly became the talk of Dublin; somebody came into O'Donnell's Court and whispered it to him. He interrupted the business of the Court for a few moments and dashed off the following, which may be pardoned upon the authority of Doctor Johnson's dictum: "Sir, it hath wit enough to keep it sweet."

> In most earthly tribunals injustice prevails;
>   But the Court of Queen's Bench is both prudent
>   and mild:
> It committed Miss A. to a prison for males
>   As the very best way of producing a child.
> How she'll do it surpasses conception to tell
>   If she cease to do evil and learn to do well;
> But if, in six months, without labour, confined,
> She produces a child, 'twill astonish mankind!

XVII

THE PRINCIPAL fault of a book written as this has been
will always be its untidiness; irrelevance is its keynote,
and even when one paragraph does suggest the next, there
is nearly always a deviation and another, and another,
until the main road has been left far to a flank.
"E. & O.E." might well be set upon the title-page.
For example, I have hitherto said hardly a word about
two outstanding figures in the old Court of Appeal, Lords
Justices Fitzgibbon and Holmes; I might be suspected of
having forgotten John Ross, the last Lord Chancellor of
Ireland; and enough has not been said about Edward
Cuming. Except Fitzgibbon, these were not members
of the Munster Circuit; but the Law Library mingled the
Circuits and allowed us to leaven the lump. I wish, too,
that I could have captured and pinned down some of the
delightful butterfly wit with which Jack Fitzgerald used
to enliven our evenings at Mess; but his comments were
as brilliant and as evanescent as soap bubbles, and just
as impossible to perpetuate. Jack Fitzgerald, with Jim
Rearden leading him on, and George MacSweeney trying
to get them both to go to bed was a delightful episode
of almost nightly recurrence, of which, alas! no phrase
or jest has lingered.

When I was a law student, Gerald Fitzgibbon was
President of the Law Students' Debating Society, and
the only time I ever met him personally was at one of
our meetings when he asked me to squire some ladies
for him. But I knew him well in Court; I never missed
an opportunity of hearing him, for never was there a man
endowed with so beautiful a speaking voice and so well
able to make use of it. He was so tall a man that he had
a lean-forward attitude that was almost a stoop. He had

an enormous head; and he had one of the most mobile faces that I have ever seen. Chaliapin frequently reminded me of him; and both were great actors. I do not know if the Lord Justice ever sang; but Chaliapin never spoke more persuasively. There was a legend that when Fitzgibbon was at the Bar he once made a bet that he would make the final speech in an important action without ever using a word of more than one syllable. His *vis-à-vis*, remembering the traditional opening phrase, "Gentlemen of the Jury," took up the bet, which Fitzgibbon won, as well as his case, the next day. His commencement was: "Now, you twelve good men and true in that box!"

An argument in the Court of Appeal when he was a member was an intellectual treat. For Fitzgibbon always argued the case with counsel; and, whereas nothing is more irritating to counsel than to be constantly interrupted by the Judge, this never applied to Fitzgibbon's interventions, for the reason that he always listened to the answer to his questions. And one could argue with him "in shorthand" as it were: an allusion to "Smith *v.* Jones and that line of case" was always sufficient to direct his mind along the path you wished it to go, although, when it became necessary to demonstrate the hair's-breadth that made all the difference between Smith *v.* Jones and the case under consideration, nobody could split the hair with greater precision or accuracy. His fault lay in being so excellent an advocate; for the advocate who is proud of his ability cannot change his character when he leaves the Bar for the Bench. Fitzgibbon had strong views about the Land Acts, which he shared with Lord Ashbourne; in a case called Magner *v.* Hawkes, they combined to defeat the tenant's claim. The case governed many thousand of others; so John Atkinson went to Gerald Balfour, then Chief Secretary, and persuaded him to bring in a Bill to get round the decision of the Court of Appeal. Mr. Balfour, always a good friend to the Nationalists, was a ready conspirator in such a cause; he called in my uncle and my father, and the four of them set to work to draft a clause that would give the benefit the original act had intended to give the tenant. The Bill became law; the tenant got his fair rent fixed; the landlord once again went to the Court of Appeal; and once again Lord Ashbourne and Lord Justice Fitzgibbon found a hole in the statute, and reversed the finding of the Land Commission. "Even the ranks of Tuscany could scarce forbear to cheer."

Fitzgibbon was a co-eval of the Lord Chief Baron's. He was called to the Bar in 1860, and appears to have been able to take silk in 1872. He was appointed Solicitor-General for Ireland in 1877, and went to the Court of Appeal the following year. His son, Gerald, was also a member of the Munster Circuit, and was one of the first Judges appointed to the Supreme Court of the Irish Free State, from which position he has just retired at the age limit of seventy, having given shrewd counsel and aid to a Bench, most members of which lacked his experience. Although the new Irish Bench has given grounds for very little criticism, Gerald Fitzgibbon was almost the only member who belonged to the old school; that is to say, he had grown up in an atmosphere which bred familiarity with the government of Ireland and with the administration of the law. He inherited his father's popularity, and, without it, would have acquired his own; he did not inherit his father's touch of partizanship, and he was a model of all that a judge ought to be.

Readers of Curran's speeches will remember that there

was an earlier Fitzgibbon, who was also a member of the Munster Circuit fated to eminence; but John Fitzgibbon, afterwards Lord Clare, was of a different family; and I believe his line died out in the Charge of the Six Hundred at Balaclava.

Hugh Holmes was short, bearded, and looked like a severe edition of Father Christmas attempting to disguise himself as a retired admiral! He was a silent man, of very deep feelings, which he rarely shewed. When Pether O'Brien used to come into the Court of Appeal to hear Appeals from Revising Barristers, he delighted in teasing Holmes by asking counsel to read out the very fine passage in Lord Justice Holmes' judgment in Someone v. Hanrahan—a passage in which the Lord Justice reverently took leave to doubt that the "service" upon which a Sister of Charity was engaged was under any but the one Master. Holmes used to wriggle uncomfortably while it was read; but it did not change his views, nor was he ever ashamed of them. He took a very severe view of agrarian crime; and he showed no pity to the perpetrators when they were convicted before him. One elderly prisoner staggered when he heard himself sentenced to fifteen years' penal servitude. "Ah! my Lord," he cried, "I'm a very old man, and I'll never do that sentence!" Most people in court were moved; not so the Judge. "Well," said he, "try to do as much of it as you can!"

Oddly enough, although his sons, Hugh and Valentine, were and are good friends of mine, I never met the Lord Justice myself. He never came the Munster Circuit in my time. Hugh, called a year ahead of me, commanded Battery Don 17 in the 29th Divisional Artillery, in which duty he greatly distinguished himself. On November 30th, 1917, he was overrun and surrounded when the Germans broke our line near Cambrai (breaking through two other divisions and not ours, let me add); but he never abandoned a foot of ground, and, with his guns pointing to every point of the compass, the gunners defending them with rifle and bayonet, he drove back the enemy and helped to restore the broken flanks in front of him. We saw a good deal of each other during the Occupation, when we found ourselves frequently opposed at courts-martial. And on February 7th, 1919, we left Cologne *en route* to Dunkirk, a journey that took us fifty-one hours, in an unheated train, across a snowbound land, while Germans, forbidden to travel more than thirty miles without special permission, passed us in each direction in comfortable steam-heated corridor trains. I was recovering from influenza; and but for Hugh Holmes and his affectionate care, I was a dead man. As it was, I had a very bad few days when I arrived home; but I was able to turn up on Circuit, as I had promised to do, on March 1st.

The Holmeses and the Murphys (Mr. Justice Murphy's family) were inter-married almost as much as the Healys and the Sullivans; and I dare not place the Lord Justice's legal grandsons with accuracy. But he has given a younger son, Valentine, to the English Bar, and also a grandson, Sir James Henry, whose father, Denis, was Attorney-General for Ireland, and afterwards the first Lord Chief Justice of Northern Ireland.

The most popular of Northern Ireland's contributions to the Bench in my time was John Ross, the last Lord Chancellor of Ireland, and in his last days a baronet, in which title he is succeeded by his son, Sir Ronald Ross, Member for Derry and a practising member of the North-Eastern Circuit in this country. When Sir John died in 1935, *The Times* was good enough to publish a letter from me, which, partly because it gave pleasure to his family and partly because I think it painted the man as well as I am likely to do it, I reproduce as it was:

"Because no tribute would have pleased him so much as one from 'the other side of the road,' I venture to add a few lines to your appreciation of Sir John Ross. Three characteristics stand out in the memory of him: his splendid presence; his beautiful use of the English language; and his extraordinary kindness to the young men who had the good fortune to flesh their maiden swords in his Court. Although he sat on the Chancery side, a shortage of judges resulted in his travelling the Munster Circuit in 1912 or 1913. The Bar anticipated heavy weather for him in the unaccustomed seas of common and criminal law; the litigants, mostly drawn from the peasantry, expected short shrift from a judge whose main duty in the Land Court had been to prevent various attempts to overreach the landlords whose estates had come under his administration. But the event was a pleasant disappointment to everybody. When he dined with the Bar at Cork he explained the reason. 'When I went down to the Four Courts for the first time,' he said, 'I looked for the largest hat I could see on the rack, and I hung up my own next to it. That hat belonged to Peter O'Brien; and what you learned from Peter you couldn't forget.' The Peter referred to was shortly to become famous as Attorney-General; and in those troubled days he put many a brief in the way of John Ross, who thus obtained as good an education in the criminal law as any man could desire. An equally pleasant surprise was his success with the small farmers, many of whom had hoped that a judge who was more accustomed to affidavits than to oral evidence would be an easy prey to the wiles so well portrayed in the pages of Somerville and Ross. But the southern Rolands were met by a northern Oliver, with a twinkle in his eye that swiftly disarmed them; and to their surprise they found that the Judge whose strong hand was so swift to commit to prison in his Dublin Court was both sympathetic and understanding when treated with open heart. So great was the success of his first Assize that Ross became a confirmed Circuiteer, to the pleasure of the Bar and the general satisfaction.

"A very hard worker, the Judge allowed himself one irregularity in the year. Usually the nominal 11 o'clock sitting of his Court was the subject of considerable margin; but on the first day of Punchestown Races he invariably took his seat as the clock struck; indeed, some say that by a strange coincidence that excellent clock would always be five minutes fast on that day. The list would be called through; no counsel would be present; 'Put them all in the list to-morrow,' the Judge would say, and five minutes later he would be on his way to catch the 11.20 train from King's Bridge. Once a turbulent barrister, heedless of the convention, became pertinacious and insisted upon opening his motion. Those in Court grinned, the Judge looked chagrined for a moment, but the twinkle soon appeared in his eye. 'Mr. Bartley,' said he, 'I suppose you are seeking to apply the decision of the Court of Appeal in Mangan's Estate?' 'No, my Lord,' said the surprised counsel. 'Ah, well, Mr. Bartley, I don't think you ought to be asked to discuss the present case without having had an opportunity of considering that decision, so I'll adjourn your application until to-morrow morning.' And before the astonished Bartley could say a word the Judge was up and away.

"Very human; and it was that humanity that made

John Ross's success. In all his opinions he was uncompromising; but he was aware of this, and never allowed it to be the occasion of bias. When he first went circuit certain counsel thought fit to wave a party flag when conducting their cases. The twinkle would at once appear; with a grave affectation of ignorance the Judge would ask for further enlightenment on the subject of this allusion, and a moment or two later the culprit would find himself driven to an admission that he had been endeavouring to load the scales of justice. We'll go on with the case now,' would be the only comment from the Bench.

"With his love of life went a love of letters; the poets were at his ready call, and many a judgment was pointed by a quotation, not of a hackneyed tag, but of some apt and remembered phrase. To the evening of such a life his beloved Hesper Phosphor must indeed have been the bringer of all desired things; nor can I think he will be unaware of all the kindly thoughts that are gathered around his bier."

I think that with John Ross I have completed the list of Judges who sat on the Bench in my own time and stamped their personalities upon their age. Sir William Moore, the late Lord Chief Justice of Northern Ireland, was appointed while I was at the war, and I am afraid I felt very bitter about the appointment; for his fame had been entirely political up to then, and he was a fierce and gallant swordsman. But he left all his political prejudices behind him when he ascended the Bench, and I returned to find him universally respected. I had, in the meantime, made the acquaintance of his brother, Colonel Moore, of the Army Medical Service, and had realised that, if blood went for anything, my fears had been ill-founded. Of the other appointments in my day, none wrote their name large. John Gordon shunned all bright colours; Arthur Warren Samuels never quite got over Professor Tyrell's reply to a query as to which of two candidates he would support for the representation of Dublin University: "I shan't vote for X, for he isn't a gentleman; and I certainly shan't vote for Samuels, for he is too much of a lady." Yet Samuels was a sincere and patriotic Irishman, and his scholarship in economics was valuable to the country in the days of Lloyd George finance. But as a Law Officer and as a Judge he was undistinguished. Jonathan Pim, who had preceded him, brought a nice bouquet of an old-world garden on to the Bench, but, alas! very little else. It was not his fault; he had modestly inquired whether his name might not be considered for a County Court Judgeship, and was asked whether he had gone mad, when a Liberal administration were in despair for the lack of Law Officers. So Jonathan found himself Solicitor-General, and subsequently Attorney-General; he continued urbane and charming, and in due course ascended the Bench. He probably had more general culture than any of his contemporaries, but he was not of the timber from which judges are carved; and I fancy that his retirement, which I trust he still enjoys, came as a relief to him.

Edward Cuming's comment upon his appointment as Solicitor-General was: "Well, why not? Lord Chesterfield was once Lord Lieutenant." As a matter of fact, Chesterfield was by no means the worst of Ireland's Viceroys; but he is remembered rather for his good manners, so admirably exhibited towards Doctor Johnson. Edward Cuming always affected to think that anyone was good enough to be appointed to an Irish office, provided the permanent civil servants continued faithful and competent. And there was a good deal of truth in it.

The first weakening of the British hold on the country came about when Mr. Birrell allowed the Irish Party to have a voice in the appointments to permanent posts. The men so appointed had neither the old loyalty nor the new; when a crisis came their grip was unsure. Had Mr. Birrell taken an occasional afternoon off to visit the Law Library, he might have received some valuable instruction from Edward Cuming's little parliament around the fire.

Cuming was unique. Tall, untidy, bearded, peering through glasses that seemed to have a year's incrustation of dust upon them, he cared for no man, and commented upon all. Mr. Justice Dodd told a story of a Catholic judge who once said: "God forgive me, but I always feel satisfaction when I am able to decide against that black-avised Protestant, Edward Cuming." "What do you mean?" cried Dodd. "He's as fierce a Papist as yourself." He was, in fact, a fervent son of the Church, although he never paraded his religion. But he had the dour manner of a covenanter, and he never smiled— which added zest to his wit. One day Johnnie Moriarty was romancing at the fireside, drawing the bow further and further, until he heard a faint sound like a snigger. "Ah! Cuming, stop laughing!" he cried, angrily. "I assure you, Moriarty, I'm not laughing," said Cuming; "at least, I'm trying not to!"

Moriarty was a favourite target of his. Once, when the irreverent started a discussion as to which had the better chance of salvation, Moriarty or Stephen Ronan, Cuming truncated the argument by saying that it reminded him of the case of a battle between two puisne mortgages where the estate was hopelessly insolvent. He once pictured Johnnie attempting to secure the spiritual aid of Saint Mary Magdalen; "but," said he, "he'd be sure to spoil it all by pretending that he had known her well in her unregenerate days!"

There was an action in Dublin about thirty years ago, in which a charming young actress named Minnie Cunningham sued the Theatre Royal for wrongful dismissal. The case turned on the fact that the lady had refused to wear a certain dress, on the ground that it was so short as to be indecent; the management, thinking otherwise, terminated her engagement. The case was tried by Pether O'Brien, who was credited with a suggestion that the plaintiff should put on the offending garment in his room, so that the jury might judge for themselves; but this, I think, was a contribution from our old friend, Ben Trovato. What was beyond question was that Johnnie, opening the plaintiff's case, thought fit to say in a far-away voice that he himself had never been inside a music-hall; astonished by the Homeric laughter which followed, he hastily added: "I mean, in Ireland!" In due course this was reported to the fireside; Edward Cuming went as near a chuckle as he permitted himself to go, and remarked: "Moriarty saying that he had never been inside a music-hall is like Pontius Pilate boasting that he had never stolen his mother's jam!"

Family loyalty forbids me to repeat his comment upon my uncle's cross-examination of the plaintiff; but I am bound to confess that I always thought it the wittiest thing Cuming ever said. But lest it should be thought that he was a mere fireside wit, it is only fair that I should repeat Mr. Justice Dodd's statement that, in a hopeless case in the House of Lords, Edward Cuming so impressed the House that he received the rare compliment of an intimation that "Mr. Cuming's argument calls for a reply."

The late Charles O'Connor was an occasional visitor to Cuming's circle, and certainly lent it grace. A more gentlemanly figure never graced the Irish Bar.   White-haired, pink-faced, dapper, he might have stepped out of an eighteenth-century play; he had been in large practice in the Chancery Courts before he became a Law Officer, and his appointment as Master of the Rolls had the approval of the profession, although he did not fulfil his promise.   But he remained popular, and would come back to the Library of an evening to talk over old times, and exchange views with his friends.   He had an amiable vanity, particularly about the greatness of the Clan Connor; and one evening, in Edward Cuming's presence, he drew attention to the varieties of spelling the name. "Yes," he said, "some spell it with an O: some spell it without the O.   Some spell it C-o-n-n-o-r: some spell it C-o-n-n-e-r.   Some spell it with one N: some spell it with two Ns."   "Yes," said Cuming, "and some of them can't spell it at all!"

Here, at last, this rambling chronicle may well draw to a close.   It has not confined itself to the Munster Circuit; but it has served to emphasise the pre-eminence of that Circuit in old days in Ireland.   I doubt that any legal body can muster so fair a roll of fame; Lords Avonmore, Clonmel and Carleton, Curran, Pennefather, Goold, O'Connell, the three brothers O'Loghlen, Jonathan Henn, Stephen Collins (the last two being ancestors of the present Mr. Justice Henn Collins), Lord Fitzgerald, Isaac Butt, Fitzgibbon, James O'Brien, William O'Brien, Peter O'Brien, John Atkinson, Edward Sullivan, Lord Justice Barry—my fingers weary before my memory fails. No higher standard of conduct has ever been set by any section of the legal profession.   It should not have been necessary to cross to Ireland to seek a defender for Roger Casement.   It well may be that the clerks to various eminent counsel had taken it upon themselves, without consultation with their principals, to decline his brief; but a system capable of such an infringement of chivalry of the profession would never have been tolerated in Ireland. It must be remembered that the second and third counsel engaged in the case were members of the English Bar; the leader was also, of course, a member of the English Bar, but had not been called within the Bar in this country, although a leader of many years standing in Ireland.

This, I think, comes from a quality associated with the English characteristic, a love of compromise. One should stick to his principles, but not to the degree of embarrassing the King's Government, which, in any important matter, must be assumed to be, not merely right, but above criticism. The King must be head of the Church. One should close one's eyes to what one cannot cure. Profess correct principles, but do not obtrude them unnecessarily. After all, the priest and the Levite who passed by on the other side of the road were men of God, and why try to be better than them?

That was not the view that prevailed at the Irish Bar, and particularly was it not the view that was held by members of the Munster Circuit. No man became really rich at the Bar in Ireland, unless he was appointed a Law Officer; the fees he then drew were supposed to be punitive, to scourge the backs of those who harboured evil-doers. I do not think that any leader, other than a Law Officer, ever made £5000 a year at the Irish Bar; I am certain that there were not ten earning £3000, and hardly a junior earned £2000, although the Counsel to the Attorney-General might make a larger income. It was generally believed that doctors in Dublin made much larger sums. The legal profession, therefore, consisted of men who had no great surplus on which to fall back if their adherence to their principles ever cost them clients; but the professional clients appreciated this, and admired them for their independence. Neither branch of the profession sought to increase costs. One member of the Bar, who was rather inclined to multiply motions in a case, caused Pether O'Brien to ask: "Who'th that fellow who keepth tinkering at a cathe and never finithheth it? He'th jutht like a plumber"; and "Plumber" remained the sobriquet of the counsel in question for the rest of his days. Yet the barrister in question was not doing this dishonestly or improperly; he was only being careful and, as we might say, pernickety. That kind of thing was not popular in Ireland. The result was that litigation remained cheaper than it was in any part of His Majesty's dominions; and I do not think that the result was any the worse.

And because of the Library system, which not only enabled us all to practise cheaply, but gave every neophyte three hundred tutors to teach him his business and knock the corners off him, we turn back to the Four Courts glances of an affection that the Temple could never inspire. The Irish Bar was a corporate body; if the soul of that body must, even in Ireland, be considered incorporate, it nevertheless had the gift of showing itself, not as a ghost, but as a conscience. Like all bodies, it had its diseases and infirmities; but it had no need to wait for another life in which to put on incorruption. The intellect that inspired the body came largely from the Munster Circuit, now, I learn, once more reconstituted, and about to enter upon another phase of service to its country. May God be with the old days, that can never be forgotten; yet may He bless that well-beloved body in its resurrection and make it once again the pride and glory of the legal profession in Ireland.